W9-BDX-708

Re-Envisioning
Education and Democracy

Re-Envisioning Education and Democracy

by

Ruthanne Kurth-Schai
Educational Studies
Macalester College

and

Charles R. Green
Political Science
Macalester College

INFORMATION AGE
PUBLISHING

Greenwich, Connecticut • www.infoagepub.com

Library of Congress Cataloging-in-Publication Data

Kurth-Schai, Ruthanne.
  Re-envisioning education and democracy / by Ruthanne Kurth-Schai and
Charles R. Green.
      p. cm.
  Includes bibliographical references.
  ISBN-13: 978-1-59311-562-3 (pbk.)
  ISBN-13: 978-1-59311-563-0 (hardcover)
  1. Education–Aims and objectives–United States. 2. Educational
change–United States. 3. Democracy–United States. I. Green, Charles
R., 1935- II. Title.
  LB41.K85443 2006
  370.973–dc22

                                                                2006021685

Copyright © 2006 Information Age Publishing Inc.

All rights reserved. No part of this publication may be reproduced, stored in a
retrieval system, or transmitted, in any form or by any means, electronic, mechanical,
photocopying, microfilming, recording or otherwise, without written permission
from the publisher.

Printed in the United States of America

For all who persist against the odds
to broaden and deepen democracy
to strengthen understanding and experience
of compassion, truth, beauty, and justice
in public schools and civic spaces.

Contents

Given the importance afforded throughout our history to foundational concepts of "education" and "democracy," why does the gap between our aspirations and our achievements persist?

Exploratory Democratic Practice: Conversational Reading

Given the exploratory nature of democratic learning and living, why do we focus our reform efforts on acquiring greater certainty and control?

Exploratory Democratic Practice: Anticipatory
     Thank You Notes

Given the daunting challenges of change, how can we draw from, yet move beyond, pivotal setbacks?

Exploratory Democratic Practice: Ethnographic
     Futures Interviews

Given the dimensions and dynamics of contemporary social and educational concerns, what, beyond rational problem solving, is ̣ ̣ ̣ary?

̣ ̣ ̣oratory Democratic Practice: Visualization

Prelude

*T*he future of public education in a democracy is everyone's responsibility. Education and democracy are inextricably linked in American social thought and practice. The core values shared by those who espouse democratic public education merge with those who attempt to enact democratic politics. Institutions developed to serve public education and those designed to realize democratic governance reflect common aspirations and experience similar constraints.

Today, the fate of public education—and therefore, the future of our democracy—is at risk. Seemingly intractable problems and heated controversies persist. The economic and cultural turbulence generated by globalization has consequences at every level and every location of contemporary life. An array of recurrent crises painfully displays the resilience of authoritarianism, the increased salience of terrorism, the widening gap between rich and poor, the undiminished rate of environmental degradation, and the persistence of racial, ethnic, and religious intolerance.

This constellation of pervasive systemic crises affects all dimensions of our personal and social lives. Democratic aspirations are deeply challenged. Impassioned critique and rhetorical repetition of familiar core values in public discourse are insufficient. Public institutions at all levels struggle to

Re-Envisioning Education and Democracy, pages ix–xxi
Copyright © 2006 by Information Age Publishing
All rights of reproduction in any form reserved.

cope, but coping alone is not enough. Comprehensive reform is required. Public education is a crucial site for systemic social transformation.

Most of what we conventionally take as 'public education' is implicitly and explicitly 'democratic politics.' From funding decisions, to the development of graduation standards, to the organization of education into districts with locally elected school boards, to the curriculum and pedagogy employed within each classroom, political processes are enacted.

Much of what we conventionally consider 'democratic politics' is teaching and learning. Positions are developed, justified, and presented; debated, compromised and sometimes implemented; always assessed and often reconsidered throughout all of the institutions of democracy.

Both public education and democratic governance are fiscally and ethically accountable to citizens. Both provide focal points for social criticism, advocacy, and reform. Both continually shape, challenge, and evolve complex approaches to power sharing—the essence of all politics. *So strong are the interdependencies that our efforts to glimpse new directions may be strengthened by treating education and democracy as one and the same.*

At the center of all democratic activity—from envisionment to enactment—is the intent to deepen and extend human potential. While expressed and interpreted in various ways throughout the American experience, the objective of democratic education, politics, and governance is to afford *all* people opportunities to pursue life with dignity, affiliation, and an ever-evolving sense of purpose and possibility.

The continuing struggle to construct policies, programs, and institutions to accomplish this, for all citizens, over the course of a lifetime, is the enduring challenge of a democratic society. This challenge is centered in public education. At the turn of the twentieth century, John Dewey argued that public schooling is a primary site of both peril and promise for revitalizing democracy and promoting social justice and compassion. His visionary assessment is even more compelling today.

Public education has become a large and complex system affecting all aspects of contemporary life. The majority of U.S. citizens are educated in public schools. Education is the largest budget item in all of the states and is perennially a central issue in local, state, and national politics. Public schooling is seen across the spectrum of ideologies as a significant social responsibility. Discussion and debate concerning specific objectives, content, and approaches to teaching and learning are prominent in public and private conversations at all levels. Public schools remain perhaps the *only* social institution that could be shaped to support and sustain purposeful interaction among citizens whose concerns and contributions vary by race, class, and cultural heritage.

More than any other social institution, public education mirrors the troubling array of global problems. Despite historic commitments to the contrary, public schools are increasingly segregated. Public support is diminishing as budget constraints and privatization drain vital resources. School policies and programs perpetuate segregation by race, ethnicity, socioeconomic background, and academic performance as gaps in achievement and opportunity continue to grow. There is persistent violence among young people. There is deep demoralization among struggling students, their teachers, and parents. There is increasing stigmatization of specific schools serving lower achieving groups of students. There is evidence of diminishing aspirations for life long learning and civic participation necessary to sustain democracy.

Well documented in the literature, and disturbingly present in the hearts and minds of those committed to egalitarian education reform, is the concern that prevailing public policy is "democratic" perhaps only in terms of the numbers of those who will be affected. The majority of America's youth, along with the majority of American educators, will find their efforts to teach and learn deeply affected by the imposition of education reform initiatives that are philosophically and pragmatically authoritarian and divisive. The majority of American adults will find themselves relentlessly shaped as political spectators and consumers, rather than supported as active citizens.

Within this context, collectively we are called to address the question:

Given challenging and uncertain times,
how can we sustain comprehensive reform
that supports broad-based participation
in democratic processes of social inquiry and civic action?

As one response, we offer this book as an invitation for continuing involvement in a complex social process that implicates education, politics, and governance—that of *re-envisioning education and democracy.*

To *re-envision*—to envision and then envision again—is to join with others in *imagining new possibilities and bringing these into existence.* The goal is to open new paths toward systemic progressive reform.

Re-envisioning is a radically *social* process. Although distinct and varied individual contributions are required, transformative visions cannot be advanced through the agency of one charismatic person, or bound by one influential perspective. The process of re-envisioning, like all forms of democratic living and learning, draws energy and insight when interaction, connection, and communion are sustained across dimensions of difference.

Re-envisioning is an intensely *creative* and *exploratory* process. It is not accomplished through careful construction of "best laid plans" aimed at attaining certainty and control. Re-envisioning is instead experienced and evolved by preparing for, and then acting on, informed and strategic *glimpses.* These brief and fleeting impressions—multi-modal and multi-sensory, incomplete and ambiguous, always in motion—offer potentials, but no definitive answers.

Re-envisioning is a profoundly *ethical* and *aesthetic* process, centered in prospects for social justice, compassion, reform, and renewal. Social movements are rarely motivated by commitments to narrow objectives aimed at solving specific problems. More often, they are compelled by *prophetic dispositions* that indicate pathways toward transformative change. Across time and cultures we are drawn to persons and processes, to ideas and images, that call us back to remember our highest principles and move us forward to respond with acts of integrity and grace. Recurrent themes of beauty and power—here mirrored in chapter titles—inspire, guide, and liberate collective vision and principled action.

Re-envisioning is a fundamental human capacity. Although accessible to all, it remains largely undeveloped and underutilized. In the process of writing this book, we have come to believe that the collective ability to realize shared aspirations for education and democracy can be significantly enhanced by integrating the process of re-envisioning along with other, more familiar, educational and political reform strategies.

*   *   *

To deepen our experience and understanding of re-envisioning, and to provide varied points of entry and engagement for our readers, we utilize three expressive forms. Within each chapter, one episode of an evolving *strategic narrative* is played out and followed by an *exploratory essay*. Key concepts raised in each essay are supported and extended by thematic references at the end of each chapter. Woven throughout each chapter is a poetic meditation stream that draws its form and function from varied conceptions of *oracles* developed historically and cross-culturally.

Strategic Narratives: A complex story line depicting reform challenges and possibilities is developed throughout the book. A purposeful narrative provides several distinctive opportunities for critical analysis and policy design. Visionary abstractions can be tested in real-life contexts that portray divergent images, voices, emotions, and events always present in democratic deliberation. Situational descriptions and dialogue on complex issues can extend consideration and conversation among readers. Carefully constructed narratives can represent less linear and narrowly rational processes along with more ambiguous and conflicted experiences characteristic of all aspects of civic life.

Exploratory Essays: Short essays are used to present glimpses of analyses and arguments linked to each chapter narrative. We understand an essay to be an interpretive composition. For the purposes of this project, the essay's function is principally neither persuasive nor prescriptive. We do not attempt to develop compelling cases or finely crafted arguments to advance specific positions or policies. Instead, we feature the tentative and exploratory characteristics of this expressive form. In each essay, we draw from the extensive literature of theory, research, criticism, and practice to prompt consideration of focal concepts and issues. Supporting references are provided at the end of each chapter.

Oracular Expressions: Brief meditations in the oracular tradition frame the essays and narratives. These are used to mark the book's priorities and preferred strategies for advocacy and action. They emphasize key concepts and relationships by foreshadowing, sometimes echoing, their expression in the narrative and essays. Our primary intent in adapting the metaphor of 'oracle' is not to advance expertise in prediction and planning. Education, politics, and governance are already replete with predictive technologies. Instead we weave a five-part oracle throughout each chapter to support efforts to imagine and enact civic visions that are possible to sustain even under challenging circumstances. Oracular expressions are also included to draw attention to the interplay among intuitive, aesthetic, emotional, kinesthetic, and ethical dimensions of educational policy and practice. In doing so, we invite exploration of what we have come to understand as a *spiritual* domain of democratic learning and life.

*   *   *

Throughout the writing process, we have struggled with the realization that each of the three expressive forms—narrative, essay, and oracle—could be developed as a literary art. Though a daunting and desirable goal, from the beginning we have known that this could not be our purpose. Our initial intentions were pragmatic and pedagogic. We wanted to develop multiple points of entry for a broad range of readers. We hoped to enhance communication by expressing key concepts in different formats. As the writing proceeded, however, we came to realize that much more was in play. Beyond their use as expressive strategies, narrative, essay, and oracle have functioned as distinctive, yet complementary "ways of knowing." Each form repeatedly challenged and extended our awareness, our understanding, and our aspirations.

Our primary goal has been to develop a book that will encourage creative but practical contributions to reform discourse and initiatives. In approaching this goal we first needed to formulate a credible reform scenario. *Narrative,* as a form of inquiry, pushed us to delve into prior research, teaching, and consulting to identify prominent issues, acknowledge a variety of troubling situations, and anticipate likely barriers. Perhaps more important, crafting a *strategic narrative* repeatedly challenged us to ground our visionary and theoretical aspirations in contexts of real world constraint and patterns of feasible response. As in real life, the issues encountered in constructing a narrative drew us into the bewildering complexity of systemic reform. This narrative with its terse situational descriptions, sparse character development, and emphasis on dialogue still touches many conflicting and dynamic possibilities.

Exploratory essay, as a mode of inquiry, better meets the need to move beyond a specific story to clarify complex conceptual patterns and articulate broadly relevant and transferable solution paths. The glimpses that permeated our emerging understanding were grounded in broadly interdisciplinary scholarship. The essays provide composite representations of problems and possibilities rather than well-formed arguments or detailed examples. Exploratory essays reflect an approach to inquiry that is tentative, multilayered, and dynamic.

As the book project proceeded, we found that the narratives and essays, while illuminating, were not sufficiently evocative. The complexities of educational and political reform require integration of intellectual, ethical, and aesthetic sensibilities. The *oracle* was initially attempted as a metaphoric frame, but soon provided a deeper conceptual structure and inquiry path. Its poetic and meditative style encouraged juxtaposition of disparate symbols and values, while eliciting aesthetic dimensions more difficult to represent in the essays and narratives. We discovered that the oracle's paradoxical tradition of broadening perspective, while focusing attention on issues of profound significance, offered distinctive insights into contemporary situations. The prophetic dispositions, used as chapter titles, provided a vocabulary signaling common emotions and critical experiences associated with the developmental stages of real world initiatives. Reform is intrinsically future-oriented and the oracle also allows us to better understand how we conceive of and move toward visions of the common good. Overall, the characteristically diffuse aesthetic quality of oracular expression extended our inquiry and shaped our advocacy.

Although different in conceptual and communicative strategy, our experience suggests that narrative, expository, and prophetic/poetic ways of knowing—particularly in combination—are well suited to the task of engaging diverse participants in processes of re-envisioning education and democracy. The integrated use of these forms is intended to serve both conceptual and civic purposes.

*   *   *

All chapters reflect a basic structure. Each begins with a one-word title followed by a meditation on its meaning. Based upon their central function, we use these key words as prophetic dispositions. Reflective of the prophetic tradition, they signal conditions of consequence, those worthy of broad-based, ethically centered, and future-oriented social deliberation. More than focal concepts, each represents a generative *field* for contemplation and action. Taken together, they mark the book's conceptual framework.

A narrative passage then follows. These are intended to support increased reader participation. Engaged readers usually enhance any story as they move through the text. Active readers embellish portrayals and situations with their own interpretations. They connect webs of imagined events, thoughts, and dialogue with their experiences and emotions. They reflect on possible applications in their own lives. Our strategic intention is to encourage and support all of these tendencies.

Each chapter narrative encompasses a second oracular feature—a brief meditation on *forces* at play in systemic reform. Here we seek insight into the kinesthetic, emotional, and sensory "feel" of the energy associated with the chapter's prophetic disposition and story line. Often linked to recurrent patterns in the natural world, this feature draws from the reflective prompts represented within several historically recognized oracular traditions. Emphasizing nonverbal symbolism, this feature invites interaction with important educational and political concepts in ways that move beyond conventional linguistic and logical analysis.

Each narrative concludes with a *query*—a complex question to be brought before the oracle. Historically, the opportunity to consult an oracle was accepted with grave responsibility. It was well understood that the nature of the question posed would shape both the quality and direction of the oracle's counsel. Informed by skilled perception of the field and the forces involved, the query was to move to the heart of the issue thus opening the way for fruitful patterns of response. In this book, we offer ten chapter queries to our readers, first for consideration in light of their own perspective, but then, more important, as catalysts for conversation with concerned others.

The chapter essay is then developed. Prompted by the oracle, these are structured to center attention on issues that both necessitate comprehensive response and open new directions for change. Connecting with the chapter narrative, the essays are intended to identify major problems, provide selected examples, and develop interpretations of research and commentary.

Contained within each essay is the fourth feature of our adapted oracular metaphor—a *response* suggesting one possible path for social reflection and reform. Similar to the chapter field, the response is framed as a prophetic disposition. Corresponding to each chapter query, we offer ten responses as invitations to extend public discourse and activism concerning challenges and opportunities facing contemporary schools and society.

Each chapter essay concludes with a *reflection*. Here we draw from the contributions of others whose meditations on similar themes have yielded eloquent expression. This fifth oracular feature emphasizes our belief that in order to be effective, the process of re-envisioning must connect and sustain approaches to inquiry, imagination, and advocacy that are profoundly social.

Comprehensive reform is a daunting aspiration. Given the barriers to enacting progressive visions in large, resource-constrained, bureaucratic and authoritarian systems, we offer our readers two additional resources. Following each chapter is an ***Exploratory Democratic Practice***—a technique that opens opportunities to construct and apply knowledge in a holistic, consensual, and strategic manner. Each practice is designed to support collective efforts to experience and evolve vibrant democratic processes in classroom and community settings. Aligned with the book's strategic narrative that traces the "life cycle" of a systemic reform initiative, exploratory democratic practices are distributed across the chapters in a developmental sequence. A brief description and rationale for each technique are accompanied by suggestions for its implementation.

Also, linked to each chapter is a collection of ***Thematic Bibliographic References***. Chapter essays explore concerns central to the task of systemic progressive reform. References are selected to ground and extend key positions raised. Included are the print-based sources that most directly shaped our understanding, and those we judge to be most useful to others engaged in processes of re-envisioning.

*   *   *

By altering our familiar patterns of understanding, discourse, and participation we *can* move beyond education, politics, and governance "as usual." This book is presented as an invitation to participate in re-envisioning education and democracy—to join in a continuous process that is *radically social, always exploratory, necessarily creative, inherently aesthetic,* and *profoundly ethical.*

Imagination is the means for going beyond our selves as presently formed,
moving transformatively toward imagined ideals of what we might become,
how we might relate to others, and how we might address problematic situations.
Moral imagination is our capacity to see and to realize in some actual or contem-
plated experience possibilities for enhancing the quality of experiences,
both for ourselves and for the communities of which we are a part,
both for the present and for future generations.

—Mark Johnson
Moral Imagination: Implications of Cognitive Science for Ethics

Thematic Bibliographic References

On education as the foundation for democracy:

Barber, B. (1984/2004). *Strong democracy: Participatory politics for a new age.* Berkeley: University of California Press.

Barber, B. (1992). *An aristocracy of everyone: The politics of education and the future of America.* New York: Oxford University Press.

Barber, B. (1998). *A passion for democracy.* Princeton, NJ: Princeton University Press.

Barber, B. (2004). *Fear's empire: War, terrorism, and democracy.* New York: W.W. Norton.

Dewey, J. (1916/1984). *Democracy and education.* New York: Macmillan.

Fields, B.A., & Feinberg, W. (2001). *Education and democratic theory.* Albany: State University of New York Press.

Fraser, J. (1997). *Reading, writing, and justice: School reform as if democracy matters.* Albany: State University of New York Press.

Green, J.M. (1999). *Deep democracy: Community, diversity, and transformation.* Lanham, MD: Rowman & Littlefield.

Gutmann, A. (1999). *Democratic education.* Princeton, NJ: Princeton University Press.

McDonnell, L., Timpane, P., & Benjamin, R. (Eds.). (2000). *Rediscovering the democratic purposes of education.* Lawrence: University of Kansas Press.

Nie, N. (1996). *Education and democratic citizenship in America.* Chicago: University of Chicago Press.

Sandel, M. (1996). *Democracy's discontent: America in search of a public philosophy.* Cambridge, MA: Belknap Press.

Sehr, D. (1997). *Education for public democracy.* Albany: State University of New York Press.

On strategic narratives:

Craig, C. (2003). *Narrative inquiries of school reform: Storied landscapes, storied metaphors.* Greenwich, CT: Information Age Publishing.

Czarniawska, B. (1997). *Narrating the organization: Dramas of institutional identity.* Chicago: University of Chicago Press.

Lightfoot-Lawrence, S., & Hoffman-Davis J. (1997). *The art and science of portraiture.* San Francisco: Jossey-Bass.

Polletta, F. (2006). *It was like a fever: Storytelling in protest and politics.* Chicago: University of Chicago Press.

Schram, S., & Neisser, P. (Eds.). (1997). *Tales of state: Narrative in contemporary U.S. politics and public policy.* New York: Rowman & Littlefield.

On exploratory essays:

We are prompted by conceptions of an "essay" that include: "a short literary composition on a particular theme or subject usually in prose and generally analytic, speculative, or interpretative."

(1998). *Random House Webster's Unabridged Dictionary* (2nd ed., p. 662). New York: Random House.

On the forms and functions of oracles across time and cultures:

Ajayi, B. (1996). *Ifa divination: Its practice among the Yoruba of Nigeria.* Ilorin, Nigeria: Unilorin Press.

Amerding, C., & Gasque, W. (Eds.). (1978). *Dreams, visions, and oracles: Handbook of biblical prophecy.* Grand Rapids, MI.: Baker Book House.

Atwater, P. (1990). *The magical language of runes.* Santa Fe, NM: Bear & Co.

Blum, R. (1989). *The rune cards: Ancient wisdom for the new millennium.* New York: St. Martin's Press.

Elliot, R.H. (1959). *Runes: An introduction.* London: Philosophical Library.

Flaceliere, R. (1965). *Greek oracles.* New York: Norton & Company.

Fontenrose, J. (1978). *The Delphic oracle: Its responses and operations.* Berkeley: University of California Press.

Grabbe, L. (1995). *Priests, prophets, diviners, sages: A socio-historical study of religious specialists in ancient Israel.* Valley Forge, PA: Trinity Press International.

Halliday, W. (1967). *Greek divination: A study of its methods and principles.* Chicago: Argonaut Press.

Howe, L., & Wain, A. (Eds.). (1993). *Predicting the future.* Cambridge: Cambridge University Press.

Jeffers, A. (1996). *Magic and divination in ancient Palestine and Syria.* Leiden, NY: E.J. Brill.

Karcher, S. (1997). *I Ching: A guide to working with the oracle of change.* Boston: Element Publishers.

King, B. (1993). *The elements of the runes.* Rockport, MA: Element Publishers.

Lipsey, R. (1995). "Ambiguous truths, true ambiguities: Utterances of the Delphic oracle." *Parabola, 20*(3), 52–58.

Loewe, M., & Blacker, C. (1981). *Oracles and divination.* Boulder, CO: Shambala.

Meadows, K. (1989). *Earth medicine: A shamanic way to self-discovery.* Rockport, MA: Element Publishers.

Peek, P. (1991). *African divination systems.* Bloomington, IN: Indiana University Press.

Pennick, N. (1999). *The complete illustrated guide to runes.* Boston: Element Publishers.

Pollington, S. (1995). *Rudiments of runelore.* Norfolk, England: Anglo-Saxon Books.

Poulsen, F. (1973). *Delphi.* Washington, DC: McGrath Publishing.

Ritsema, R., & Karcher, S. [trans]. (1994). *I Ching: The classic Chinese oracle of change.* Rockport, MA: Element Publishers.

Smith, R. (1991). *Fortune-tellers and philosophers: Divination in traditional Chinese society.* Boulder, CO: Westview Press.

Turner, V. (1975). *Revelation and divination in Ndembu ritual.* Ithaca, NY: Cornell University Press.

Wilhelm H., & Wilhelm R. (1960). *Understanding the I Ching: The Wilhelm lectures on the I Ching.* Princeton, NJ: Princeton University Press.

Wilhelm, H., & Baynes, C.F. [trans]. (1960). *I Ching: Book of changes.* Princeton, NJ: Princeton University Press.

Reflection:

Johnson, M. (1993). *Moral imagination: Implications of cognitive science for ethics* (p. 209). Chicago: University of Chicago Press.

c h a p t e r   1

Reform

Scattered, then drawn together and formed again
causes and challenges, cautions and dreams
revisited, reconsidered
then carried forward, but never the same
new patterns, new processes, new life
fear and exhilaration
all is in motion.

He was alone, awake, and reflective. It was an unusual moment. Ordinarily, he was seldom alone, awake too much, and thoughtful too little. With two hours before his first campaign event, Jonathan Caine paused. Since the campaign began in full fury last spring, fatigue had become his daily companion. Rarely had he time to think beyond the next speech, the next interview, or the next urgent request for funds.

Today, his disconnected thoughts cascaded over aspects of his career as a lawyer, as state senator, and touched mostly on this intense struggle for re-election. As he poured his first cup of coffee, his thoughts gathered around education policy issues.

Education was his, and almost everyone's, number one theme in this election. Other issues were prominent—deficits, affordable housing, tax

Re-Envisioning Education and Democracy, pages 1–14
Copyright © 2006 by Information Age Publishing
All rights of reproduction in any form reserved.

reform, environmental policy, economic development, and gun control. Yet, it was again a very important political time for public education. All the school failure talk, education crisis scenarios, and proposed responses crossed party lines. Reform ideas were being pushed by a broad array of interest groups and media attention to the campaign often centered on the candidates' stances on public schools.

Caine had built much of his political career on education. It was the state's biggest budget line and an issue that seemed to touch every voter he had talked with. As a well-known state senate incumbent, he was again running in a high profile election. He knew he had achieved much in his public life. He had a well-publicized record of legislation, especially on education policy. He had been a key figure in several important coalitions that pushed for progressive change. With his experience, political skills, and his very powerful senior position he felt poised for even deeper democratic reforms of public education.

But a journalist reporting on a recent campaign debate pointed out that he seemed "a little vague." Caine and his opponent, the reporter claimed, "mouthed the usual clichés and were fuzzy and unspecific about an issue that both claimed was their main concern."

"Come on," he thought impatiently. "That article reported on one of those oddly formatted television encounters misnamed 'debates.' Trying to score points, project sincerity, provide sound bites, smile a lot, differentiate yourself from your opponent, and not fall into the traps the journalists set could never result in a 'fuzz free' focus." Sure, he used catch phrases, hot button words, well-rehearsed short stories, and promises. So did his opponent. She was an articulate and energetic campaigner and had actually fared somewhat better in the media's performance ratings. But she was also criticized for her lack of substance. Even though he took some of the criticism seriously, Caine knew that his views on public education actually represented a coherent plan with feasible proposals necessary to move ahead. His job was to make those proposals understandable to the voters and fashion them into public policy. He had done that in the past and he would do it again!

Why, then, was he uneasy and uncertain this morning? That was neither his self- nor his public image. He had been a powerful Chair of the Senate Education Committee for the past four years. Before that he had been an ambitious and increasingly influential ranking member. He had emerged as "Mr. Education" in reform circles. Think tank 'talking heads' regularly identified him as the pivotal figure in key legislation. Caine had taken significant time and effort to keep informed and involved with diverse education policy constituencies. His name was on the reform legislation that had facilitated charter schools, shifted school financing from property to more equitable tax bases, and supported teachers' professional development. He was a prodigious coalition builder and outspoken in attempts to deal with racial and class inequalities in education.

Caine knew that there was a genuine "education crisis"—it was not just a bumper sticker slogan. He knew from experience and with conviction that resolving that crisis was necessary to sustain a deeper democratic life in his state. He believed that public education and a truly representative democracy were inseparable. He was convinced that he was more informed than most. He knew he was more strategically effective than any of his legislative colleagues. He was certain that he was the best candidate.

His opponent featured a "no new taxes" pledge linked to a long list of state tax-cuts. She advocated budget caps, and "less government and more private responsibility" before she even got to any of her campaign items on education. In those, she emphasized "holding the line on school budget increases," "tighter fiscal accountability," "getting rid of bad teachers," and "bringing more discipline into the classroom." She had sketched a voucher plan for all students and, in line with national policy mandates, advocated more intensive standardized testing across the grades. Caine had countered her positions throughout the campaign. He readily brought to mind fragments of his speeches on education that he knew met her head-on. But this morning he couldn't quite reach the sweep of a broader democratic reform vision that he knew was at least as important as this election.

"Don't worry about it," he thought as he reflexively stirred his coffee. "This is the height of the campaign. OK, so I can't think clearly this morning. I'm tired and overworked. I'll have time to think all this through after Election Day."

Rising energy
gathering power and purpose
creativity converges
awareness and responsibility align.

Caine's thoughts continued to cascade, but they didn't converge. "What is it about education that engages almost everyone who participates in politics? It's got to be more than the perennial budget hassles, special interest pressures, and the dramatic school crisis fireworks.... Of course, candidates are expected to say that education is important—that our children are our future—that none should be left behind—that our democracy depends on sound public education." He had said all that, and more, and believed all of it—voters seemed to expect it from him—but yet....

"There are a lot of important policy issues besides education. There are significant political and ideological differences across the campaigns nationally, in this state too, and in my race—why do we center politics on education? Is education any more vital than the other major issues in this campaign—in our society? Is it really more complicated than say, civil rights, or taxes, or economic development? Well, nothing in politics is simple. It's not just politicians who seem to only support uncomplicated proposals—from charter schools to privatization to smaller class size to improved teacher salaries to a particular curriculum to dress codes to standardized testing to more rigorous teacher training to comprehensive assessment to ... to so many, many more."

"Why do these seemingly simple reform proposals satisfy most citizens but seem so partial and inadequate to me?" Many people had voiced their education concerns at his town meetings across the district. "Crisis" was again the framing term in most of their compelling presentations. Some expressed urgency about violence in the schools and others complained about deteriorating buildings. Strong views were expressed on the chronic property tax burden, unsatisfactory test scores, uneven teacher quality, class size, vouchers, and special needs students. Their stories were about very specific problems, usually expressed in moving personal accounts. Almost always they came down to a single highly focused proposal, usually phrased with a supremely confident "if we only did *this*" enthusiasm.

Caine could often identify with their stated problems, even if he couldn't always share their specific enthusiasms. He accepted some of their analyses, and he usually agreed on the value of what they proposed. But he knew that piecemeal approaches were insufficient in the face of this poorly understood "education crisis."

Now nearing the end of a grueling campaign, there was so little time to think, listen, and talk through all the important issues. He sensed he wasn't fully connecting his constituent's concerns with his own broader, but still scattered, vision of necessary systemic reform. Soon, after re-election, he would have time to shape perspectives that could go beyond this campaign language and move toward more complex policy conversations. Election campaigns were never big picture events. Yet, Caine also knew that legislative sessions could be as hectic as this campaign. Well, after the election he would find a way.

But what if he lost? That would give him time to think. Lose? Ha! There is no time for doubting now. He was the well-known incumbent with a powerful committee chairmanship. Sure his opponent was raising money and working as hard as he was. But he was the more experienced politician and an energetic campaigner. Of course he was going to win! Again he promised himself that right after his victory, he would engage others in thinking, listening, and talking about what was required to educate for democracy.

Caine heard faint radio sounds upstairs. Soon his wife would be up and he would need to get ready for the teachers' union breakfast that would begin another long campaign day. What could he say to those teachers about education? He was sure he had most of their votes. Could he really move beyond the expected clichés? This morning, he wasn't quite sure.

Given the importance afforded throughout our history
to foundational concepts of 'education' and 'democracy,'
why does the gap between our aspirations and our achievements persist?

Strongly held aspirations for public education in a liberal democracy have shaped American public policy for more than a century. We have experienced widespread consensus on the need for an accessible and effective system of state-funded education. There has been sustained support for the preparation of well informed and socially responsible citizens who will contribute to a free market economy and participate in an individual rights-based representative polity.

Beyond these basic aspirations, visions of deeper, more expansive and inclusive forms of education and democracy have also enriched our cultural heritage. Educational and political theorists, philosophers and policy makers, influential critics and activists, educators and citizens have focused public attention on a wide array of challenging reform assumptions and ambitions.

Assuming that as individuals we find meaning and fulfillment in social responsibility and solidarity, we emphasize educational and political experiences that compel collaborative inquiry in response to significant public concerns. Knowing that deeply democratic learning and living are inherently complex, dynamic, and exploratory, we seek and support principled questioning, compassionate critique, and strategic creativity. Understanding the primacy of an evolving civic vision and its expression through acts of civic virtue, we aspire toward deeper purpose, equity, and activism across all educational and political institutions.

Prevailing attempts at comprehensive change, however, are *not* structured to promote more deeply democratic forms of social inquiry and public life. Systemic approaches to educational and political reform are fueled and financed largely by government and corporate interests. Expertly

driven and centrally mandated, these efforts are responsive to the perceived necessity of promoting very limited forms of academic achievement
and political participation in order to ensure market advantage in a competitive, consumer-centered global economy.

Movement toward deeper democratic aspirations is continually
impeded by over-reliance on change strategies that are highly *individualis-
tic*, unproductively *elitist*, intensely *oppositional*, and narrowly *rational*. Passive acceptance of public educational systems and political processes that
emphasize individual merit, competition, and conformity narrows conceptions of 'excellence' and 'accountability', constrains learning, and hinders
the development of civic participation. Tendencies to concentrate scarce
resources on the preparation of a select *few*, discourages contribution that
could be provided by a more equitably resourced *many*. Resigned participation in oppositional politics emphasizing sharp critique, campaign-style
persuasion, special interest advocacy, and quick closure severely limits
opportunities for sustained deliberation and creative compromise. Tendencies toward narrow rationality, economic determinism, and unnecessary risk avoidance prevent fuller integration of emotion, aesthetics,
intuition, and spirit. Visions of reform thereby loose their capacity to
inspire and sustain principled social action. In spite of widely shared goals
and genuine resolve, a sharp divide remains between the 'American
dream' and the 'American experience' of deep democracy.

> *Radical . . .*
> *to move to the source, to move to the heart*
> *to seek fundamental changes in orientation, in character*
> *to liberate and to focus imagination*
> *to challenge boundaries*
> *to shift patterns of interdependence*
> *to alter the rules of engagement and accountability*
> *move together, move to the heart, move to the source.*

'Radical' is not a positive term in American public discourse about education and governance. The word is often used dismissively to label opponents' positions and tactics. 'Reform' is a more ambivalent concept. As a

noun, the term is used to describe almost any modest change in policy, practice, or organization. As a verb, 'reform' refers to any intended or enacted attempt to correct an identified 'problem.' Rarely do these 'problem solutions' culminate in deep modifications of the structures and processes of education and democracy.

Resistance to radical change is understandable. Incremental change characterizes the adaptive development of all human systems including democratic education and governance. Typically, significant change processes involve several institutions and many competing interests. Most result in compromises that have modest effects and do little to raise public awareness or involvement.

Public education and democratic civic participation—as fundamental social processes—do capture attention from time to time, but with limited depth or duration. Public attention is most often centered on specific policies or special interests. Public concerns are most often raised when functions taken for granted appear to have broken down—declining test scores, contested election results, or an allegedly failed school.

Both advocates and proponents dramatize policy responses and situate the associated controversies as the dominant ones in our political lives. Campaign finance reform and extensions of standardized testing in public education represent this common phenomenon. The quite strenuous politics accompanying such changes are reported in familiar conflict terms. Resulting minor modifications are characterized as comprehensive reforms. Yet restrictions on soft money contributions for election campaigns will not substantially reduce the risky dependence on special interest donors. Annual standardized testing of public school students will not transform schooling, nor will it enhance democratic civic engagement.

But there have been instances of deeper and wider change. Important efforts on local, state, and national levels have resulted in greater inclusion of, and more substantive support for, historically under-served populations. Improved processes protect individual students from varied forms of neglect or abuse. Initiatives promoting public school decentralization and innovation in curricular and instructional design have yielded enhanced student performance.

Over the years and across society, there have been important shifts resulting in somewhat more equitable access to social services, job opportunities, and voter rights. While voter turnout has generally drifted downward and declines have been noted in several forms of social association, community-based initiatives, grassroots mobilization, and emerging Internet approaches to political involvement have enjoyed some success.

Yet, while most modern educational, social, and political movements include the language of broad democratizing objectives, their implemented reforms are typically fragmented, emphasizing economic rather than philosophic or participatory changes. In the economy, education, and politics, fundamental forms of interaction and opportunity are rarely altered in deeply structural ways. Barriers imposed by race, class, and gender remain significant in current educational and political life.

There is some consensus on aspirations for education and democracy, and there have been some important moments of change in our social experience. Critical imagination and creative strategies are necessary to move on. Reform efforts must embrace deeper visions, bolder proposals, and more innovative enactments. Radical changes—those that are deeper and more systemic—are necessary to realize human development with greater equity and effectiveness, across all aspects of an aspirant democratic society. Institutions and processes integral to public education and civic participation will require continuous re-envisioning.

> *"Education is the primary method of social progress and reform."*
>
> —John Dewey
> *Education & Democracy*

Exploratory Democratic Practice: Conversational Reading

Reading is fundamentally a social act. It carries strong potential not only to affect the course of our personal lives, but also to enhance the quality of our collective experience. Although *Re-envisioning Education and Democracy* can be read independently, it is designed for reading as part of an ongoing conversation with others. To begin collaborative consideration of the book, we recommend reading in a manner that is *resonant*, *recursive*, and *responsible*.

To read *resonantly* involves attuning increasingly skilled attention to possibilities and relationships that most immediately hold personal meaning or draw personal interest. In reading this book resonantly, participants are encouraged to be mindful of two questions:

- What aspects of my personal knowledge, feelings, values, and experience are most strongly engaged by each of the three expressive forms—oracle, strategic narrative, and exploratory essay?
- What aspects of my personal knowledge, feelings, values, and experience are most strongly engaged by the reform issues and analyses raised?

To read *recursively* entails reconsidering the same piece of writing at different times, at different stages of inquiry and deliberation. Readers are encouraged to continually weave backwards and forwards through the experiences they bring, to revisit assumptions at various points, and to refine expectations as the process evolves. In reading this book recursively, participants are encouraged to individually and then collectively consider:

- In what ways are my personal opinions, feelings, values and experiences changing throughout the reading and conversations, particularly in response to insights and interpretations provided by others?

Perhaps most important is the challenge to read *responsibly*. In order to explore reform prospects democratically, participants cannot read for themselves alone. Reading to advance personal skills and understanding, or to support one's initial position, is necessary but not sufficient. In reading this book responsibly, participants are encouraged to reflect upon, and then to discuss together:

- What have I come to understand that holds the greatest potential to advance our shared vision and support continued participation?
- What needs to be voiced in order to sustain respectful and compassionate consideration of the implications of our work for broader civic aspirations, and for the lives of those who will be most profoundly affected?

Through this process, the act of reading retains its power as a private endeavor aimed at enhancing self-awareness and personal comprehension of pivotal reform issues. Beyond this, participants develop conversational skills necessary to express ideas of personal significance while engaging and extending those presented by others. Reading becomes a *public practice* aimed at envisioning and enacting an evolving conception of the common good.

Thematic Bibliographic References

On competing aspirations and agendas for public education:

Adler, M. (1983). *The paideia proposal: An educational manifesto.* New York: Macmillan.

Anyon, J. (2005). *Radical possibilities: Public policy, urban education, and a new social movement.* New York: Routledge.

Apple, M. (2001). *Educating the "right" way: Markets, standards, god, and inequality.* New York: Routledge Falmer.

Cutler, W. (2001). *Parents and schools: The 150-year struggle for control in American education.* Chicago: University of Chicago Press.

Danzinger, S., & Waldfogel, E. (Eds.). (2001). *Securing the future: Investing in children from birth to college.* New York: Russell Sage Foundation.

DeBray, E. (2006). *Politics, ideology, and education: Federal policy during the Clinton and Bush administrations.* New York: Teachers College Press.

Detweiler, F. (2000). *Standing on the premises of god: The Christian right's fight to redefine America's public schools.* New York: New York University Press.

Finn, C. (1993). *We must take charge: Our schools and our future.* New York: Simon & Schuster.

Hirsch, E. (1988). *Cultural literacy: What every American needs to know.* New York: Vintage Press.

Hochschild, J. & Scovornick, N. (2003). *The American dream and the public schools.* Oxford: Oxford University Press.

Kahlenberg, R. (Ed.). (2000). *A notion at risk: Preserving public education as an engine for social mobility.* New York: Century Foundation Press.

Kozol. J. (1992). *Savage inequalities: Children in American schools.* New York: Harper Collins.

Manna, P. (2006). *School's in: Federalism and the national education agenda.* Washington, DC: Georgetown University Press.

McGuinn, P. (2006). *No child left behind and the transformation of federal education policy, 1965–2005.* Lawrence, KA: University Press of Kansas.

Mondale, S., & Patton S. (Eds.). (2001). *The story of American education.* Boston: Beacon Press.

National Commission on Excellence in Education. (1983). *A nation at risk: The imperative for educational reform.* Washington, DC: U.S. Government Printing Office.

Pignatelli, F. (1993). Toward a post-progressive theory of education. *Educational Foundations, 7*(3), 7–26.

Ravitch, D. (2000). *Left back: A century of battles over school reform.* New York: Simon & Schuster.

Ravitch, D. (2001). *Making good citizens: Education and civil society.* New Haven, CT: Yale University Press.

Reese, W. (2005). *America's public schools: From the common school to "no child left behind."* Baltimore, MD: Johns Hopkins University Press.

Rury, J. (2002). *Education and social change: Themes in the history of American schooling.* Mahwah, NJ: Lawrence Erlbaum.

Shipps, D. (2006). *School reform, Chicago style, 1880–2000.* Lawrence, KA: University Press of Kansas.

Spring, J. (2001). *American education.* New York: McGraw-Hill.

Tyack, D. (1974). *The one best system: A history of American urban education.* Cambridge, MA: Harvard University Press.

U.S. Department of Education. (2002). *No child left behind act.* Washington, DC: U.S. Government Printing Office.

U.S. Department of Education. (1994). *Goals 2000: Educate America act.* Washington, DC: U.S. Government Printing Office.

Wagner, T., & Vander A. (2001). *Making the grade: Reinventing America's schools.* New York: Routledge.

Weiner, L. (2000). Democracy, pluralism, and schooling: A progressive agenda. *Educational Studies, 31*(3), 212–224.

Weltman, B. (2002). Praxis imperfect: John Goodlad and the social reconstructionist tradition. *Educational Studies, 33*(1), 61–83.

West, E. (1994). *Education and the state: A study in political economy* (3rd ed.). Indianapolis, IN: Liberty Fund Books.

Yecke, C. (2003). *The war against excellence: The rising tide of mediocrity in America's middle schools.* New York: Praeger.

Zimmerman, J. (2002). *Whose America?: Culture wars in the public schools.* Cambridge, MA: Harvard University Press.

On politics and processes of education reform:

Borman, K. et al. (Eds.). (1996). *Implementing educational reform: Sociological perspectives on educational policy.* Norwood, NJ: Ablex Publishing.

Brerkman, M., & Plutzer, E. (2004). *Ten thousand democracies: Politics and public opinion in American's school districts.* Washington, DC: Georgetown University Press.

Cross, C. (2004). *Political education: National policy comes of age.* New York: Teachers College Press.

Deckman, M. (2003). *School board battles: The Christian right in local politics.* Washington, DC: Georgetown University Press.

Elmore, R. (2004). *School reform from the inside out: Policy, practice, and performance.* Cambridge, MA: Harvard Education Publishing Group.

Fink, D. (2000). *Good schools/real schools: Why school reform doesn't last.* New York: Teachers College Press.

Fullan, M. (2001). *The new meaning of educational change.* New York: Teachers College Press.

Fullan, M. (1993). *Change forces: Probing the depths of educational reform.* New York: Routledge Falmer.

Gittell, M. (1998). *Strategies for school reform.* New Haven, CT: Yale University Press.

Gordon, D. (Ed.). (2003). *A nation reformed: American education twenty years after A nation at risk.* Cambridge, MA: Harvard University Press.

Grindle, M. (2004). *Despite the odds: The contentious politics of school reform.* Princeton, NJ: Princeton University Press.

Hayes, W. (2004). *Are we still a nation at risk two decades later?* Lanham, MD: Scarecrow Press.

Hess, S. (1999). *Spinning wheels: The politics of urban school reform.* Washington, DC: Brookings Institution.

Hess, F. (2006). *Common sense school reform.* New York: Palgrave Macmillan.

Johnson, J. et al. (2003). *Where are we now: 12 things you need to know about public opinion and public schools.* New York: Public Agenda Press.

Jossey-Bass (2001). *The Jossey-Bass reader on school reform.* San Fransisco, CA: Jossey-Bass.

Kennedy, M. (2005). *Inside teaching: How classroom life undermines reform.* Cambridge, MA: Harvard University Press.

Levin, B. (2001). *Reforming education: From origins to outcomes.* New York: Routledge Falmer.

McAdams, D. (2005). *What school boards can do: Reform governance for urban schools.* New York: Teachers College Press.

McDermott, K. (1999). *Controlling public education: Localism versus equality.* Lawrence, KS: University of Kansas Press.

Mirel, J. (2001). *The evolution of American schools.* New York: Fordham Foundation.

Plaut, S., & Sharkey, N. (2003). *Education policy and practice: Bridging the divide.* Cambridge, MA: Harvard Education Publishing Group.

Ravitch, D. (2005). *Brookings papers on Education Policy 2005.* Washington, DC: Brookings Institution Press.

Sarason, S. (1996). *Revisiting the culture of school and the problem of change.* New York: Teachers College Press.

Sarason, S. (1998). *Political leadership and educational failure.* San Francisco: Jossey-Bass.

Smith, M., Fey, P., Heinecke, W., & Miller-Kahn, L. (2003). *Political spectacle and the fate of American schools.* New York: Routledge Falmer.

Spring, J. (2002). *Political agendas for education: From the religious right to the green party* (2nd ed.). Mahwah, NJ: Erlbaum Associates.

Stone, C. et al. (2001). *Building civic capacity: The politics of reforming urban schools.* Lawrence: University Press of Kansas.

Tyack D., & Cuban, L. (1997). *Tinkering toward utopia: A century of public school reform.* Cambridge, MA: Harvard University Press.

Tyack, D. (1974). *The one best system: A history of American urban education.* Cambridge, MA: Harvard University Press.

Wirt, F., & Kirst, M. *The political dynamics of American education* (2nd ed.). Richmond, CA: McCuthan Publishers.

On the need for systemic reform of public education and democracy:

Anyon, J. (2005). *Radical possibilities: Public policy, urban education, and a new social movement.* New York: Routledge.

Arnot, M. (1997). *Feminist politics and education reform.* London: Taylor & Francis Ltd.

Barry, B. (2004). *Sounds...: Traditional American education reform from the steps of the United States capitol.* Frederick, MD: Publish America.

Berube, M. (2004). *Radical reformers: The influences of the left in American education.* Greenwich, CT: Information Age Publishing.

Burbules N., & Torres C. (2000). *Globalization and education, critical perspectives.* New York: Routledge.

Cossentino, J. (2004). *Talking about a revolution: The languages of education reform.* Albany: State University of New York Press.

Cuban, L. (2003). *Why is it so hard to get good schools?* New York: Teachers College Press.

Evans, R. (2000). *The human side of school change: Reform, resistance, and the real-life problems of innovation.* San Francisco: Jossey-Bass.

Fullan, M. (2001). *The new meaning of educational change.* New York: Teachers College Press.

Furlong, J., & Phillips, R. (Eds.). (2001). *Education, reform and the state.* New York: Routledge.

Goodlad, J. (1997). *In praise of education.* New York: Teachers College Press.

Gordon, D., & Gordon, D. (Eds.). (2003). *A nation reformed: American education 20 years after a Nation at Risk.* Cambridge, MA: Harvard Educational Publishing Group.

Grindle, M. (2004). *Despite the odds: The contentious politics of education reform.* Princeton, NJ: Princeton University Press.

Grubb, W., & Lazerson, M. (2004). *Education gospel: The economic power of schooling.* Cambridge, MA: Harvard University Press.

Gunderson, L., & Holling, C. (2001). *Panarchy: Understanding transformations in human and natural systems.* Washington, DC: Island Press.

Hess, F. (2004). *Common sense school reform.* New York: Palgrave Macmillan.

Jervis, R. (1997). *System effects: Complexity in political and social life.* Princeton, NJ: Princeton University Press.

Leonardo, Z. (2003). *Ideology, discourse, and school reform.* Westport, CT: Praeger Publishers.

Lummis, D. (1996). *Radical democracy.* Ithaca, NY: Cornell University Press.

Macedo, S. et al. (2005). *Democracy at risk.* Washington, DC: Brookings Institution Press.

Nur-Awaleh, M. (2005). *International education systems and contemporary education reforms.* Lanham, MD: University Press of America.

Nussbaum, M. (1997). *Cultivating humanity: A classical defense of reform in liberal education.* Cambridge, MA: Harvard University Press.

Oakes, J., Hunter, Q., Ryan, S., & Lipton, M. (1999). *Becoming good American schools: The struggle for civic virtue in education reform.* San Francisco: Jossey-Bass.

Oshry, B. (1996). *Seeing systems: Unlocking the mysteries of organizational life.* San Fransisco: Berrett-Koehler Publishers.

Owens, R. (2003). *Organizational behavior in education: Instructional leadership and school reform* (8th ed.). Boston: Allyn & Bacon.

Petrovich, J., & Stuart A. (Ed.). (2005). *Bringing equity back: Research for a new era in American educational policy.* New York: Teachers College Press.

Postman, N. (1996). *The end of education: Redefining the value of school* (reprint ed.). New York: Vintage Books.

Rotberg I. (Ed.). (2004). *Balancing change and tradition in global education reform.* Lanham, MD: Rowman & Littlefield.

Rothstein R. (2004). *Class and schools: Using social, economic, and educational reform to close the black-white achievement gap.* New York: Teachers College Press.

Schlechty, P. (2004). *Shaking up the schoolhouse: How to support and sustain educational innovation.* Hoboken, NJ: John Wiley & Sons, Inc.

Schwartz, J. (2005). *Freedom reclaimed: Rediscovering the American vision.* Baltimore, MD: The Johns Hopkins University Press.

Sterling, S. (2001). *Sustainable education: Re-visioning learning and change.* Devon, UK: Green Books.

Reflection

Dewey, J. (1916/1984). *Democracy and education* (p. 83). New York: Macmillan.

c h a p t e r   2

Crisis

A time of consequence and change, challenge and choice
anticipating, opposing, then engulfed in the loss
drawn to the call to conserve and retreat
as trusted paths are now blocked
the way is not clear.

He lost. A poll in the last week of the campaign indicated that Jonathan Caine could "suffer a surprising major upset." He had campaigned nonstop, approaching the limits of his stamina and coherence. But in that last week he didn't close the predicted gap. He wasn't sure he'd taken seriously the opinion poll predictions that dominated the media and panicked his advisors. He wondered about the polls and their predictions. Later he could sort out what any prediction, not only election forecasts, actually meant.

He had told himself over the last weekend that he was prepared for a loss. But when the result became apparent early Tuesday evening, it brought surprising feelings: deep disappointment, an inescapable sense of humiliation, flooding regret, and maybe even a little suspicion of betrayal. While he gave a graceful speech later that night congratulating his opponent, Jonathan Caine had not yet begun to accept defeat.

Intellectually, he knew that even partially expected losses are displacing. But this feeling state was strange to him. The words he heard from others

Re-Envisioning Education and Democracy, pages 15–26
Copyright © 2006 by Information Age Publishing
All rights of reproduction in any form reserved.

and those he uttered in public places and in private conversations over the next few days sounded odd. They were more like echoes of someone else's voice: words, sentences, even paragraphs. Somehow they were not connecting directly to his intentions or especially to his emotions. All the post-election analyses with their second and third thoughts and second and third guesses about strategies, tactics, and detailed meanings of the results did not reach him. The intensity of planning sessions that had so absorbed him during the campaign was distant for him as his staff and others tried to make sense of the election and fix blame.

He read. He listened politely. He conversed. He even joked. But he was nearly numb about reconstructing the past and was increasingly disinterested in pouring over the numbers. He was tired, hurt, and confused.

Later that week, Caine approached an interview with reluctance. Karla Morgan was an experienced political reporter who also wrote a weekly editorial page column read by everyone in politics. They met in a downtown coffee shop where Karla began with an expected question: "Senator Caine, does this loss mean you're through with public life? I hear you're going back to lawyering, but only for half time at first. Right?"

He nodded and then put up his hand. He tried a smile that he hoped looked sincere. "Let me talk with you off-the-record for a little while. I'll go on the record later if you wish."

She nodded slowly, tried a smile, and hoped she didn't look too skeptical. "Fine," she said as she put down her pen and notebook and looked at him intently.

"Yes, of course I'm disappointed. I feel, well, humiliated. I know I'm still the better person to lead the Senate on education for these next few years."

Karla let his pause linger and then prompted quietly, "The new Chair of the Education Committee will be less experienced and certainly more to the right than you were. But maybe he'll be closer to where the citizens seem to be."

She wasn't sure Caine had actually heard her as he continued, "Look, we all know that public education is in crisis. It's not just campaign rhetoric! We were ready to move on some important policies and now all that's completely out of reach. There are a hundred, maybe more, little and big tactical things that keep popping up from the campaign, mostly as "We should haves" or "We shouldn't haves." All along I told myself that I was running because the agenda was important, especially the public education issues. I was confident that I could continue to make a difference. But I lost by almost three percent. I know, that's not exactly a landslide, but it wasn't really that close either. Look, I couldn't get even half of the voters to acknowledge my record, understand my vision, and then vote for me."

"Well, consider what was happening around the country and the state-wide shift away from your party in this election," Karla said. "You weren't the only incumbent upset."

"Sure there are trends, but this was my race and I lost it. Katherine Hart-man didn't raise much more money than I did. I probably should have responded more sharply in the debates and especially to some of her TV spots—especially the ones she ran during the last week. Maybe there was also a gender thing. . . ."

"Well, you did look a little uncomfortable sometimes at your joint appearances, but then that's true for all you guys of a certain age. She didn't once say, "it's time for an experienced, qualified woman to represent this Senate District." Besides, you agree she is qualified and politically skill-ful, and she did offer direct, simple positions on things most voters seem to care about."

"But education and all the other issues aren't simple. They're really complicated!" he retorted. "She made it sound like we could make a few changes and solve everything. It sounded like a 'one size fits all' appeal. There really is a crisis and it is really complicated!"

"Yes it is complicated, but you sent all sorts of signals of ambivalence and uncertainty. No matter what you said in speeches about your policy record, it's how you framed your ads that probably mattered most. You told voters that you wanted to explore issues with them and she told them about clear, direct positions. You talked a lot about 'process' and she called that kind of talk 'just more politics as usual.'"

"She just told voters what they wanted to hear!" he snapped.

"Maybe not—I'm not so sure she did. You know what the exit polls showed in your district and across the state about the late deciding voters and all those new, first time voters. Most felt you were too vague and, well, indecisive. Strong political leaders don't leave the impression that they don't know exactly what to do. To a lot of the voters—the majority—you were probably seen as just another incumbent; another "bleeding heart, tax and spend, old fashioned fuzzy minded liberal."

"I suppose so," he muttered. "I should know politics is always about ste-reotypes. But the polls showed that swing voters and the new voters gener-ally agreed that education is a high priority. Hell, Katharine and I even agreed, during those so-called debates your paper staged on public televi-sion, that education was the main issue."

Karla thought about responding to his media attack diversion, but thought it better to keep Caine on track. "Sure," she continued, "but she gave the impression she knew what to do. Even though her main theme was to cut state and local taxes, she came off as credible, sincere, and practical on education. Hartman delivered punchy advocacy on school vouchers, cor-porate–public partnerships, some very good stuff on school violence, a tough line on classroom discipline, the need for a core curricula, and more rigorous test-based standards for students and for teachers too."

Caine stared down at his coffee. "I know that there will be a huge conflict around those issues in both houses. And I know they'll probably be able to push some of that stuff through." He slumped over the table as he continued, "They make it seem so simple. Like the shootings in the schools around the country—as if all that could be stopped with slogans! And standardized tests? Testing is painfully complex and "results" aren't so easy to interpret. In the Senate we were beginning to shape more research-based, more community connected, more bottom-up accountability policies. What will become of all that?"

Picking up her notebook and pen, Karla said firmly, "Let's go back on the record now, I do have a deadline—yours may not be so pressing."

He looked at her warily.

"Some have said that you now face three choices, Senator Caine. First, you could pack-up all those shiny appreciation plaques you've received over the years, put them in your attic, and leave public life. Your law partners would like that."

"Second, you could gear up to rerun for the legislature, maybe for a house seat in two years. But you'd need to move more toward the center—where this, and most, elections are won."

"Third, you might find another way to continue with the education issues you care about by writing and speaking out. You could easily join one of the public affairs think tanks around town."

"I've always hated multiple choice tests," Caine tried to joke.

"And now I have the lead for my story," Karla concluded.

> *The energy explodes, then forcefully contracts*
> *propelled into heightened awareness*
> *of pain, paralysis, confusion and doubt*
> *amid the sharp edges of shattered dreams*
> *paths toward stagnation or transformation are chosen.*

While he had picked up pieces of his law practice with little effort, Caine was deeply preoccupied with what was to become of his public life. He had been in the Senate for twelve years and active in civic affairs long before he first ran for office. "That's a lot of momentum," he thought. While education had become his political identity partly out of opportunity and ambition, he came to realize that his concerns for education and democracy were deeper and more resonant than his recent campaign.

The disappointment of his defeat lingered. Cleaning out his senate office and saying "See you soon!" to his former staff and colleagues was more wrenching than he let show. In his head, he often found himself beginning to plan an Education Committee meeting or starting to rehearse what he would say to his party colleagues in the Caucus. Acknowledging that those were no longer his places for action came with agonizing slowness.

As he was putting the last box of office things into his car in the Capitol Parking Ramp, Jim MacIver, an important campaign supporter, drove by. Barely slowing, he leaned out of the window of his aging van and shouted, "Jon, we have a lot to talk about. Things have really changed!"

Before he could even acknowledge the rapid-fire bursts, MacIver drove off. As Caine turned to close the trunk, he noticed his parking sticker was no longer valid.

Later that week he sat down with Jim at the Lifelong Education Advancing Democracy offices. Caine wondered if he had become overly sensitive. Were the smiles on the familiar faces of the people in the outer office a bit strained? Were their friendly greetings a little hollow? Did they turn back to their desks a bit too quickly?

LEAD was a coalition of progressive groups that had initially formed as a broad social reform organization with advancing democracy through education as its overarching objective. Over the years it proposed many wide-ranging programs in the metropolitan area and had become identified as a highly visible advocate for social justice. Jim MacIver has been Executive Director for the past eight years. He was an imaginative and energetic coalition leader who had been instrumental in bringing LEAD into direct involvement with election campaigns that shared the coalition's objectives.

Jim characteristically minimized opening small talk and polite regrets over the election results. His eyes did not immediately meet Caine's. They seemed to wander over the colorful LEAD posters on the walls as he quickly reverted to his rapid-fire, list-like speaking style.

"OK Jon, so you weren't the only educational reformer who lost. We're in for serious trouble with the next Legislature—probably in for even bigger trouble now with the bureaucracy—and it's happening to progressives all around the country.

"You already know about your successor as Chair of the Senate Education Committee," Jim rushed on. "He's really bad news! The likely appointee for State Commissioner of Education is about as close to a complete privatizer as we can imagine. Vouchers, more testing, and contracting out for services are only the start for him. He's going to be even worse news!"

"And the Governor has painted the Teachers Union into a corner—with a lot of help from them, I must say—now their salaries and benefits are their only visible issues. They're below the horizon for us—at least for a while."

"And our Governor, who ruled out any tax increases, has already begun to detail his tax cuts that would freeze education funding at current budget levels. And you know he'll try to pour big money into one of the voucher schemes. That leaves us with '*nada*' to show for the initiatives we've been killing ourselves over all these years."

Pointing in the direction of the Capitol, Jim hurried on. "Just about everyone over there is fixated on the testing—tests for students' promotion and graduation as well as much stiffer testing for teachers when they are first licensed as well as throughout their careers—even tests for principals."

"Maybe testing principals is not such a bad idea," Caine joked with a small smile.

Jim didn't smile back. "And a good number of them up there, maybe even a majority now, want to end district-wide desegregation and, as they say, "return to neighborhood schools." Not only do the polls show a lot of support for that retreat statewide, some really prominent people in our own communities-of-color think so too.

"Then, there is the rejuvenated 'back to basics' crowd... I'm still not sure exactly what 'basics' are supposed to be." Now he was smiling tensely. "They sure are eager to go back: back before sex-education, back before site councils, and, for sure, back before any programs on 'diversity.'"

He seemed to pause for effect, and then said, "Zero-tolerance in this legislature probably means far more than an attitude toward school violence or drugs. Teaching evolution is being contested again. And even the school prayer advocates are getting respectful media attention as if the Bill of Rights was just one obsolete point of view."

"Look, I tried to deal with those in the campaign...." Caine muttered. Jim interrupted immediately. "Stop. Let's not talk about the campaign. Karla Morgan's column on you this morning puts all that behind us. You did have a good legislative record. You really did have what she called a "broad vision for public education." But, as she wrote, in this last campaign you seemed unsure and ambivalent. Katherine Hartman beat you. Morgan is right—the choices between you two turned out to be pretty clear. And you lost. And a lot of us, and not just in your district, lost a lot too. It was not just you, Jon—all of us lost!"

"You make it sound like I should apologize." Caine murmured.

"Nope! It's just time to find other ways to do what we care about. We probably should have started sooner, even before this last election. I know now that we put way too much of our effort into electoral politics; too much into trying sounding good to everybody; too much appeasing and not enough confronting. I also know now we're really not cut out to be a campaign and election shop. We were trying to do too much on too many fronts. We've got to focus, and keep LEAD moving ahead."

Jim turned back to Caine and asked, "So, Jon, what do you plan to do now?"

"I really don't know . . ." Caine said slowly. "The things that used to make so much sense just don't seem to connect with me now. I think I need to talk around some more. I'd like to consult with some of your coalition members who have held LEAD together all these years."

"Of course. But remember, the election is the past, Jon. LEAD is going to do some other things—we have plans—like picking up the ball on a really important charter school idea. We need to move on recruiting and training leaders for social reform."

"Yeah, I guess you're right Jim. I've got to move on. We all must move on."

Given the exploratory nature of democratic learning and living,
why do we focus our reform efforts on acquiring
greater certainty and control?

In education, as in other policy areas, we experience loss of certainty and control as unexpected and undesirable. When confronted with complex public concerns, our governing impulses are to limit forms of thought, expression, and activity. There are so many claims voiced and so many possibilities to consider. Options are elusive and consequences unpredictable. With the stakes so high and projected impacts so pervasive, we can afford neither to hesitate nor to err. We acquire both a heightened sense of urgency and reduced tolerance for ambiguity. We tell ourselves that such responses are necessary because we have reached a point of crisis.

On a personal level, we respond to crises by struggling to restore balance—to reduce feelings of uncertainty, even panic. We seek solace and shelter. On a societal level, our responses to crises feature attempts to simplify causes, to fix blame, to advance our skills in prediction and prevention, to collect information and exercise caution. We seek decisive leadership and straightforward solutions.

Crises are particularly challenging for democracies. The resonating tension in democratic education, politics, and governance revolves around *who* gets to shape the response. As we broaden the scope of participation to include diverse visions and voices we find ourselves confronted with many contradictions but little consensus; with many tangents but little time. We struggle to restore balance by reverting to habitual preferences for centralized authority and control. "Somebody needs to take charge!" is the dominant advice. Usually, the 'somebody taking charge' turns out to be a small few—experts sometimes, central political leaders more often, and charismatic types occasionally. During turbulent periods, advocates for specific solutions—from privatization, to back to basics, to particular testing programs—become visibly active. School administrators attempt to exert greater control over the agenda as resources diminish. The mass media seeks out the more articulate or the most controversial players such as a school superintendent, an influential board member, or a political figure. Journalists then focus on personalities and conflicts.

We have often been told that times of crisis are times of significant change. The evidence indicates that this is rarely the case. Restoration—emotionally, intellectually, and institutionally—is the dominant response. Familiar structures and strategies are sought and quickly imposed. While crises can inspire visionary thought and action, most often we attempt to restore—we seek to reclaim the clarity and confidence we thought we once had.

Ambiguity...
to explore, to gather, to hold, to engage
dynamically varied and valid truths
multiple meanings, dimensions, possibilities and plans,
though confronted with confusion and doubt
principled action is still required
moving beyond illusions of certainty, of fully formed understandings
we learn to seek glimpse gates.

Especially during times of stress, we turn to centralization and standardization as means of restoring *social unity*, achieving *efficacy*, and regaining a sense of *security*. We entrust our public institutions with the highly complex tasks of clarifying communal priorities and then implementing reliable processes through which we may pursue our shared aspirations with confidence. We claim that we want equality and fairness as standards of opportunity and performance in all aspects of our lives.

Social unity is established through efforts to cultivate and sustain a sense of shared purpose that transcends differences in background, experience, and perspective. In democratic societies, unity of purpose is primarily centered in the concept of "equal rights." Given a rights-based emphasis, we look to public schools, political processes, and government agencies to ensure that all are treated in a manner that is fair, respectful, and responsive to individual needs and interests. Standardization is alleged to promote social unity because it promises equal access, treatment, and interpretation of results.

Political centralization facilitates many aspects of social unity by preempting the expression of diverse or antagonistic values in public policy. Nationally mandated school desegregation plans and state legislated performance standards are major examples of this process. Some localized discretion always remains—at the school district level, at each school site, and even in individual classrooms. And central authority—from federal mandates to state guidelines to school district directives—is always contested. Nonetheless, there is often at least 'official consensus' on primary objectives, on programs targeted to achieve these, and on outcome measures deemed appropriate for assessment. Broad societal consensus, however, is always fragile and especially unstable during times of acute challenge.

In democratic societies, *social efficacy* is approached by developing efficient and reliable processes that are described and managed in mostly economic terms. Standardized approaches to accountability, managed by central authorities, are justified politically and operationally as the most effective and efficient ways to administer public policy. We look to government agencies to ensure that human service systems—including public education—run smoothly, predictably, and in a cost-effective manner. Issues and opportunities are driven by "the budget" and in times of fiscal constraint, increased centralization is the dominant response. Despite public declarations to the contrary, intensified competition for limited funds is often managed by shifting money away from classroom instruction to fund administrative imperatives to document performance. This tactic is assumed to be necessary to improve fiscal accountability and to enhance school productivity. It is usually accompanied by attempts to simplify priorities, reduce variation, and provide assurance that nothing frivolous or wasteful will be tolerated.

Standardization is alleged to promote social efficacy because it assumes the possibility of collecting the information necessary to support the careful design of solutions that can be predictably and routinely applied. But information is always incomplete and complex implementations are agonizingly difficult to measure. Changing life contexts and circumstances defy attempts to attain simplicity and permanence in policy or practice. Genuine accountability practices are not yet realized in our public institutions. Still, we persistently seek to resolve ambiguities through standardization.

Experience teaches, however, that providing access to the same resources and judging all in relation to the same criterion does not result in similar opportunities for, or experiences of, success. Personal, cultural, and economic differences sharply challenge efforts to realize social justice through standardized opportunities, programs, and assessments.

Particularly during times experienced as 'crises', we return to our well-rehearsed rituals of redefining objectives, narrowing standards, and looking to centralized authority in part because each offers a sense of *security*. We attempt to reduce variation in interpretations and to concentrate authority for action. In our political and educational lives, we do not tolerate ambiguity well.

Yet ambiguity is a constant reality. It can become a source of strength. Working through crises in education and democracy requires shifting our expectations and patterns of participation. Ambiguity is an indispensable resource for re-envisioning. Certainty and control are never simple and always elusive.

> *"Without uncertainty,*
> *love,*
> *which always entails risks*
> *as well as the joys of discovery,*
> *loses its sharp edge."*
>
> —Jacque Dreze
> *Essays on Economic Decisions Under Uncertainty*

Exploratory Democratic Practice: Anticipatory Thank You Notes

In the urgencies and uncertainties of a crisis, it is useful to think backward and forward in time about causes, consequences, and opportunities. One productive direction for strategic conversation is the mutual acknowledgement of principal actors—the institutions, organizations, groups, and persons involved.

Participants might begin by discussing:

- Who were, are, and could be the key players in the crisis and its possible resolution?
- What roles did, do, and could they enact?

Given this preliminary identification, it is then useful to envision possible avenues for future action. In conversation, participants are encouraged to draft and edit brief *anticipatory thank you notes* to those who could contribute to resolving the crisis.

For each note it is useful to:

- Identify the role, and for what contribution, this anticipatory gratitude is to be expressed.

An appreciative understanding of supporters as well as opponents, and even those indifferent to a particular policy, program, or reform initiative, is useful in crisis resolution.

Thematic Bibliographic References

On complexity and ambiguity in public policy:

Connolly, W. (1991). *Identity/difference: Democratic negotiations of political paradox.* Ithaca, NY: Cornell University Press.

Cross, C. (2004). *Political education: National policy comes of age.* New York: Teachers College Press.

Gregg, B. (2004). *Coping in politics with indeterminate norms: A theory of enlightened localism.* Albany: State University of New York Press.

Heck, R. (2004). *Studying educational and social policy: Theoretical concepts and research methods.* Mahwah, NJ: Lawrence Erlbaum Associates.

Holland, J. (1996). *Hidden order: How adaptation builds complexity.* Cartersville, GA: Addison Wesley Publishing.

Leonardo, Z. (2003). *Ideology, discourse, and school reform.* Westport, CT: Praeger Publishers.

Loveless, T. (2002). *Conflicting missions: Teachers' unions and educational reform.* Washington, DC: Brookings Institution.

Lowi, T. (1979). *The end of liberalism: The second republic of the United States.* New York: Norton.

Paris, D. (1995). *Ideology and educational reform: Themes and theories in public education.* New York: Perseus Books.

Petrovich J., & Stuart, A. (Eds.). (2005). *Bringing equity back: Research for a new era in American education policy.* New York: Teachers College Press.

Seashore, K. (1998). A light feeling of chaos: Educational reform and policy in the United States. *Daedalus, 127*(4), 13–41.

Stein, S. (2004). *The culture of educational policy.* New York: Teachers College Press.

Wallace, M., & Pocklington, K. (2002). *Managing complex educational change: Large scale reorganization of schools.* New York: Routledge Falmer.

On conceptualizations of and responses to crisis:

Glickman, C. (Ed.). (2004). *Letters to the next president: What we can do about the real crisis in public education.* New York: Teachers College Press.

Isaac, J. (1998). *Democracy in dark times.* Ithaca, NY: Cornell University Press.

Reflection:

Dreze, J. (1987). *Essays on economic decisions under uncertainty* (p. 63). Cambridge: Cambridge University Press.

chapter 3

Reflection

Looking forward and looking back
while holding fast to what still remains
brief alignments yield fleeting insights
voices, images, feelings and thoughts
focus and fade
lingering just beyond reach
but not beyond hope.

As the next week passed, Jonathan Caine discovered that his defeat was not as isolating as he had feared. Campaign workers sent regrets and reassurances. A few former Senate colleagues called for advice. Old coalition partners invited him to meetings.

Of these, one meeting in particular turned out to be pivotal. Caine met with Althea Putnam and May Haun-Crawford at Partners in Participation just north of the downtown business district. Putnam was the Executive Director and Haun-Crawford the Board Chair. PIP housed and attempted to integrate a number of government agencies and nonprofit organizations that provided programs for welfare-to-work transitions and addressed the special problems of the working poor. Caine had called Putnam to confirm the appointment and said he might be able to help PIP, maybe with legal work or with advocacy.

Re-Envisioning Education and Democracy, pages 27–46
Copyright © 2006 by Information Age Publishing
All rights of reproduction in any form reserved.

"May is running late again," Althea said as she motioned Caine toward a worn-looking but comfortable chair. Although he had worked with several people in the agencies that occupied the building, this was his first visit.

It was not his first visit with Althea. They had known each other for years, going back to when, as a relatively young preschool teacher, Althea emerged as a gifted advocate for early childhood education. About that time, she became the director of a school-based demonstration project in the same neighborhood where she and Caine now met. That early childhood program, largely due to Althea's expressive skills, grabbed considerable publicity for its innovative strategies and impressive success. The media attention for the program also featured her as a bright, effective administrator deeply connected to her African American community. Althea won a "young leader" fellowship to do graduate work and after getting her degree, she returned to her model preschool project. Two years later she joined others in conceiving, funding, and now directing Partners in Participation.

PIP evolved out of a convergence of frustration and opportunity. Activists in several community organizations and directors of public agencies had found coordinating programs for individual clients to be nearly impossible. Public and non-governmental policies and service programs seldom meshed to provide the needed comprehensive support for people moving, as the politicians liked to put it, "from welfare to work." The agencies were scattered across town. Clients had to arrange many trips, mostly on erratic mass transit. However well motivated, the programs were designed and delivered almost entirely by professionals largely distanced from the communities, the lived experiences, and the particular situations of the clients they worked so hard to serve.

Partners in Participation had been formed in part to include those who were not only under-served but also under-represented. Its goals included reforming decision-making and program implementation to be more inclusive and representative of the 'targeted working poor.' PIP now provided a central location for all of the largest public assistance providers. Most clients now had a one-stop location for almost all of their services. Communication between the organizations was in principle much easier with everyone at the same site. A coordinating council with agency administrators and client representatives met monthly.

"May is hung up with her county human services buddies downtown," Althea announced. "She'll be here as soon as she can. Jon, we're both really sorry you lost and very interested in what you want to talk with us about. So, you'd like to be a lobbyist?"

Caine looked startled and said, "I'm not sure I had that in mind."

In Althea's mind, a jumble of things—shifting thoughts and feelings— were still eluding words and some semblance of sentence structure. She wasn't sure that lobbying would be Caine's best move. But why had he looked surprised when she mentioned it? Lobbying could exploit his impressive political connections and his formidable skills. Why, then, were both of them now hesitant about that prospect? Caine could do a lot of good for PIP. But what was PIP good for? She couldn't seem to focus on that, so she said, "Then what else do you have in mind, Jon?"

As she listened to Caine repeat and then elaborate on the familiar goals they shared, the snarled web in her head continued its pre-verbal spinning. Why was she identifying with what seemed to be Jon's drifting uncertainties? Why did PIP seem such an uncertain prospect for her today? Caine was saying that PIP was an important accomplishment with lots more potential. Of course! Was that right? Why did she now find herself questioning the value of a program she'd worked so hard to build? As Caine concluded recounting his commitments, Althea asked: "So, are you still making campaign speeches Jon?"

"Give me a break, Althea. I'm still smarting from the election. I'm not used to losing. I still think there are important things to do—not just coping, but some significant changes."

"Big job, Jon. Doesn't coping usually mean pulling in and trying to re-energize our existing strengths? Getting back to where we were? Beyond coping? Oh? Is that really the path you want to go down?" She paused to smile, "You know better than I do that deep thinking doesn't get us very far politically. Everything moves pretty slowly and on the surface, right? Rocking the boat at times like this is pretty risky. All of us activist types agree that we benefit from not thinking too much . . . at least out loud and never in public. We never want to be labeled too 'intellectual,' 'too far ahead of the times,' and certainly never as a 'liberal.'"

"Yeah, but I've got to do something besides being another rainmaker for my law partners. OK, so I know my way around the capitol. Maybe I can be of some use to PIP up there. I've also begun talking with Jim and the folks at LEAD. He's thinking about some new education initiative and wants me to part of that."

"As a lobbyist?" Althea asked.

"I don't know. Well, I just don't like the sound of the word 'lobbyist.' But I can't let go of all the things we all were working on . . . the things we sacrificed for . . . all the things we still need to defend . . . all those things we know are at risk!"

With just a hint of irritation in her voice that was more for herself than for him, Althea said, "You seem to want to continue your focus on education, right? What is it about public education that separates this particular time, right now, from our long history with it? Why is it more important now than what we do here at PIP with our welfare-to-work programs—most of which, Jon, are in their own way about education? Why do you think this is a decisive time or even a good time to advocate for public education? Is education really in crisis? Or is education a 'just coping' opportunity for you now?"

Her scatter of direct, almost impertinent questions silenced him and gave Althea a moment to attend to her own thoughts. PIP was really mostly about coping. Yes, it enabled some more tightly integrated services and provided a little more interaction among all the players—from policy makers to the administrators to the clients themselves. PIP was widely seen as a successful demonstration project. Oh, that word: 'demonstration!' Her preschool initiative had been called that too. But it hadn't spread much beyond that site. It had been visited, written up in professional journals, featured on local television, and even won several national prizes. It was still operating a few blocks down the street from PIP—still struggling and still coping. She had hoped for a *movement* to develop from what she began as a creative collaborative approach to early childhood teaching and learning. But it hadn't changed much, nor had it been adopted as a model elsewhere. The program had achieved a kind of stability—nearing institutionalization. It was a good place. She was proud of it. Yet after the kids went into the elementary grades, there was nothing like it to support them and their struggling families. Sure, not all of them needed such labor-intensive attention, but many of them still did. And she knew they weren't going to get it. The fate of those kids she first knew as toddlers troubled her.

Putting PIP into motion was about the fate of those kids and their families. It was really hard work—all the effort, all the hours, and all the disappointments. But there were some amazing successes. The clients were better off. The agencies were more satisfied. So why all these feelings of doubt? So much was going on! Was PIP still moving forward? Or was it just hovering?

Caine brought her attention back to the conversation, as he spoke again, "Typical tough questions from you Althea! That's what old friends are for. Maybe I am in some kind of recovery period, I don't know. Maybe it's just a longtime habit to be concerned and wanting to stay active. I've always been involved in civic life. In politics, it seems, we are only drawn into action when issues are said to be "in crisis." And we both know there are urgent chronic problems with big consequences if we don't solve them. Public education is surely one of those—and I think it's the most important one. Some of us always try to fix the important things we know are broken." He paused. "And I do know how to do some things—even though I lost the election."

"Yes, you do, Jon," Althea said soothingly. "You have an enviable record. But all of us, not just you politicians and lawyers," she continued quietly, "talk policy talk, including education policy, in a kind of "we professionals can fix it" language. I find myself doing that all the time here too. We move in a pretty top-down 'walk' despite all of our self-righteous 'talk' to the contrary. Sure, we really do want to be more inclusive, more democratic . . . but we are professionals . . . we do know important things and have experience . . . and we have authority. We take and maybe make opportunities to act on what we think we know. All of our democratic talk about being inclusive and especially about such things as 'citizenship' and 'rights' and 'empowerment' . . . all that's truly complex! I wonder if even here, at PIP, we can do much along those lines. We have the structures to support broader representation and input, but I don't know if we really are more inclusive. PIP still has a lot of top-down movement. We began with a big vision but we always seem to be stuck with small changes that don't seem to matter that much beyond a particular problem or a particular client. Maybe that's the real 'crisis'."

May Haun-Crawford breezed into the room and landed in a chair between the two.

"Crisis? You people talking crisis? Crises! What else is new besides crisis in our business?"

May was a co-founder and now the Chair of the Board of PIP. While Althea had resigned from the public school system to help establish the program, May had kept her position with the county's Human Services Department. She insisted that a partnership meant bridging several organizations. She was good at bridging—at crossing generations in her work with all age groups, and she was good at building bridges to connect races, classes, and cultures including those three tensions in her own marriage.

May continued briskly. "Besides our perennial crises, guys, where are we? So, Jon, you've agreed to help us?"

Caine said nothing but looked through window into the late November gloom.

"Jon's thinking of lobbying for us," Althea said with a small smile.

May looked intently at him. "Great! You know everybody who counts in and around town and in government. You sure you want to lobby? Of course you do and we sure need your help. PIP always needs more help!"

Both Althea and Caine remained silent.

"PIP needs lots of help," May repeated. "We're doing so many good things and we have a lot to protect—including protection from those people in power in Washington and now back here too. And Jon, you have the smarts, all the moves, all that experience, and a great network. You'll be a dynamite lobbyist."

Althea looked troubled. "Before we do our well-rehearsed PIP welfare-to-work counseling job on Jon, let's consider a few things."

May and Jon looked at her expectantly.

"I love PIP and am just as proud as you are, May, of what we've done and what we're doing. You're right, of course, PIP does need protection and continuing development. Everything valuable always does. But PIP is pretty stable, pretty well accepted now. It's really part of the 'system' even though we don't like to think so. What we like is to feel righteously embattled most of the time. . . ."

"Althea, get real!" May exploded. "We *are* under attack! We're *not* part of the system! Jon here just lost big in an election about the very things we care about most. The people who won this election are out to get us!"

"Hold on May. We can march to the battlefield later. I still need to think out loud. PIP has positive inertia and of course there is always opposition. Maybe worse, there's a lot of indifference. PIP is working, with a constant struggle. Still, we're accomplishing a lot. But our 'get-out-the-vote' effort only got a few more of our clients to the polls. Too bad they didn't all live in Jon's district. Sure, we need preventative maintenance that a good lobbyist could help with. Yes, we do need real expertise, maybe like Jon's, and a lot of new energy too."

"So . . . what's the point, Althea?" May asked as she reflexively looked at her watch.

"The point is, May, that for all of the uncountable hours, all of everyone's amazing efforts, and even with what we think of as our success, we aren't getting anywhere close to real reform."

"But of course PIP has been a successful reform," Caine stated confidently.

"You bet we're successful," May broke in. "But we're also fragile."

"I worry about our fate, too," Althea said to May, "and I always wonder what else needs to be done that PIP can't quite get at. Look, the agencies here are busy doing their thing and protecting their turf. We've got a little more cooperation, but we're a long way from changing the system. We said we'd work toward that—toward structural reform—when we started PIP. What we have at PIP are many good people doing many good things, but they are still isolated and often self-regarding. Our Coordinating Council looks good on paper, but it's not very influential. We got the agencies and their clients into the same building, but not into the same program."

"I don't believe this, Althea," May said disgustedly. "The feds talk up our approach all around the country. The state and county agencies are ecstatic. The agencies here are more satisfied, and the clients have easier access to what they need. What's with you?"

"Look May, I agree we've had some success. We're certainly accepted. Maybe PIP is about as good as it can get. But maybe I just want more. I don't know."

Caine used his lawyer voice to say, "PIP is successful and there is much yet to be done. Just look at the lack of affordable housing and the erosion of desegregation. We must keep moving on with what already works. This place works. We've got to keep at it!"

"And keeping at it is a battle!" May added.

"Jon, you mentioned some of Jim MacIver's LEAD programs. Jim always talks about deep democracy and radical reform. But do even his impressive programs add up to something like comprehensive change?" Althea asked urgently. "Sure all of us, LEAD and here at PIP too, have some niche successes."

May exploded again. "Niche successes? Althea, you sound like one of those MBA types babbling about some retail mall strategy or positioning one of those dot.com start-ups they used to love so much. I don't like this talk."

Althea paused. "Well, this is kind of a campaign isn't it? Not the type of campaign Jon is used to...not something that can be seen very well through market lenses. Maybe there is a new set of openings that wasn't there before—something like what the Internet is supposed to represent in the global economy. Maybe there's a different way to connect. Perhaps we need new kinds of persuasion. Maybe we need new kinds of organizations, with new approaches and different tactics. I don't know. I really don't! Sorry, I just feel unsettled today. I don't think Jon is the only one who needs to consider new ways of getting things done."

May cut off what looked liked a response from Caine with characteristic swift intensity. "All right, let's get back on task, people! PIP still deserves our best shot. Much of this place is your vision and a result of your incredible work, Althea. Take your little philosophy break or whatever this has been, but keep your eye on the ball! This is definitely not the time for job counseling for any of us. We've got a lot more work to do! PIP is one of the most important programs around and we all know it! Hey, we'll plan on you lobbying for us, right Jon? See you guys, I gotta run!"

And she did.

Before the winter, after the storm
energy still focused, convergent, contained
evolves within existing constraints
hesitant strivings
gently push the boundaries.

"As I said, Jon, you can still be useful," Jim MacIver noted as he looked around the table in LEAD's scruffy conference room. "I think you'll want to join LEAD's Charter School Board, but it'll be great if you can also lobby for us." He looked at Althea and added, "And, oh, its all right if you lobby for PIP, too."

"I'm not sure about the lobbying," Caine murmured.

"Thanks for allowing Jon to help PIP, too," Althea interjected with a slightly sarcastic smile.

"We're all in this together," Jim responded without a smile.

Two others sat at the table. Roberta Williams was LEAD's Educational Programs Coordinator. She had worked on many progressive education projects with LEAD's coalition partners, including two now housed in Althea's Partners in Participation building. Bobbi (don't call me Roberta!) had produced most of the background materials now stacked in neat piles in front of MacIver.

The second person was new to both Caine and Althea. "You'll like Kirk," Jim had said earlier. "He talks a little weird—drives Bobbi nuts! But he's a genius . . . a real artist with his videocam, or whatever, and a wonder with those kids."

'Those kids' referred to middle school students at the Building Visions Workshop—a joint venture between the public schools and the county's Juvenile Justice Department. Kirk Peterson was the 'video artist in residence' who worked with 'kids at risk'—those who had been identified either in their school or through the courts as youth with difficult behavior problems, particularly those prone to violence.

Slouched in his chair, Kirk seemed amused by the situation as he said quietly, "Would you like me to talk weird now, Jim?"

"In a minute." Jim said again without smiling. "First I want to make sure that we all understand the 'basics' of charter school legislation. First, in this state anybody can propose a charter school, including established coalitions like LEAD. Second, a complete program proposal must be submitted and reviewed by the School District and then by the State Department of Education. Third, if our proposal gets approved by the bureaucrats, then the new school gets some start-up money, plus about the same annual per student allocation as any other public school. A charter school can also apply to our legislature for a year or two of supplemental program money. Fourth, the charter school gets a little elbowroom in and among all those rules and regulations handed down by the state education establishment. But while it can have an emphasis, it can't just select students on narrow criteria. Fifth, that flexibility includes more control over hiring, like not having to hire a lot of supporting staff, or hire only licensed teachers or union members."

Althea looked at Caine and with a small smile said quietly to him, "Didn't you write that legislation Jon?"

Caine returned the smile and nodded. Jim ignored the byplay, but before he could resume Caine spoke. "This charter school idea is interesting, Jim, but isn't it a kind of departure for LEAD?"

"What do you mean? The 'L' in LEAD can also mean 'Leadership'. That requires recruiting and training leaders for progressive community action.

We've always had that in our mission. Our coalition members and other groups desperately need to cycle in new leadership and this charter school will do that."

Caine nodded as he said, "Well, this does look a little self-serving, maybe even a lot narrower than what LEAD has done in the past."

He tried to continue but Jim rushed on, "LEAD must focus! We and our member organizations are being crunched. We lost big time in that election you were part of Jon. Election campaigns are a lost cause for LEAD. Funds are being drastically cut. Deficits at all levels are used to purge progressive programs. We should continue to complain, loudly, but this charter school is something we can do right now. The opposition has all those elite private schools where they send their kids. There'll probably be a big voucher program in the next couple of years to cream off still more kids. Well, we can cream too . . . we have to! We have to find and support the next generation of progressive leaders. A charter school is doable. It will enable us to fight back!"

Everyone at the table except Jim looked a bit puzzled. He continued, "Now, I'd like Bobbi to fill you in on where we are with our LEAD Charter School proposal."

Bobbi made eye contact with everyone around the table before beginning. "All the preliminary applications have been filed. That was routine. We hit all the marks. What we need now is a compelling mission statement and a detailed proposal right down to curriculum, staffing, scheduling, physical plant, and budget. We have to show that we can meet the state's performance and graduation standards—although we don't have to do it exactly the same way as the regular schools do. We need to name a Board for the LEAD School—which will include Althea and Jon, we hope. We have to have our LEAD faculty in place—which we hope includes Kirk. And we're planning to be up and running in September. So we have to deliver the full proposal package to the School Board by the middle of January!"

Jim picked up as Bobbi stopped for breath. "We'll also need to get additional funds from the legislature. The start-up money that goes with a charter school will not be enough. Jon, you'll help with that!"

"Hold on a minute," Caine said. "While this is all highly informative, I do have some concerns. We paved the way for some important new possibilities by pushing through the charter school's legislation—that was one of my own 'pet projects' as you may remember. But I'm also aware that charter schools, however well intentioned, can drain vital resources needed to support other public schools. Some argue, rather persuasively I think, that charter schools typically are designed to cull specific students—what you called "creaming" Jim. And they may even end up re-segregating—by race, by class, by interests, by abilities. There's a lot to be concerned about."

"Yes, there are a lot of minefields around charter schools," Althea broke in. "Of course I like most of what Jim sent us as the mission statement draft, but I too think there are some dangers. Even if we think this is a plausible thing for LEAD to do—and I'm still not sure—how can LEAD put together a complete, detailed, responsible, and feasible proposal in the next six weeks? Where's the school to be located—do you have a building? Who will be the students? How will you recruit them? I know there may be flexibility with staffing, but how can we even think about hiring unlicensed, non-union teachers when the Teachers' Union is a founding member of the LEAD coalition?"

"The Teachers Union is pretty isolated now," Jim said dismissively. "Look at their limited role in the last election or their bad press generally."

A long silence followed Jim's assessment.

"Maybe staff flexibility could be an advantage," Kirk said quietly. "I am an unlicenced, non-union teacher now at Building Visions."

He looked around, but no one spoke so he continued: "I've sort of been inadvertently involved in art education most of my life, even though I didn't get officially certified by anybody for teaching. Now I get to work with these really tough kids in a program housed in a public school. Most of my colleagues are official teachers or whatever—probably union members too. Some are not. I can't tell the difference and I bet our students can't either."

The people around the table were now paying close attention to Kirk.

"I don't know anything about LEAD's history and this political stuff," Kirk continued. "As Jim said, I'm the 'video artist in residence.' It's both a lot like and nothing like anything I've ever done before. But I know more can be done with kids—all kids. I'm not exactly sure why, but this charter school sounds like something I'd really like to be part of."

Jim nodded vigorously.

"And what did you do before Building Visions?" Caine asked

"Well, I grew up in Detroit, in a neighborhood sort of like this one. You know, like a mix of races and new immigrants and a lot of families like mine who'd lived there quite awhile. I was into drawing and painting early, before school, and then got into art things at the community center. I did graffiti before it was, well, trendy. It got me into a ton of trouble! I also liked to do electronic stuff—build gadgets that worked or not, fix things other people threw out. I scavenged a lot. Somewhere along the line a video camera landed in my hands and I have never let go."

"Didn't Jim say you were in art education?" Althea probed.

"Yeah, not like through an official school—you know, through a degree program. I always liked learning but I never liked school. I'm not sure how to say this... hey, I do images, not words. But really early on, even when I was doing graffiti and learning how to make prints, and then later, after I started doing mostly video, I never wanted to do any of it just by myself. I know, I know, art is supposed to be about individual expression and all that. Well, I guess it can be—it is for some. But me, I like putting images and ideas together with other people. I found out that we could learn more about all sorts of things doing art that way. As I told Jim and Bobbi when they asked me if I might be interested in this charter school scheme, I think art—my kind of art anyway—is all about what somebody told me once is called 'social learning.'"

When Kirk concluded, Jim let the silence continue for a while before riveting his gaze on Althea and Caine. "Very soon," he said, "I'll need to know whether I can count on you two. The remarks you made earlier about charter schools are disturbing. How can you even imply that LEAD's core progressive democratic values are not in line with this project? You know better than that! We don't need wasteful diversions here. We need to crank-out a killer proposal and get our school going. This is our big opportunity! This school is far too urgent to quibble about imagined risks."

Then pointing at Kirk, he said to Althea and Caine, "I expect you both to see him at work with his students. I want you on this board and Kirk at the LEAD Charter School."

Given the daunting challenges of change,
how can we draw from, yet move beyond, pivotal setbacks?

The quest for deep democracy and the experience of deep disappointment are often closely linked. Despite sustained commitment and often-valiant efforts, we have yet to accomplish a profound and integrative restructuring of public education and civic participation. Perceived failure to move public institutions toward more genuine and expansive expressions of social justice and compassion is intensely felt. On a personal level, we grapple with both anger at the sources of resistance and despair at the consequences. Confronted with feelings of inadequacy and doubt, we tend to act more energetically along familiar solution paths. We resolve to work harder to protect what we hold dear. We move more assertively to define and attack the opposition. We narrow our focus and redouble our efforts to defend any gains made. We consider compromises that will make our initiatives more acceptable within the systems we seek to reform. We reassess our ambitions and resign ourselves to 'do what's doable' under persistently difficult circumstances.

When attempts to enact deeper forms of democracy are repeatedly blocked, there is a risk of withdrawing from collaborative change. The task of widening and maintaining coalitions is very demanding, and at times when prompt action is urged, participation may be narrowed. Engaging in the strenuous politics of crisis takes focused energy. Sharply targeted opposition, highly assertive strategies, and relentless competition are reinforced. "Politics as usual" is mostly carried out by small groups of skilled activists—decision-making elites, interest group lobbyists, campaign professionals. Our democratic political systems at times even reward participants who play by less-than-democratic rules, usually justified by asserting that broad democratic ends can only be accomplished through less-than-democratic means.

When public concern is focused on education, the intensity of adversarial politics increases. Mobilization tactics that feature a clear enemy, blame fixing, and scathing critique become commonplace. Discourse between political activists and the attentive public becomes oversimplified and increasingly dependent upon negative slogans. Opportunities for collaboration are quickly narrowed by the rhetoric of intense opposition. Even among actors whose intentions are similar, defensive wariness of cooperation often develops, resulting eventually in political isolation. This pattern of response is understandable and strongly reinforced in our political culture. But it diminishes generative reflection, forecloses opportunities for genuine collaboration, and sharply reduces possibilities for progressive reform.

As advocates of democratic reform are resigned to be more pragmatic and more protective, there is also a risk of giving in to pressures to reduce aspirations and narrow the scope of implementation. Coping strategies vary across a continuum emphasizing *compromise and assimilation* on one end, and *distancing or withdrawal* from involvement with the larger system on the other.

In public school systems expected to respond to a wide range of conflicting community values, it is not uncommon to back away from more creative and controversial aspects of curricular reform in order to ensure at least partial adoption. Reform aspirations are also compromised, often unintentionally, by district policies intended to cope with increasing mobility and changing demographics. Most innovative programs begin with a well-integrated team of teachers, parents and administrators dedicated to a specific educational philosophy or approach. Program coherency is diminished as continuity in staffing and student populations becomes impossible to maintain.

Two approaches dominate attempts to narrow the scope of implementation and distance reform efforts from challenges that characterize public school systems. Demonstration projects, such as charter schools, offer significant opportunities to experiment and extend educational theory and practice. Freed from many of public education's important constraints (e.g., class size, instructional standardization, and unwieldy administrative structures), charter schools are allowed greater discretion and flexibility. They can pursue carefully focused missions, support imaginative curriculum and instruction, enable deeper parental commitment and participation, and provide motivating settings for selected teachers and students. These thematically centered initiatives are now widely embraced as integral to large-scale attempts at education reform. Yet the 'lessons learned' seldom transfer or generalize beyond their initial context and affect relatively small numbers of students, their teachers and their families. While valuable in many ways, charter schools contribute little to systemic progressive education reform.

A second approach involves policies and programs designed to provide focused treatment for specific concerns. From teenage single mothers struggling to continue their education while learning to navigate a complex array of early childhood assistance programs, to 'exceptional' students struggling to cope with disabilities in starkly insensitive social settings, the spectrum of challenges affecting school age youth and their families is daunting. Small, intensive, carefully targeted programs can play a crucial role in responding to basic survival needs. But highly specialized projects lacking resources necessary either to provide sufficient follow-up, or to develop connections with broader communities and concerns, can unintentionally place participants in learning and life situations that are unrealistic and isolating. At best, such programs create 'pockets of humanity' for a limited number of young people, for a limited time. Fundamental changes in social awareness, responsiveness, and resource distribution are not accomplished.

Democratic reform in schools and society is hard won and difficult to sustain. Struggling to cope with persistent and significant setbacks, advocates too often find no options other than to engage in the alienating politics of opposition or to settle for small victories. Adopting either strategy, we move farther from our aspirations and risk reiteration of the *progressive tragedy*—moving tales of idealism and activism ending in isolation, cynicism and defeat. Too often, democratic reform initiatives on all levels result in disillusionment, disengagement from social institutions, and abandonment of further attempts at comprehensive change. The fate of public education and the future of democracy will depend on our collective capacity to envision and enact alternative, non-tragic endings.

Preparation . . .
to sustain a broad and inclusive state of anticipation
finding faith and trust
in resources not immediately apparent nor completely understood
heightened awareness, practiced willingness
to be moved by, and to move with others
proceeding with care and discernment
by unspecified means, toward indefinite ends.

When initiatives and imagination are blocked, reform activists often feel compelled to fall back on strongly reinforced individual and social strategies. One common strategy centers on *intense critique*, another is preoccupied with the *reiteration of higher order values*. Both responses can be partially, but never completely, useful in avoiding the progressive tragedies of oppositional politics, diminished aspirations, defeat, or withdrawal.

While critical evaluation is necessary to respond productively to setbacks and to keep systemic reform moving, strategies of intense critique entail several risks. Identifying significant and justifiable complaints can be emotionally satisfying, but can constrict focus and result in confusing 'complaint' with 'causation.' In response, for example, to perceived dissatisfaction with teacher quality, state legislators have often assumed lack of preparation as a primary causal factor. They have concentrated their efforts on escalating teacher education requirements and linking certification to performance on standardized tests. Through political rhetoric that combines some worthy intentions with stereotypic "teacher bashing," advocacy for tougher certification for beginning teachers is paradoxically joined with lenient access to the profession by those seeking entry at mid-career from other occupations. Teachers are understandably angered by unchallenged negative stereotypes and frustrated by the imposition, without consultation, of what they see as arbitrary standards and complicated procedures. But close attention to such immediate and exasperating circumstances can dim perspectives on current conditions and future prospects.

Reform initiatives operate in large and complex contexts with many factors affecting eventual success or failure. Opportunities to consider alternative policy directions are limited by early closure on causal explanations grounded in broader ideological objectives that are seldom publicly stated. Regulatory policies deployed to "teacher-proof" public school curriculum exemplify targeted remedies embedded within more extensive movements toward centralization of authority and limitations on teacher discretion. Teachers and students are disadvantaged as singular attention to such policies precludes possibilities for enhancing the profession by other means—e.g., through mentoring of new teachers, improved opportunities for continuing professional development, and union activity regarding education issues that move beyond valid concerns for conditions of work.

Complaint-driven reflection also risks centering analysis on aspects of programmatic success or failure associated with the highest levels of negative emotional energy. The persistently demeaning language of a hostile critic or the deliberately distorted interpretation of a piece of educational research cited during a legislative process, can bring intense responses from teachers and their allies. While highly salient to reform participants, these affronts may not be the most important considerations for understanding what has actually happened, or for devising effective plans for response.

Re-emphasizing a reform initiative's higher purpose and core values is another frequently encountered response to blocked initiatives. It is important both for situational analyses and for longer term planning to keep core values and objectives in mind. Movements that advocate policies not aligned with progressive reforms goals routinely evoke virtues and values both to justify their programs and to shape their efforts. To engage in discourse on higher-order objectives is necessary, but also carries risk. Opportunities for public deliberation are limited when restatement of values and purposes takes place at a high level of abstraction. Concerns, for example, about 'character education,' and the difficult tensions entailed in the 'separation of church and state' can become incomprehensible when framed as arcane philosophy and dense jurisprudence. Public consideration is also constrained when complex purposes are reduced to familiar pieties. Public discourse aimed at character development through civic education is confined to an exchange of clichés and platitudes concerning recitation of the pledge of allegiance as a mandated display of patriotism.

Of equal importance is the closely related risk of confusing a high purpose with wishful thinking. Merely affirming a desired premise or forcefully stating a valued objective is not sufficient to transform teaching and learning. Elegant expressions of student-centered models of curriculum and instruction made by the most passionate advocates often stop short of proposing effective implementation strategies. Assertions such as "we must educate the whole child" or "children are our future" do not necessarily lead to smaller class sizes, adequate facilities, or support for deepening civic involvement. However abstractly coherent, intellectually compelling, and emotionally resonant with participants, high purpose and core values alone are programmatically insufficient.

Developing a pragmatic understanding of pivotal setbacks, and arraying resources needed to continue systemic reform, requires close critical analysis of complex situations and reflective attention to core values and broad purposes. Yet the inherent hazards of both 'complaint' and 'wish' driven conceptual strategies must be addressed. Preparation that draws from and moves beyond these habits of mind and response is necessary.

> *"So may we, in this life*
> *trust*
> *to those elements*
> *we have yet to see*
> *or imagine,*
> *and look for the true . . . "*
>
> —David Whyte
> *Teaching with Fire*

Exploratory Democratic Practice: Ethnographic Futures Interviews

To enhance policy imagination while providing opportunities to extend and connect insights through strategic conversations, we have adapted an interview technique developed by Robert Textor.

Ethnographic futures interviews are designed to elicit probable, possible, and preferable policy scenarios in a contextual manner. Participants in pairs or in triads are first asked to remind each other of their personal reform interests. Then, in reference to a specific reform initiative or policy concern, they are asked to take turns responding in detail to the series of interview prompts below. During the interview session, participants are encouraged to focus not only on specific reform goals and concerns, but also on the on the broad societal dimensions of the issues raised.

Interviewees are asked to speak for at least five minutes on each prompt. The interviewer is asked to keep time, take notes, and offer probing questions if necessary to encourage the interviewee's continuing response. A five minute shared preparation and reflection period should precede each set of responses as indicated below:

Five minute preparation and reflection period

- Very pessimistic scenario (five minute responses)

Five minute preparation and reflection period

- Very optimistic scenario (five minute responses)

Five minute preparation and reflection period

- Change model identifying strategies for movement in a desirable direction

Five minute preparation and reflection period

- Three questions you would most like to have answered regarding your proposed reform initiative. [This prompt is referred to by Textor as an "Imaginary Consultation with an Omniscient Clairvoyant."]

Five minute presentation and elaboration on questions

Upon completion of the process, results can be pooled and analyzed, question-by-question, in small groups. Interpretive summaries—identifying both common themes and unique or thought-provoking insights—are developed and shared for continuing collective consideration.

Involvement in systemic progressive reform requires us to see beyond debilitating personal or institutional experiences that animate the past, to move beyond fears of personal inadequacy or political limitation that constrain the present. Ethnographic Futures Interviews can be shaped to engage reform participants in a social process that demonstrates and extends individual and collective imagination and expertise.

Thematic Bibliographic References

On responses to the challenges of progressive reform:

Barr, R., & Parrett, W. (1997). *How to create alternative, magnet & charter schools that work.* Washington, DC: National Educational Service.

Brouillette, L. (Ed.). (2002). *Charter schools: Lessons in school reform.* Mahwah, NJ: Lawrence Erlbaum Associates.

Bulkley, K., & Wohlstetter, P. (Eds.). (2004). *Taking account of charter schools: What's happened and what's next.* New York: Teachers College Press.

Carnoy, M., Jacobsen, R., Mishel, L., & Rothstein, R. (2005). *The charter school dust-up: Examining the evidence on enrollment and achievement.* New York: Teachers College Press.

Chavous, K. (2004). *Serving our children: Charter schools and the reform of American public education.* Wellington, VA: Capital Books.

Cookson, P., & Berger, K. (2002). *Expect miracles: Charter schools and the politics of hope and despair.* New York: Westview Press.

Finn, C., Manno, B., & Vanourek, G. (Eds.). (2001). *Charter schools in action: Renewing public education.* Princeton, NJ: Princeton University Press.

Fuller, B. (Ed.). (2000). *Inside charter schools: The paradox of radical decentralization.* Cambridge, MA: Harvard University Press.

Gitell, M. (Ed.). (1998). *Strategies for school equity.* New Haven, CT: Yale University Press.

Hill, P., Lake, R., & Celio, M. (2002). *Charter schools and accountability in public education.* Washington, DC: Brookings Institution Press.

Miron, G., & Nelson, C. (2002). *What's public about charter schools?: Lessons learned about choice and accountability.* Thousand Oaks, CA: Corwin Press.

Murphy, J., & Shiffman, C. (2002). *Understanding and assessing the charter school movement.* New York: Teachers College Press.

Nathan, J. (1998). *Charter schools: Creating hope and opportunity for American education* (new ed.). San Francisco: Jossey-Bass.

Nehring, J. (2002). *Upstart startup: Creating and sustaining a public charter school.* New York: Teachers College Press.

Rofes, E., & Stulberg L. (Eds.). (2004). *The emancipatory promise of charter schools: Toward a progressive politics of school choice.* Albany: State University of New York Press.

Sarason, S. (1998). *Charter schools.* New York: Teachers College Press.

U.S. Department of Education. (2004). *Successful charter schools.* Stockton, CA: University Press of the Pacific.

Vergari, S. (2002). *The charter school landscape.* Pittsburgh, PA: University of Pittsburgh Press.

Wells, A. (2002). *Where charter school policy fails: The problems of accountability and equity.* New York: Teachers College Press.

On the 'progressive tragedy':

Carlson, D. (2002). *Leaving safe harbors: Toward a new progressivism in American education and public life.* New York: Routledge Falmer.

Hart, S. (2001). *Cultural dilemmas of progressive politics: Styles of engagement among grassroots activists.* Chicago: University of Chicago Press.

Norris, N. (2004). *The promise and failure of progressive education.* Lanham, MD: Rowman & Littlefield Education.

Osterman, P. (2003). *Gathering power: The future of progressive politics in America.* Boston: Beacon Press.

Semel, S., & Sadovnik, A. (Eds.). (1999). *"Schools of tomorrow," schools of today: What happened to progressive education?* New York: Peter Lang.

Tanner, D. (2002). *Crusade for democracy: Progressive education at the crossroads.* Albany: State University of New York Press.

Tomasky, M. (1996). *Left for dead: The life, death, and possible resurrection of progressive politics in America.* New York: Free Press.

Reflection:

Whyte D. (2003). "Working together." In S. Intrator & M. Scribner (Eds.), *Teaching with fire: Poetry that sustains the courage to teach* (p. 29). San Francisco: Jossey-Bass.

Exploratory Democratic Practice: Ethnographic Futures Interview

Poolpatarachewin, C. (1980). Ethnographic Delphi futures research: Thai university pilot project. *Journal of Cultural and Educational Futures* 2(4), 11–19.

Textor, R. (1978). Cultural futures for Thailand: An ethnographic inquiry. *Futures* *10*(5), 347–360.
Textor, R. (1979). The natural partnership between ethnographic futures research and futures education. *Journal of Cultural and Educational Futures 1*(1), 13–19.

chapter   4

Intuition

Seeking, calling, listening, receiving
perceptions surprising though not unexpected
complex truths, varied interpretations, generative ambiguity
apparently sudden, sources unknown,
these gifts of disciplined openness.

*C*aine and Althea were wary, each for different reasons, about the LEAD Charter School. They were curious about the Building Visions Workshop Kirk Peterson had described at their first meeting, but were unclear about what it meant for LEAD's charter school proposal. Now in its first year, the Workshop provided young adolescents thought to be "incorrigible" in the public schools with a "last chance" option before expulsion or incarceration. The LEAD staff had arranged for them to observe Kirk and his students on site.

They met at the control desk just inside Jefferson Middle School's main entrance. A uniformed security officer checked their identification against the appointment sheet on his clipboard and politely inspected their briefcases before issuing them brightly colored visitor badges. A student monitor escorted them to the Building Visions program housed on the third floor of one wing of the building.

Re-Envisioning Education and Democracy, pages 47–61
Copyright © 2006 by Information Age Publishing
All rights of reproduction in any form reserved.

As they waited to be buzzed through the Workshop's door, Caine remarked, "I think they have more security here than up at the capitol."

Kirk greeted them warmly. "We have a few minutes before we can walk you through the place, meet some kids, and show you what we're trying to do." They followed him into an alcove, the only place that seemed unoccupied by students or staff.

"Look, I do want to show you what we're up to," Kirk said after they sat down. "But I also want to talk more about the LEAD Charter School thing."

"I understand that Jim and Bobbi are recruiting you to be one of the LEAD teachers," Althea said.

"Yeah, well they think I could be a 'LEAD Leader!' Right? Let me try to say why I'm really interested. First off, I'd like having a regular income. Artist types—even so-called video artists like me—aren't always on a salary. But I'm also convinced that I could make a difference for most kids if I could just have more time with them. I mean, have more time than I get here. Here, I get at most four maybe five weeks and no follow-up with them later."

Althea said encouragingly, "But from what I've heard about Building Visions, the program does make a difference. Some of the students have committed acts of violence, right?"

"Maybe so. That's what our PR materials say anyway. I don't ask. The kids don't tell. But yes, I believe we do make some difference for them. But we're only beginning. What I do is probably seen as some kind of art therapy. I don't really know what that's supposed to mean. But I do know that just about when we get things a little more in sync here, boom! These kids get sent right back to where they screwed-up in the first place. Their experiences here have a whole lot to compete with once they leave the building. I worry a lot about that. Out there, for most of them, Building Visions probably just ends up like some sort of painful reminder. Maybe some hidden talents and aspirations are uncovered and begin to flourish. Art can do that, you know. But then they're thrown right back into places where they're told that they are 'the problem' and that they'll never amount to anything."

Althea looked especially thoughtful. Kirk resumed after glancing first at Caine and then looking more intently at Althea. "OK, so we get plenty of interruptions all the time. Kids are always going off to do all sorts of other stuff with other programs. They're dragged out for court appearances, for all kinds of re-hab sessions, or whatever. What I try to do here is done in small groups, you know, in teams. It's nearly impossible to keep those art project teams together for long. So LEAD, as Jim tells me, is shaping up like at least a semester, maybe a whole year, to work with the same group of kids."

"Jim's curriculum and calendar are still not clear to me," Caine said cautiously.

"Right, it's all under construction with lots of options still open. We all are building visions, right? So, let me tell you why I'm interested in LEAD—why *I* want in!"

Althea interrupted. "Neither Jon nor I have even agreed to be on the LEAD Board. This is not a job interview."

"Yeah, right," Kirk continued. "I like MacIver's charter school idea. You know, lots of flexibility—not as many layers of people to go through to get things done. Now this shop is pretty good—you'll see that in a minute. There are amazing people around here—teachers and social workers and counselors. But we've got bureaucrats too—all over the place—with forms to complete and junk they want from me for their endless reports. We're always doing reports! Like even *I* am getting real sympathetic with all those doctors who complain about their HMO's."

Caine said, "It can become burdensome, Kirk. But a lot of paperwork comes with collaborations, right Althea? Besides, we do need accountability—or call it transparency—in all our public programs including public schools." Althea nodded but said nothing.

"Yeah." Kirk muttered and paused. "Well, listen . . . ah, I think I've never said what I'm about to say . . . at least not out loud to anyone else. So, I'm going to need your tolerance, or something like that. So look, I think art, the kind of art I do, is part of democracy. Sounds strange? But I don't think you can get to justice and equality and truth, good things like that, without . . . I don't know what to call it . . . maybe without an aesthetic dimension. I don't mean decorations or ornaments or symbols like flags and that kind of thing. I mean a shared feeling; something like, well, almost a spiritual sense of community. I know some of that comes best through artistic expression and all the really hard work that must go into it. I know that everyone—even these kids here who are labeled 'at risk'—needs art in their lives as a part of being well, being human. But even more . . . for being social. Creating, struggling together . . . building visions together . . . changes respect levels, responsibility, and understanding. I know it does. I see it happen every day. Am I making any sense? What do you think?"

Althea and Caine remained silent and thoughtful.

"OK, so here at the Workshop," Kirk began again, "art is pretty important. But it's a kind of last resort for these kids. They can't hack it in the mainstream we're told. Almost all of them here are in big trouble with their families, with the law—and all of them are big problems for the school system. So an art-centered 'immersion' program is acceptable here as a last ditch effort to prevent more trouble, more violence. Art therapy is the so-called "plan." But this isn't a clinic. I am *not* a shrink with a videocam. Here, art is merely tolerated. I don't want art to be tolerated. I want what I try to do to be seen, be understood, as *necessary!* You know, as a central part... not just some 'alternative program' for a few weeks, for a bunch of kids in trouble. Not just my kind of video art—but all kinds of art. Art is essential, not only when we think we can afford it, or, like here, when nothing else seems to work. I think the other kids in schools where art is mostly a joke, if it exists at all, are the ones really at risk. And I don't know all the theory involved, but I think democracy is at risk too. There... now I've probably blown my cover."

Caine and Althea looked at each other, each seeming to wait for the other to speak first. Althea said quietly, "I think John Dewey said something like that. . . ."

Kirk said, "Who?" Then he looked quickly at the clock, stood up, picked up his digital video camera and said, "Let me show you what's up around here. Like we say, to new kids and especially to visitors: 'it's time to build a vision.'"

> *Fluidity, quickening energy*
> *the winds move over the water*
> *rising mists, dispersed sunlight*
> *expansion and uncertainty create active space*
> *inviting interaction and exploration.*

Kirk spoke quietly as they moved into the brightly lit workshop area. "What's really awesome for me is not just what we can do with the video—which has become sort of the center piece of Building Visions—it's the way it affects most kids... something inside them just seems to shift. I can see it in their faces and eventually it shows up in their art."

"Oh?" Althea sounded skeptical. She was mindful of all the important ambitions in the many projects in which she had been involved. Echoing were thoughts about PIP and about LEAD as she listened to Kirk.

"Well, we're only into our second set of students, and each bunch of kids is only here for about six weeks before they go back to their regular schools. All the kids that started with us back in September are still in school."

"So, they've stayed in school for a few weeks—is that what you mean by 'success'?" Althea said rather sharply.

Kirk paused to look at her and continued carefully, "I didn't say "success." I said we may make "a difference." I think that small classes and a lot of personal attention matters to them. I know the video art matters."

"I'm sure it does," Althea said. "And so do the small classes. The students get a lot of individual attention, and it looks like you've got plenty of resources. The kids get to play with slick technology. Individual attention in a resourceful setting usually works."

Caine tried to break what seemed to him like growing tension by asking, "What's a typical day like for these students?"

Kirk, looking away from Althea, answered rapidly. "A group of six or eight starts with me right after their orientation and daily check-in session. They hang out with me in this workspace, which we call "the studio," or over in the editing room, or we build stuff downstairs in the shop. The kids are with me until around noon. Right after lunch I get another bunch for about the same amount of time, but they work on different projects."

Glancing around, Caine watched two students adjusting a lighting bridge, four others who seemed to be puttering with what looked like scene backdrops, and the rest tinkering with racks of technical equipment. "What do they do when they're not with you?" he asked.

"Like I said, in the morning they check in and have an orientation period. There's an 'exit session' right before they all leave in the afternoon. About half of them start with me while the other half take two 'basics' courses and maybe catch up in one-on-one tutorials, depending on what they need. One of their courses is intensive reading and writing and the other is science and math, but I think it's mostly math. The reading-writing course, I know, works at getting them to do a bunch of writing on some of the things that got them sent to us. They write letters, essays, poems, plays, and short stories. I think the point is to work out their anger, or whatever is bugging them, as well as learning how to read and write better."

"And during their time with you?" Althea prompted.

"They learn how to operate these mini-digital cams, do video and sound mixing, learn some of the basics of scripting, editing, lighting, scenery design and construction, directing. . . ."

"Sounds like fun," she said, "but what's educational about that?"

Kirk waited awhile. "It's not all fun. What's really different here is that all of our video projects are joint efforts. We produce them as a group. In the other two classes the kids work on individual things—what they might need in writing or reading or math. There, they work individually and do assignments and tests by themselves. Here, we try to do almost everything together. We create art together—and that's really hard work! We don't just provide some break from the usual classroom regime. It's different, sure, satisfying most of the time—but it is not just fun."

He turned away expecting more questions but Althea and Caine both remained quietly attentive.

"While each of them begins by learning the fundamentals more or less by herself or himself, all of our projects soon become mutual efforts. I know that most of the kids come in preferring to work by themselves. They get all excited about playing with these computers and especially the video toys. At first they want to make music videos, show-off, or say dumb things and do outrageous stuff on tape to show their friends. But that doesn't go on for long. We work on creative presentations together—just about from start to finish."

He waited a moment, but Caine and Althea still said nothing.

"It's really hard for all of us. It's hard because everyone thinks 'art' is exclusively an individual process. It's hard when I work at not letting them fall into too much specialization—you know, just doing the things they think they're good at, or only doing what they *want* to do. That's really tough. But it all seems to come around as we approach deadlines. It's important for these kids to see and hear that they all have talent. It's really tough for them to learn together. It's really important for them to learn that art is social—not just for private or personal gratification."

"And...?" Althea prompted.

Kirk looked intently at her as he resumed. "And...we begin with some 'trial and error' early learning in our first week and then put together a video collage of what each of them has created. Then we work out a short production with everyone involved and make copies to show to the other video art group for their comment and criticism—you know, something like peer review. After that, we do some tweaking and make enough copies so each student can take one copy home. They have to bring back written comments from at least one parent and one peer from outside the Workshop. That requires us to focus on what we all want others to see and hear. All that feedback is sometimes hard to take...for me too. Parents can be very demanding."

Before continuing, Kirk stopped to answer a student's question about a piece of equipment. "We do another round of that to learn and practice some more. Then in the last ten days or so, together we conceive, write, arrange, tape, edit down, and produce a fifteen-to-twenty minute piece of video art. That gets another peer review from the other student group. We cut a final and give it to the Building Visions' Director, to the School Board, and also to the foundation that helps fund this place. A copy also supposedly goes into the Workshop archives, along with the best writing and science/math projects from the other classes. And of course all the kids get to keep a copy for themselves."

"And how have these video art pieces been received?" Caine asked.

"Well, I hear that most of the kids from our first session have shown their video art in one of their classes at their schools when they returned. That's pretty impressive. Comments from a few parents who responded have been positive. But I haven't heard a thing from the foundation or the School Board staff or, honestly, from our Director."

"As I understand it then," Althea said, "you're not exactly like the other teachers. You're more like what—a director or a technical advisor?"

"I don't know that any one description fits. I do a lot of things here and the actual 'what' and 'when' changes over time, in each situation. Maybe teaching is always like that. But what might be different is that I have no idea when we start each project how it will turn out. Everything is put together by all of us—the students and me. I'm not trying to get them to match some plan, or fit into some template I have in my head."

"But they can't do just anything they want," Caine stated.

"No, of course not. We negotiate all the time. And it gets really hot sometimes. But art is like that. Sometimes their creative vision exceeds our technical range here, or the time we have—you know, they may want on-site shots of jungles or interviews with rock stars or something happening way downtown at rush hour. We're restricted by how much time we can be out of the building, and by what they have to do in their other two classes."

"Your projects sound, well, different, as you say." Caine commented.

Kirk broke in. "Sometimes, it can get pretty noisy around here. We argue because we come to care about sharing a vision and putting it into some creative form that satisfies a lot more than just meeting a deadline. A lot of what we are trying to do doesn't fit well into words. There are limits, sure, but I know that we all feel pretty good about what we end up doing. I know there's some real understanding and real pride in our creativity. I think that's the difference for most of these kids."

"So what do others think of all this?" Althea asked.

"I think that some of the original sponsors and the administration expected what I told you earlier—you know, that we'd do something like art therapy. We'd probably end up with tapes with each kid acting out the things that made them such disasters at school. Maybe they wanted confession and contrition bits, or testimonials, or even a "scared straight" piece to show in classes. But it doesn't work that way here. What these kids thought up and were able to produce in the end is art—some really impressive art. The videos are artistic rather than like some cliché public service spot. They are more powerfully expressive than any little message piece we could possibly do."

"Can we see some of it?" Caine asked.

"Let's go to the video tape," Kirk responded.

Given the dimensions and dynamics of contemporary social and educational concerns, what, beyond rational problem solving, is necessary?

We are taught that to be responsible in our personal and public lives, we must be both rational and realistic. With individual choice portrayed as the essence of both democracy and the economy, it is important to consider the 'realism' and 'rationality' of prevailing approaches to personal and social decision-making.

Public choice in education policy is situated in complex social institutions (e.g., legislatures, school boards, and administrative bureaucracies) and in complex civic processes (e.g., public discourse, campaigns, and elections). Shaped by their particular histories and operating rules, social institutions make decisions that must be publicly justified as 'realistic' and 'rational.' Civic processes are framed as opportunities for citizens to become informed, weigh alternatives, and arrive at rational choice.

In everyday life, politics, and markets, 'realism' and 'rationality' are neither as simple nor as straightforward as popular portrayals contend. Tension is felt between what is asserted by others to be 'real,' and what is actually experienced. Advice on being 'realistic' usually means accepting a hierarchically determined framing of a context or a specific situation. Education reformers, for example, are advised to shape their proposals within the "rules of game" and to accept what they are told is "acceptable." Being 'realistic' in these ways reinforces elite positions and practices. It also limits social imagination and innovation by labeling alternatives as "unrealistic" and therefore beyond consideration.

Most normative models of decision-making assert that 'rationality' is grounded in 'reality'. It is accepted as 'objective' and justified on the basis of quantitative analyses. Theoretical and empirical research on 'rationality' in individual and social choice, as well as many anecdotal accounts, however, paint a more complicated picture. Most decisions are embedded in dynamic and ambiguous situations. Reliable information is often scarce, and the cost of acquiring more can be steep. Recommended decision rules, structured to simplify and direct choice, frequently exclude important values and variables. Important assumptions are left unexamined in order to fit a preferred quantification procedure. This strategy is then justified as a "rational necessity." While it is understood that not all things of importance can be quantified, measuring the conveniently mea-

surable is accepted as a "best practice." Personal and organizational decisions can also be compromised by flawed sampling and by unreflective
wishful thinking.

Personal choice has also become a focal attribute of public education.
In the politics of school vouchers, for example, advocates assert that parental choice to use public funds to pay for private schools trumps constitutional limitations, enhances student performance, and actually strengthens
democracy. The growing practice of home schooling has been justified by
its proponents as a reasoned choice that meets individual family needs.
Most debates on school vouchers and home schooling feature the central-
ity of personal choice, while muting important distinctions between private
and public purpose, between sectarian and secular domains, and between
individual and social welfare in a democracy. This tendency reinforces a
broader trend toward privatization of public services, justified as more economically efficient. The overall shrinking of the public sector, judged to be
more rational in a market economy.

Limiting public consideration to what is conventionally or conveniently
labeled as realistic and rational is not necessary. While the material
resources available to support public education and democratic political
participation are always scarce, the conceptual resources are nearly boundless. Gaining access to these conceptual assets, however, requires both 'letting go' and 'trying harder.' We can let go of the assumption that
oversimplified rational decision-making models capture everything worth
knowing. We can come to know that formulaic strategic planning and simple cost-benefits analysis are not the only realistic and responsible ways to
act on behalf of the public good. At the same time, we can try harder to
develop a deeper understanding of choice, to explore added dimensions
of inquiry, and to find deeper forms of accountability that advance reform
efforts aimed at addressing our most pressing social concerns.

Enchantment . . .
to experience enhanced understanding
acquired not through deliberate effort, planning, or intent,
drawn to, prepared for, then received as a gift
profound and elegant integration
of emotion, insight, sensation, ethics
illumination accompanied by deep mystery
the complex interplay of fear and joy, doubt and wonder
that challenges our carefully reasoned assumptions
and compels us to expand, to enrich, or to abandon these.

Intuition and inspiration, prophecy and poetry, enchantment and emotion, mystery and movement, silence and spirit are concepts seldom associated with problem solving in education, politics, and governance. This is
understandable. While the experiences and possibilities these terms represent are widely recognized as important avenues for human development,
long-standing social conventions relegate their influence strictly to the personal realm.

Civic processes are shaped to limit expression of emotion, to prevent
infringement on personal privacy, and to protect each individual's freedom
to pursue spiritual beliefs of their own choosing. Governance is to be
accomplished through the implementation of carefully reasoned decisions
formulated by persons in positions of power. Political processes are to
orchestrate negotiations that advance individual and special interest group
ambitions. Social services, including public education, are to be judged
based on records of demonstrable performance that assist informed citizens in selecting the resources best suited to their individual needs.

At times, however, the most compelling rationale for a social policy or
practice does not lend itself to empirical verification or logical interpretation. Teaching, learning, and decision-making for public purposes involve
and require much more than objective analysis and linear problem solving.
Inseparable, rather than distinct from highly individualized cognitive processes, are human capacities for social *empathy, intuition,* and *artistry.*

Our emotions shape our thinking, often focusing attention, sometimes
exerting decisive influence. Empathy, a feelings-based capacity, makes it

possible to establish meaningful connections. Its continuing development allows us to sustain collaborative relationships not only with like-minded others, but even more important, with those whose experiences and commitments are quite different from our own.

At times, we are moved by awareness that is surprising. A strong sense of understanding or direction suddenly appears; comprehension precedes its validation. Intuitions, like emotions, can help to mobilize, connect and extend divergent conceptual resources. Shifting time, space, speed, pattern, and perspective, intuitive processing can break down conceptual barriers and signal new pathways.

At other times, we are moved by awareness of beauty. The need for aesthetic experience and expression is active in all aspects of our lives. To engage artistry in the domain of public policy is to extend beyond valid concerns for efficiency and utility, to add priorities for balance, movement, resonance, and grace.

Strategic and developmental attention to intuition, empathy, and artistry—as public processes for public purposes—can enrich our efforts toward democratic educational and political reform. The invitation to incorporate 'non-rational' ways of knowing, however, is not a call to abandon well-refined research methods or to ignore widely utilized planning techniques. Instead, it is an opportunity to acknowledge the central importance of attempts to synthesize diverse and complimentary approaches to social inquiry. In the absence of such efforts, re-formation of contemporary approaches to social problem solving, policy design, and institutional practice cannot be accomplished.

Neither is the invitation to move beyond over-reliance on what we usually understand to be rational resources a call for superficial experimentation with 'soft' strategies that offer little more than temporary escape from tough challenges. Social intuition, empathy, and artistry require sustained and mindful grappling with highly problematic personal and public realities. Seeking wisdom—deep understanding that is fundamentally *expansive* (across domains of self, society, environment, time, space, and spirit) and *integrative* (across dimensions of truth, beauty, and justice)—requires discipline, humility, and persistence.

> *"Suddenly things snap into focus.*
> *I've been pursuing unity all my life,*
> *But could only glimpse the monstrous vision in fragments;*
> *It has haunted me for years.*
> *Each time I sighted it, I struggled to make it concrete.*
> *At first, it seemed I only had a sculptor's yard of unfinished figures*
> *Then it slowly began to make sense,*
> *Gathered from glimpses and inferences.*
> *More and more, this mysterious life comes together.*
> *It may take years more to reveal the whole.*
> *That's all right.*
> *I'm prepared to go the distance."*
>
> —Deng Ming-Dao
> *365 Tao: Daily Meditations*

Exploratory Democratic Practice: Visualization

Many important aspects of social inquiry and democratic deliberation are not primarily linguistic. Attending to visualized understanding and communication in policy and pedagogy is imperative. On one hand, citizens need to be wary of the seductions of visual eloquence, to be sensitive to non-obvious emotional triggers, and to exercise a rich multiplicity of perspectives in expression and interpretation. On the other hand, citizens, researchers, and policy actors need to become more strategic and skillful in the use of visual representations that goes beyond immediate persuasive objectives and familiar graphic conventions. We seek new and perhaps deeper ways of seeing at different levels of abstraction (e.g., macro-micro, whole-parts). We see flexibility to understand, express, and manipulate (e.g., search, query, compare, represent) several visual symbol systems.

We encourage participants to sketch—first by themselves and then in small groups—visual representations of significant aspects of their reform initiative using either pen/pencil drafting tools or computer-based graphics.

Initially, these may take the form of:

- *simple diagrams* (e.g., depicting basic relationships in a policy context);
- *flow charts* (e.g., indicating temporal sequences for an initiative);
- *cognitive maps* (e.g., spatial representations of focal concepts); or
- *sketches* (e.g., snapshot representations, cartoons).

We encourage consideration of the *form* as well as the *content* represented. Guiding questions include:

- How are elements positioned relative to the designers' points of view?
- How is interaction expressed?
- How are desired outcomes represented?
- How are directionality and causality expressed?
- How are designers' and viewers' expectations about information and interpretation entailed in the representations?
- What emotional loadings are detectable?
- How do expectations among participants and among various forms of representation influence design, expression, and understanding?
- How do the goals and the tasks interact to shape the way graphic information is selected, abstracted, and organized?

Through this *exploratory democratic practice*, participants encounter the visual challenges of representing increasing complexity. They explore structures and relationships, and discover existing or missing patterns in the objects, attributes, and connections portrayed. The goal is to develop greater tolerance for complex designs that incorporate more variables, include richer relationships, and demand multidimensional imagination—all necessary to sustain systemic democratic reform.

Thematic Bibliographic References

On the limits of normative rationality:

Elster, J. (1999). *Alchemies of the mind: Rationality and emotions.* Cambridge: Cambridge University Press.

Mero, L. (2002). *Habits of mind: The power and limits of rational thought.* New York: Springer-Verlas.

Willinsky, J. (2000). *Public knowledge and the social sciences.* New York: Routledge.

**On personal choice in the public sphere
(privatization, school choice, vouchers):**

Abernathy, S. (2005). *School choice and the future of American democracy.* Ann Arbor, MI: University of Michigan Press.

Betts, J., & Loveless, T. (2006). *Getting choice right: Ensuring equity and efficiency in education policy.* Washington, DC: Brookings Institution Press.

Brighouse, H. (2003). *School choice and social justice.* Oxford: Oxford University Press.

Dwyer, J. G. (2001). *Vouchers within reason: A child-centered approach to education reform.* Ithaca, NY: Cornell University Press.

Feuer, M. (2006). *Moderating the debate: Rationality and the promise of American education.* Cambridge, MA: Harvard Education Publishing Group.

Fusarelli, L.D. (2003). *The political dynamics of school choice: Negotiating contested terrain.* New York: Palgrave Macmillan.

Gill, B., Timpane, P., Ross, K., & Brewer, D. (2001). *Rhetoric versus reality: What we know and what we need to know about vouchers and charter schools.* Santa Monica, CA: RAND.

Godwin, R. (2002). *School choice tradeoffs: Liberty, equity, and diversity* (1st ed.). Austin: University of Texas Press.

Good, T., & Braden, J. (2000). *The great school debate: Choice, vouchers, and charters.* Mahwah, NJ: Lawrence Erlbaum Associates.

Goodwin, K., & Kemerer, F. (2002). *School choice tradeoffs: Liberty, equality, and diversity.* Austin: University of Texas Press.

Henig, J. (1995). *Rethinking school choice* (reprint ed.). Princeton, NJ: Princeton University Press.

Howell, W., & Peterson, P. (2002). *The education gap: Vouchers and urban schools.* Washington, DC: Brookings Institution.

Kahlenberg R. (Ed.). (2003). *Public school choice vs. private school vouchers.* New York: Century Foundation Press.

Moe, T. (2001). *Schools, vouchers, and the American public.* Washington DC: Brookings Institution Press.

Peterson P. (Ed.). (2003). *The future of school choice.* Stanford, CA: Hoover Institution Press.

Schneider, M., Teske, P., & Marshall, M. (2000). *Choosing schools: Consumer choice and the quality of American schools.* Princeton, NJ: Princeton University Press.

Scott, J. (2005). *School choice and diversity: What the evidence says.* New York: Teachers College Press.

Scott, J., & Levin, H. (Eds.). (2003). *School choice and student diversity.* New York: Teachers College Press.

Smith, S. (2001). *The democratic potential of charter schools.* New York: Peter Lang.

Stevens, M. (2001). *Kingdon of children: Culture and controversy in the homeschooling movement.* Princeton, NJ: Princeton University Press.

Sugarman, S. (Ed.). (2000). *School choice and social controversy: Politics, policy, and law.* Washington, DC: Brookings Institution Press.

Van Dunk, E., & Dickman, A. (2004). *School choice and the question of accountability.* New Haven, CT: Yale University Press.

Wang, M., & Walberg, H. (2001). *School choice or best systems: What improves education?* Mahwah, NJ: Erlbaum.

Wolfe A. (Ed.). (2003). *School choice: The moral debate.* Princeton, NJ: Princeton University Press.

Zuckerman A.S. (Ed.). (2005). *The social logic of politics: Personal networks as contexts for political behaviour.* Philadelphia, PA: Temple University Press.

On emotion and intuition in education policy and pedagogy:

Abbs, P. (1994). *The educational imperative: A defense of Socratic and aesthetic learning.* New York: Falmer Press.

Beyer, L. (2000). *The arts, popular culture, and social change.* New York: Peter Lang.

Boler, M. (1999). *Feeling power, emotions, and education.* New York: Routledge.

Bourdieu, P. (1998). *Practical reason.* Stanford, CA: Stanford University Press.

Bresler, L. (2004). *Knowing bodies, moving minds: Towards embodied teaching and learning*. New York: Springer-Verlag.

Curtis, K. (1999). *Our sense of the real: Aesthetic experience and Arendtian politics*. Ithaca, NY: Cornell University Press.

Dewey, J. (1934). *Art as experience*. New York: Perigee Books.

Fleener, M. (2002). *Curriculum dynamics: Recreating heart*. New York: Peter Lang.

Goleman, D. (1997). *Emotional intelligence: Why it can matter more than IQ* (reprint ed.). New York: Bantam Dell Publishing Group.

Halpin, D. (2003). *Hope and imagination: The role of the utopian imagination*. New York: Routledge Falmer.

Kelley, R. (2002). *Freedom dreams: The black radical imagination*. Boston: Beacon Press.

Marcus, G. (2002). *The sentimental citizen: Emotion in democratic politics*. University Park: Pennsylvania State University Press.

Noddings, N. (2005). *The challenge to care in schools: An alternative approach to education*. New York: Teachers College Press.

Reeve, J. (2000). *Understanding motivation and emotion*. New York: John Wiley & Sons Inc.

Schutz P., Lanehart S., Corno, L., & Winne, P. (Eds.), (2002) *Emotions in education*. Mahwah, NJ: Lawrence Erlbaum Associates.

Seeburger, F. (1997). *Emotional literacy: Keeping your heart, educating your emotions, and learning to let them educate you*. New York: The Crossroad Publishing Company.

Taylor, J. (1998). *Poetic knowledge: The recovery of education*. Albany: State University of New York Press.

Torff, B., & Sternberg, R. (Ed.), (2001) *Understanding and teaching the intuitive mind: Student and teacher learning*. Mahwah, NJ: Lawrence Erlbaum Associates.

Weems, M. (2003). *Public education and the imagination-intellect: I speak from the wound in my mouth*. New York: Peter Lang.

Zembylas, M. (2005). *Teaching with emotion: A postmodern enactment*. Greenwich, CT: Information Age Publishing.

Reflection:

Deng Ming-Dao. (1992). *365/Tao: Daily Meditations* (p. 346). San Francisco: Harper-San Francisco.

Exploratory Democratic Practice: Visualization

Sless, D. (1981). *Learning and visual communication*. New York: Wiley & Sons.

Tufte, E. (1983). *The visual display of quantitative information*. Cheshire, CT: Graphics Press.

Tufte, E. (1990). *Envisioning information*. Cheshire, CT: Graphics Press.

Tufte, E. (1991). *Visual explanations: Images and quantities, evidence and narrative*. Cheshire, CT: Graphics Press.

chapter   5

Inquiry

Questions of consequence center shared purpose
to search, to examine, to interpret and appraise
across varied perspectives and tentative positions
explore, persist, surprise and connect
new alliances of awareness emerge to evolve and inspire movement
toward comprehension and compassion that is always social.

When Althea and Caine met again a few days after their visit to Building Visions, they were eager to discuss their experience. As they left Kirk Peterson, they had promised to read as much as they could and begin to talk with as many people as possible before they decided whether to join the LEAD Charter School Board. They now sat in PIP's conversation room where Caine had talked with Althea and May Haun-Crawford a few days after the election.

"I can't get Kirk and those kids out of my mind," Caine began. "They were so skillful with all that video technology they get to use...I'm amazed!"

"They're good," Althea agreed. "Visual media are a big part of their lives. But as a mother of children who make electronic gadgets do things I can't begin to describe, I'm not so amazed. My kids play their complicated

Re-Envisioning Education and Democracy, pages 63–83
Copyright © 2006 by Information Age Publishing
All rights of reproduction in any form reserved.   63

computer games at blinding speeds and zip around the Internet in ways that frighten me. So, maybe I'm a little less impressed with Kirk's students' technical feats. Besides, Kirk's really smart about getting user-friendly graphics software. What I can't get out of my mind are the pieces of real collaboration they pull off. Sure they were showing off a little and maybe acting out for visitors. But, Jon, did you see them work together? I mean, they took care that everyone got involved. These are kids—and I've known kids like them all my life—these are the ones we say *can't* get along. That's part of why they're at Building Visions."

Caine nodded. "It was not what I expected. Well, I don't know what I expected. Those kids casually told us about how they settled on an image and then composed it with their computer graphics, or whatever that is called. Then how they hassled out a script segment for the image—very impressive—I could go on and on. . . . "

"You remember that skinny little girl in the baggy black sweatshirt?" Althea asked. "She was explaining to two or three others why colors and emotions are really close and that they had to work that into the piece they were doing. I leaned over and asked her if Kirk had taught her that. And she frosted me with 'Like look lady, everybody knows about colors—here we get to do it!'"

Caine wrinkled his brow and said, "When we were leaving I asked Kirk what he'd been reading about technology and art education, especially about video projects. He said that he actually hadn't read much that helped him with his teaching. What he had learned had been with the kids. He insisted that it was 'with the kids'—not 'from' or 'for' but 'with.' Later he told me what he does read is mostly on-line and mostly about digital technology. He said he doesn't know if there's been much written about the things that he's discovered to be most effective."

"Right," Althea said. "Kirk told me that linking the group's video projects up to other projects at the Workshop—you know, to students' writing and their math/science—just seemed to make sense to him. Jim was right. Kirk is really good with those tough kids. He is obviously a talented guy. But maybe his genius, or his artistry, or whatever it is, really is in the collaborative teaching/learning he does with them. I remember some of that working back at the preschool. . . . "

"Yes, I think there is an awareness of the social aspects of learning that seems unavoidable for everyone at Building Visions. Kirk was right when he said that learning *with* is at the heart of their success."

"That doesn't exclude the learning *for* and learning *from* either," Althea broke in. "So what's really striking about Building Visions for me is something like a blending of the intellectual-academic with the emotional-aesthetic. I don't know how to say this—I'm swirling with things I've heard and been trying to read the last couple of days."

"Me too. Some of the language I've come across does seem pretty vague. Sometimes it's even a little trite. OK, I know, we all have trouble talking and writing about these things. Whatever the words are, both Kirk at Building Visions and Jim at LEAD, along with the rest of us who are struggling over this charter school idea, have a sense of how important it is to support each student's full range of possibilities. So many kids in our public schools, not just those over at Kirk's Workshop, feel disconnected. And, as adults, many will stay disconnected."

"Oh yes, connections! Here at PIP we tried one simple strategy to connect," Althea said. "Putting most of the services and resources in one place is a big help. But it isn't much more than a physical convenience for the agencies and organizations, or for their clients. Public schools are like that too, you know. Everything is in one building. Still that doesn't necessarily connect the teachers, or the students, with opportunities, nor with each other. . . . "

Caine broke in with some intensity, "One thing that seems to work for Kirk, and maybe could work at LEAD, is providing situations in which kids do connect, and as you said, become responsible and helpful to each other . . . And . . . "

"And . . . " Althea picked up the thought, " . . . and work together on things that connect with their real world too. Kirk's kids are accomplishing things that go well beyond their classroom assignments. I mean their audience goes beyond the teacher—to their peers and their families, and I'm betting it'll go on right into their later lives. Some of the pieces I've been reading call things like what we saw, "powerful learning experiences," and "pedagogies for civic engagement." Those kids at the Workshop sure weren't headed toward responsible citizenship when they started there. Now, maybe they've gained a slightly different momentum."

"Yes, there's some real promise in all this for a better all-around education and maybe for more active citizens." Caine paused and then said, "Isn't that what we say public education should be about?"

Both were silent for a long moment. Then Althea said quietly, "What would it take to provide this kind of experience for everyone? What could we do to get beneath the surface of 'public education as usual'? You know Jon, we should go for something deeper—a more connected learning."

"Yes, but I don't know how to do that. I'm not ready to commit to the LEAD charter school just yet," Caine said slowly. "Let's read and talk around some more."

"I'm not ready to decide now either," Althea agreed. "I need to talk to a lot of other people. Jon, I still don't know what to think. Even worse, I don't know what to do."

Faint fires waver in the mist
elusive, obscured, yet calling to be revealed
energy moves within and among
crossing forms, dimensions, boundaries, beliefs
all are needed for none are the same.

When they met again a few days later, they tried to make sense of what each had read and what they had heard in their many conversations.

As he settled back in his chair, Caine said, "Maybe Kirk hasn't found much to read that's useful, but I sure have. I asked people for book recommendations and did my usual bumbling search on the web. I've got a huge stack of books and articles and a really long list of other possibilities. There's just so much. I don't know where to begin."

"OK, then I'll begin," Althea said. "I confess I have trouble staying interested for very long in the abstract philosophical and theoretical positions on both education and democracy. I know they're important, but I had this problem all the way through school. I think once I've made up my mind about what's important, I need to know how to get on with it! When I read, I want to get to ideas about what to *do* right away."

"I understand how you feel. There's a real sense of urgency about public education right now—not just the deadline for this LEAD project. Everyone is eager to talk about education. I hope they're ready to do something about it too. It's not just the politicians or the public policy intellectuals or the professional schooling communities who are talking. Maybe it's pushed by news events—the way the media covers them—and by all the talking heads, the columnists, and commentators who focus, mostly negatively, on education issues. I don't know, but I had absolutely no trouble getting the subject engaged with anyone."

"Yes, everyone was ready to talk," Althea agreed.

"All the issues that I thought were central to my campaign—you know, about the "crises in the classroom" and about how "kids are our future"— pop up right away."

"But here again, what's important depends on who you talk to," Althea continued. "People are upset with specific things like schools running out of supplies before the year's half done. Or they're angry about a particular requirement, or disciplinary rule, or person—an insensitive teacher or tyrant as principal. Or they're ambivalent about school choice and all the pressures from testing."

"The policy people mentioned those concerns too, but they were especially vocal about school finances," Caine said. "The state's brutal fiscal crisis, the general economic situation and prospects, particular tax strategies, the legislature's budget games and the school bonding issues coming up were all part of the pessimism I heard. With a lid on state taxes, and a shift back to property taxes to support schools, as well as growing constraints on local government, there's just no room to move. Increases in property taxes and local sales taxes are not experienced equitably. And a couple of my former Senate colleagues are now pushing to devote all of the state lottery revenue to education. They claim they can turn 'vice into virtue.' I can no longer tell the difference between paradox and hypocrisy."

Althea smiled as she replied, "But what I heard wasn't only about money. A number of people who are community leaders here in PIP's neighborhood were intense and articulate about the achievement gap between the races. I don't need to tell you about that, but their patience as parents and as activists is long gone—it's not just fierce rhetoric. They see a persistent segregation of access to excellence—gross inequalities not being addressed in, and by, public schools. They are truly angry and very serious about finding something that works for their children. In this part of town, there are more "failing schools" on the superintendent's report card. These struggle to survive with fewer teachers, fewer effective programs, fewer resources, and barely functional school buildings. They are fed-up to here with programs that are full of promises, but in reality are superficial and end up dividing communities-of-color. And Jon, they know deeply as you and I do, that public education is about the *only* hope for our communities and for our country."

"It is! It really is. I've read and heard a lot again about how racism and classism are built into our public schools. No news for us there, but it was a jolting reminder of the complicated problems and all the dug-in positions. I heard much the same thing in my years in the Senate. Some of that also gets expressed, heatedly, about special needs. There are plausible claims about special needs for kids of different races and ethnicities. And the needs of kids with various disabilities—the whole range from physical to emotional to intellectual. There are big unmet needs for the newly arrived immigrant kids, and then there's all the attention to the needs the variously identified 'gifted and talented.' Althea, this 'most urgent list' gets longer and longer."

"Yes it does! And the list should include disruptive youth and the sometimes violent ones like Kirk has over at the Workshop. And, it must include the kids on drugs, the kids who are chronically truant, the kids in gangs, and the kids who are in their fifth school this year. Most often this was said to me in a sort of despairing, "What can we possibly do?" tone of voice. I sure know that feeling."

Caine nodded as he said, "Then there's also the perennial concern about the preparation, recruitment, and continuing development of teachers. Everybody can provide good teacher/bad teacher stories and quite a few authors proposed this as *the* fundamental crisis—that really good teachers are essential to all school reform efforts and we simply don't attract and keep enough of them."

"Yes, teachers were always mentioned in my conversations too. And I heard plenty of individual problems. Parents are worried about their own kid's performance and about the reality of opportunities. They are uncertain about whether schools are preparing their kids for the competitive world they will face. They wanted "excellence" across the board for their children and I understand that. I didn't hear much about contributing to society, or building community, or educating citizens. The new immigrant families were really pointed, almost single minded, about schooling and economic opportunity. To get ahead is what schools are for—and they meant that in economic terms. So, public education must prepare new citizens to be competitive in a really tough economy."

"Right, there's plenty about employment-ready education and the schooling needs of a world class, globally competitive work force," Caine said. "I talked with several guys who are energetically into privatizing schools and having "smart management companies" do school administration, purchase off-the-shelf, ready-to-use technologies, "run a tight ship" and give teachers monetary incentives for results. They gave me slick brochures on a couple of for-profit companies that have already approached the School Board here to provide programs anywhere from a single building all the way up to district-wide. These materials stress economic competition, with order and discipline in the schools. They promise jobs before they get to the paragraph on academic achievement. They have loads of great colored pictures of orderly, serious, poster-child kids—either alone in front of a computer or with a caring teacher or a business community volunteer working with them one-on-one."

"Hey, we should get their ad agency to do our PIP brochure—we're serious, we have poster kids, but we're probably not orderly enough!" Althea said with a smile.

Caine smiled too. "Some other people talked about school-business partnerships and gave me some more reading on examples around the country. Of course, I agree with them about the need for a network of partners. But with LEAD's progressive position and the type of partners in their coalition, their charter school may not be attractive to most corporate and small business types."

"Wait Jon, let's not close those doors yet. I know a lot of business people, many of them small business owners, who have given us great ideas for PIP. Their values about democratic communities and processes can be pretty close to ours. I don't have to agree with them all of the time to appreciate their worth. I don't agree that capitalism equals democracy and that economic competition and efficiency should be the central values for schools. But they too care about broader inclusion and participation and are not simple minded about accountability."

Caine nodded as he looked again at his notes. "We do ask a lot from public education don't we? Just like that long list of needs everyone is talking about, there's a shopping list of goals that keeps getting added to—and how we respond to 'needs' and 'goals' is complicated. I know that in the Senate we usually settled on simply stated goals we could more or less easily reach. And we talked about them as if they really were deeper basic needs. Still, the key questions are about *what* gets the most attention, and *who* gets to decide."

"Yes Jon, it's hard to know where to begin. Almost every day, my kids bring home handouts about their schools' problems—sometimes school specific stuff, but also things that clearly come down from the School Board and the superintendent. The day before yesterday it could have been reading. Yesterday, maybe it was drugs and smoking. Today, bullies and school violence . . . tomorrow it might be multicultural harmony and next week, recycling. I'm not cynical but it seems that beyond scoring on the state tests, our schools can't focus on broad objectives for very long. We're continually bombarded with some new or imagined crisis. And, I don't recall seeing much about democracy or citizenship lately."

"But there is a big emphasis on civic education, Althea. At least it seems that way in the reading I'm doing. I find eloquent calls for broader participation in schooling as a way to prepare students for involvement in civic life. Many authors make compelling cases for more parental engagement, more transparency in school board and administrative activities, and more democratic practices in the classrooms. They see all this as a necessary dimension of academic excellence—not just some add-on frill."

"The people I've been listening to, Jon, may not be as eloquent as your authors, but they are *very* concerned about schooling and social injustice. As I said before, my community leader friends are skeptical about public education's willingness to confront racism. The LEAD proposal itself was almost unanimously dismissed as deeply irrelevant to what is personally, socially, and economically necessary to the people they represent—just another band-aid fix at best. They kept coming back to the achievement gap between white kids and kids-of-color."

"But there's only so much that public schools can do," Caine said with a sigh.

"Yes, I heard that often too, Jon," Althea nodded. "But my feeling now is that we could do more by involving *everyone* in working to improve public education, not just those who self-select to support some special program. Look Jon, I have a strong feeling that our main goal should be something like doing democracy *everywhere* and doing democracy *now*. Public education isn't just for some future time—you know, later in life when kids, as adults, should be active in their communities organizing campaigns, or voting, or being financially responsible. Sure, that's important. Still I think public education should be about 'right now' too—you know, about how we learn together, and make a difference for each other and for society."

"We really don't have many large scale models of equity and democracy in public schooling, at least not in the way we're thinking, do we?" Caine said thoughtfully. "Democracy does mean, at least for me, including a lot more people in a lot more places and a lot more often than we do now. There is a big gap between our high-sounding democratic rhetoric and what we actually do. I heard a lot about that over at the university."

"You heard what?" Althea asked.

"Well, there were two very informed but skeptical profs. They laid out the usual objections to charter schools—their uneven records of accomplishments, the financial glitches, and the growing number of failures not only in this state. They also talked about some impressive successes, and what charter schools could accomplish. They did a lot of 'on the one hand but on the other hand' talk that I loathed as a Senator. If you call for expert testimony, you should at least get clear declarative sentences, even if there are no clear conclusions!"

"They know who you are, Jon. No one wants to be cross-examined by you!" Althea said with a smile.

"Point taken. But they were generous with their time and both gave me a lot more to read. One of the senior fellows at the research center put it this way. He said that regardless of the specific innovations attempted, most education reforms at the core remain locked into an "industrial assembly line model"—you know, in our culture we've turned everything into a commodity—including education. Public schools in general, even new learning initiatives, are seen as production technologies for a consumer economy. Schools are understood as social functions shaped by the market. They are essentially consumer focused, and most often assessed with economic cost–benefits standards. But that's the model for all our social services— right? I'm not talking only about the 'profit sector', but also about the so-called 'public sector' including healthcare, welfare, the courts, and even the political system."

Althea nodded.

"Democracy," Caine continued, "or even 'citizenship' usually ends up like some afterthought—at best centered on decision making or conflict resolution. If we manage to hold a few public meetings and take votes using majority rule, that's sufficient for 'democracy.' As one policy analyst suggested, democracy is now understood as mostly about individuals making personal choices as *active* consumers and *passive* citizens. What's stressed is our individual rights—and that's good! But our democracy talk seems to focus less and less on the importance of being collectively involved in developing strong communities."

"But maybe here, maybe this time, maybe with this LEAD initiative, we can push for something more," Althea mused.

"But I'm still uneasy about this initiative, Althea," Caine said. "I felt that ambivalence in the Senate and often during the campaign. The lofty objectives would glimmer and sound great when I spoke them. And then I would be brought right back to the practical necessities of doing public policy. Getting what you can get is the way it works—it's frustrating to do politics that way. But then 'politics as usual' is not just about one emotion."

"Politics as usual, at all levels, right Jon?" Althea interjected. "We both do politics as usual. We push a little, but as May pointed out to us a couple of weeks ago, we end up devoting most of our energies to defending past gains, or to managing all the operational details for the next agenda item. That's what 'reform as usual' is all about too."

"Yes, May was right. We have to sustain even the incremental progress we've made. That takes incredible effort. It takes winning elections. It takes bureaucratic tenacity. Reform, or maybe what we call 'progress', isn't about a few of us getting what we want. It's not about just one well-stated goal. It's not about one organizational achievement or one piece of important legislation," Caine said forcefully. "We've got to build a broader base for reform."

"So where do we begin?" Althea continued. "Maybe the 'deep democracy' we are dancing around here requires something more like 'deep social learning.' I don't know what that means either, Jon."

Given prevailing philosophic and pragmatic commitments to individualism, what is the meaning and purpose of social learning?

Most systemic attempts at public education reform have centered on improving the academic performance of individual students. Performance is assessed through standardized testing, indicated by graduation rates, and confirmed by readiness for post-secondary education and the job market. This predominant pattern rests on the widespread assumption that academic progress is most effectively realized through individualized, competitive, and convergent approaches to teaching and learning. Benchmarks of minimum competency and standards of excellence are identified and sanctioned across traditional bodies of knowledge (e.g., mathematics and science) and inquiry skills (e.g., critical thinking and literacy). Individual students and their schools can then be evaluated, compared, rewarded or targeted for necessary improvement based on a set of shared criteria. School rankings are well publicized and carefully scrutinized when making important decisions ranging from voting for school board candidates to choice of residential neighborhood. Parental choice is further supported by open enrollment, and families feel pressured to compete for the limited number of slots available in the most successful local schools.

In doing so, we explicitly and implicitly impose a *market economy metaphor* on the process of public schooling. Knowledge is treated as a commodity available for acquisition in a free market of educational opportunity. The goal is to accumulate as much as possible in a manner that ensures both personal advancement and attainment of the social status necessary for effective participation in a competitive, credential-driven society.

Culturally dominant market values shape all aspects of public education. Policymakers and administrators are understandably engrossed in the demands of the material culture. Much of their perspective and most of their decisions are framed in budgetary terms, calculated as economic cost-benefits, and executed through bureaucratic organizations that are continually admonished to be more "business like." Much needed flexibility is restricted in response to political pressures that advocate centralized control and feature financial imperatives as the driving rationale. In some cases, school administration is "contracted out" to management firms in accordance with mandated privatization programs.

Parents, politicians, and corporate constituents of public education, along with most mass media, also develop their judgments in terms of economic choice. During political campaigns and local school district bonding elections attempts are made to persuade with simplistic economic slogans. "No new taxes" is a familiar and effective theme. The actual uses of tax monies—old or new—usually receive less attention.

Options such as charter schools, service learning, or specific literacy approaches, are also framed predominantly in terms of their projected financial implications. Teachers are sometimes treated as "cost centers" and regularly urged to become more "efficient." In their public conversations, teachers are often positioned to defend their conditions of work (e.g., 9–10 month contracts), or their salary and benefits (e.g., merit pay versus traditional salary schedules). Overall, forms of quantification that involve risky oversimplification impose deep social consequences.

As the largest state budget line, public education should be assessed in complex cost terms—not in relation to some single figure that purports to be the crucial summation or the most compelling comparison. Over-reliance on economized forms of reflection restricts policy analysis and imagination. Economic efficiency (i.e., more for less), understood largely in terms of personal impact, becomes the dominant decision criterion. In an array of multiple paths to diverse objectives, effectiveness (i.e., goal achievement) collapses into measuring the readily measurable. Our actions as voters are persistently represented as simplistic economic choices between alternatives generated by others.

This pervasive outlook casts all individuals as competitive consumers in all aspects of their lives. For students, even though their identities are multifaceted and socially constructed, their prospects are narrowly scripted as opportunities to exercise individual choice in pursuit of personal ambitions. Gaps in achievement are to be expected based upon differences in academic interest, motivation, and merit. Segregation by ability is accepted as the most efficient way to provide specialized support both for students demonstrating the highest levels of performance and for those facing significant challenges. Separation by economic background occurs as families willing and able to make additional financial sacrifices, seek out more heavily resourced public schools in affluent neighborhoods or opt for more selective and directly accountable private schools. Segregation by cultural, civic or spiritual belief is accepted as a particularly important expression of individual choice. Differences in gender, class, race, ethnicity, language proficiency, and other factors likely to affect academic performance are treated as inconsequential, evaded, or targeted for remediation.

Although applying market metaphors to public schooling may serve current cultural and economic expectations, it impoverishes student opportunities to develop the dynamic and multidimensional identities necessary for full democratic participation in a diverse society. Something more, something different, is required if public schools are to provide broad access to knowledge that is of deep personal meaning and profound social value. Something more, something different, is needed if we are to renew resources of shared experience and social inquiry, within common schools for the common good.

Composition . . .
to creatively integrate
experience, expressions, emotions, beliefs
beyond simple combination or resigned compromise
insights offered, interwoven, adapted, arranged
are joined in radical grace.

Movement toward deeper, more inclusive forms of social inquiry and civic participation could be facilitated by extending our gaze beyond the market economy as the focal metaphor guiding public education reform. In principle and in practice, it is useful to explore the possibility of re-envisioning teaching and learning as an *economy of gift exchange.*

Metaphorically, in a gift economy goods and services flow through the community as contributions rather than commodities. As needs and desires are dynamic, context-specific, and unlimited in variety and number; so too are the ideas, objects, and actions that may function as gifts. The value of a gift is defined in terms of the quality of relationships established through its exchange. To be classified as a gift, the relationship must be characterized by mutual affirmation and benefit. If the exchange is experienced as negative or neutral, there is no gift.

Gifts are interpreted neither as entitlements nor as just rewards. In a sense, they are bestowed as blessings, received through grace. Once acquired, the value of a gift can only be sustained through its development and donation. As a gift is first enhanced and then strategically shared, its value to the individual releasing it increases. In this vision, individual gain is acquired through acts of benevolence and humility rather than achieved through maintaining competitive advantage and a strong sense of personal security. When gifts move, community is created—community that emerges not in response to joint efforts of those promoting similar interests, but instead through acts of giving and receiving among those possessing diverse needs and potentials. Knowledge is understood as a gift to be received, deepened, and shared by all members of a learning community.

Learning is fundamentally *relational*. It is centered on the discovery of new, often surprising conceptual patterns that provide broad direction in contexts of complexity and uncertainty. It finds and sustains connections across cognitive, emotional, intuitive, aesthetic, and kinesthetic ways of knowing. Learning is best supported through interpersonal relationships that are close, continuing, and egalitarian. The focus is not only on preparing learners to derive personal meaning, but also on determining how gifts of knowledge might be made accessible and beneficial to others. Roles and responsibilities of teacher and learner continually shift as individual contributions are collectively considered, enriched, and refined.

Learning is *conversational*. Instructive exchanges are characterized by open and exploratory query and response. The goal is to continue, complicate, and extend consideration rather than to move as quickly as possible toward resolution. Careful attention is devoted to both speaking and listening. Development of skill in self-expression is balanced with preparation to listen actively and respond with respect and creativity to the concerns of others. Conversational interactions do not necessarily lead to a sense of complete agreement, but often instead to experiences of 'resonance'— shared awareness that a particular path reflects genuine commitment to and possibilities for amplifying the common good.

Learning is *integrative*. Learning, as life, is sustained not when interaction across difference is actively restricted or merely tolerated, but instead when those possessing distinctive attributes interact and evolve together. Diversity is sought and supported because it provides opportunities for creative synthesis and renewal. Varied insights are carefully arranged in multifaceted compositions that compel reflective action. In this manner, new gifts of knowledge are continually developed and dispersed.

In a gift economy of teaching and learning, it is through full engagement in relational, conversational, and integrative processes that each individual's unique form of *giftedness* emerges. Academic excellence is multidimensional, inclusive, and defined within the context of significant social relationships. Excellence is understood not only as cumulative, defined as expanding expertise, but also as connective, developed by extending one's relationships within, among, and beyond prior boundaries.

Guided by the metaphor of gift exchange, the landscape of public education reform can be altered. Educational policy could shift to emphasize student proficiency in social adaptation and innovation rather than in competitive acquisition. The well-established practice of allowing parents and students to join with like-minded others in choosing specialized instruction, could be balanced with incentives for involvement in programs that support interaction across differences in position, experience, aptitudes and interests. Curriculum and pedagogy, along with school and classroom populations and environments, could be configured to assure experience of varied worldviews and lifestyles, with special attention devoted to differences known to elicit fear and discrimination.

Assuming the instructional primacy of establishing egalitarian relationships, educational policy could shift to actively counter school-based expressions of social injustice. Predictable gaps in performance and opportunity based on race, class, gender, or handicapping condition would not be tolerated. Private consideration of test scores for diagnostic purposes would continue to be important. Public reporting, however, would feature longitudinal district-level comparisons aimed at assessing communal progress and decreasing gaps among specific student populations. Published interpretations would emphasize *public responsibility for the welfare of all students.* The current assumption that individual families should be responsible for acquiring educational services for their own children, regardless of whether or not they have the resources necessary to do so, would no longer be considered appropriate. School based comparisons would be utilized internally to shape patterns of resource distribution so that the highest levels of support are provided for students, teachers, families, and communities struggling together to raise academic achievement under the most challenging conditions. Initiatives designed to secure opportunities for all young people to learn and grow within the context of caring peers and adults would be developed. Possible examples might include division of large impersonal schools into small learning communities and full integration of social service professionals and programs within schools. Increased public support could also be provided for public schools actively engaged with community constituents in addressing social justice concerns.

Understanding that the pursuit of knowledge is advanced through divergent and dynamic patterns of exchange, approaches to inquiry and related pathways toward academic success would diversify and deepen. Standardized assessment, used to measure acquisition of content knowledge and basic academic skills, would be complemented by those used to identify and document the broadest possible range of learning styles and forms of contribution. Research-based strategies for self-reflection, along with peer and teacher evaluation, would be implemented to extend and refine awareness of learning processes, challenges, and assets specific to each learner.

Collaboration is necessary to teach and learn as *social selves*. By centering on the potential and purpose of social inquiry, just and affirming communities can be established and sustained. Exploring the metaphor of public schooling as gift exchange expands our vision and directs our action toward reform that yields more inclusive, expansive, and enduring forms of personal growth and social progress.

> *"Knowledge emerges only through invention, and re-invention,*
> *through the restless, impatient, continuing, hopeful inquiry*
> *human beings pursue*
> *in the world, with the world, and with each other."*
>
> —Paulo Freire
> *Pedagogy of the Oppressed*

Exploratory Democratic Practice: Cultural Futures Delphi

The Cultural Futures Delphi is a deliberative survey technique designed to engage diverse constituencies in *social inquiry and imagination* (i.e., developing a shared vision of possible, desirable, and sustainable reform) linked to *collaborative policy design* (i.e., identifying strategies and resources necessary to enact that vision). The technique is rooted in a method of technological forecasting designed to elicit sound predictive judgments from technical experts. It has emerged as a particularly promising tool for systemic democratic reform due to its demonstrated capacity to support and extend social discourse, understanding, coalition building, decision-making, and principled action in relation to complex and controversial issues. Cultural Futures Delphi is distinctive as a deliberative method in that it provides opportunities for clarifying and evolving consensual knowledge through a process that is socially interactive, yet protects individual privacy.

Cultural Futures Delphi is a flexible technique that can be creatively adapted to specific reform contexts ranging from classroom applications, to school and district level analyses, to more extensive state, national, and international projects. Promising examples might include:

- supporting collaborative research and reflection in a secondary social studies class leading to the development of school policy to address issues such as youth alienation or the rise of violence on school grounds;
- orchestrating broad-based participation in the design of a charter school;
- informing a statewide debate on the restructuring of graduation standards or fiscal policy to support public education;
- deepening and extending a national discourse on topics ranging from science education, to community service, to teacher preparation; and
- providing an international forum for addressing challenges to public education posed by globalization.

The Cultural Futures Delphi proceeds in four phases:

Phase 1—*Preparation:*   A core design group is convened to assume responsibility for orchestrating the process. Their first task is to identify and engage members of a much larger response group inclusive of all constituencies that will affect, and be affected by, the proposed initiative.

Phase 2—*Questionnaire Development:*   Delphi participants are first asked individually and anonymously to share relevant insights concerning the design of a reform initiative through focused yet open-ended interviews. These are conducted by members of the core design team utilizing, for example, the Ethnographic Futures Interview process described in Chapter 3.

Core design members then work to identify both common themes and distinctive insights represented in the interview responses. These resources—along with concerns and issues drawn from relevant theory and research, media representations etc.—are used to construct a series of forced choice statements to be included in a questionnaire. The statements are carefully and collectively constructed, ordered and refined; then organized into a comprehensive questionnaire that represents the complexity of perspectives on the reform task under consideration.

Phase 3—*Questionnaire Response/Analysis/Feedback.*   The Delphi questionnaire is distributed to core design team members and all those interviewed for their private response. Questionnaire participation may also be extended to a larger community of respondents, again attempting to involve as many potentially interested or affected parties as possible.

Questionnaire responses are analyzed by members of the core design team. A comprehensive summary of the results is presented to all questionnaire respondents so they might reconsider, and possibly revise, their initial judgments in light of the opinions of others. The process of questionnaire response/analysis/feedback/response is continued until an acceptable level of agreement is reached regarding key design directions and strategies.

Phase 4—*Continuing Design/Evaluation/Revision of Reform Initiatives in light of Questionnaire Results.*   Questionnaire results are used to determine design tasks and to guide working groups in the development of specific components of the reform project. Throughout the reform process, priorities and approved strategies identified through the Cultural Futures Delphi can be considered collectively to assess the quality of the project components and the extent to which the initiative addresses aspirations determined democratically among diverse participants.

Broad-based participation and 'ownership' in the selection of focal intentions, priorities, and strategies are essential to ensure the sustained success of any progressive reform initiative.

The Cultural Futures Delphi supports these democratic aspirations by providing a forum capable of accommodating both private reflection and social inquiry, expressions of diverse perspectives as well as consensual agreement.

Thematic Bibliographic References

On the market exchange metaphor in politics and public education:

Ball, S. (2003). *Class strategies and the education market: The middle classes and social advantage.* New York: Routledge Falmer.

Belmonte, D., & Ayers, W. (2001). *Teaching from the deep end: Succeeding with today's classroom challenges.* New York: Corwin Press.

Benveniste, L., Carnoy, M., & Rothstein, R. (2002). *All else equal: Are public and private schools different?* New York: Routledge Falmer.

Boyles, D. (2000). *American educational corporations: The free market goes to school.* London: Falmer.

Bracey, G. (2002). *The war against America's public schools: Privatizing schools, commercializing education.* Boston: Allyn and Bacon.

Chubb, J. (Ed.). (2005). *Within our reach: How America can educate every child.* Stanford, CA: Hoover Institution Press.

Chubb, J., & Moe, T. (1990). *Politics, markets and America's schools.* Washington, DC: Brookings Institute Press.

Coulson, A. (1999). *Market education: The unknown history.* Somerset, NJ: Transaction Publishers.

Engel, M. (2000). *The struggle for control of public education: Market ideology vs. democratic values.* Philadelphia, PA: Temple University Press.

Fiske, E., & Ladd, H. (2000). *When schools compete: A cautionary tale.* Washington, DC: Brookings Institution Press.

Gorard, S., Fitz, J., & Taylor, C. (2003). *Schools, markets and choice policies.* New York: Routledge Falmer.

Grubb, W., & Lazerson, M. (2004). *The educational gospel: The economic power of schooling.* Cambridge, MA: Harvard University Press.

Henig, J. (2001). *Rethinking schools choice: Limits of the market metaphor.* Princeton, NJ: Princeton University Press.

House, E. (1998). *Schools for sale: Why free market policies won't improve America's schools and what will.* New York: Teachers College Press.

Ladd, H. (2002). *Market-based reforms in urban education.* Washington, DC: Economic Policy Institute.

Langer, J. (2004). *Getting to excellent: How to create better schools.* New York: Teachers College Press.

Levin, H. (2001). *Privatizing education: Can the marketplace deliver choice, efficiency, equity, and social cohesion?* Cambridge, MA: Westview Press.

Loveless, T. (1999). *The tracking wars: State reform meets school policy.* Washington, DC: Brookings Institution.

Lowe, R., & Miner, B. (1996). *Selling out our schools: Vouchers, markets, and the future of public education.* Milwaukee, WI: Rethinking Schools, Ltd.

McNeil, L. (2000). *Contradictions of school reform: Educational costs of standardized testing.* New York: Routledge Falmer.

Molnar, A. (2005). *School commercialism: From democratic ideal to market commodity.* Oxford: Routledge.

Orfield, G., & Kornhaber, M. (Eds.). (2001). *Raising standards or raising barriers?* New York: Century Foundation Press.

Packer, M. (2000). *Changing classes: School reform and the new economy.* Cambridge, MA: Cambridge University Press.

Sacks, P. (2001). *Standardized minds: The high price of America's testing culture and what we can do to change it.* New York: Perseus Books.

Saltman, K. (2000). *Collateral damage.* Lanham, MD: Rowman & Littlefield.

Saltman, K. (2005). *The Edison schools: Corporate schooling and the assault on public education.* London: Falmer Press.

Spring, J. (2003). *Educating the consumer citizen: A history of the marriage of schools, advertising, and media.* Mahwah, NJ: Lawrence Erlbaum Associates.

Walberg, H., & Bast, J. (2003). *Education and capitalism: How overcoming our fear of markets and economics can improve America's schools.* Washington, DC: Hoover Institution Press.

Witte, J. (1999). *The market approach to education: An analysis of America's first voucher.* Princeton, NJ: Princeton University Press.

On the gift exchange metaphor in public education:

Adams, M., Blumenfield, W., Castenada, R., Hackman, H., Peters, M., & Zuniga, X. (Eds.) (2000). *Readings for diversity and social justice.* New York: Routledge Falmer.

Adams, M., Bell, L., & Griffin, P. (Eds.). (1997). *Teaching for diversity and social justice: A sourcebook.* New York: Routledge Falmer.

Banks, J., & Banks, C. (Eds.). (2001). *Multicultural education: Issues and perspectives* (4th ed.). New York: John Wiley and Sons.

Berends, M. et. al. (2002). *Challenges of conflicting school reforms: Effects of new American schools in a high poverty district.* Santa Monica, CA: Rand.

Boyer, J., & Baptiste, P. (1996). *Transforming the curriculum for multicultual understandings: A practitioner's handbook.* San Francisco: Caddo Gap Press.

Bray, J., Smith, L., Lee, J., & Yorks, L. (Eds.). (2000). *Collaborative inquiry in practice: Action, reflection and meaning making.* Thousand Oaks, CA: Sage.

Cazden, C. (2001). *Classroom discourse: The language of teaching and learning.* Portsmouth, NH: Heinemann.

Chang-Wells, G., & Wells, G. (1992). *Constructing knowledge together: Classrooms as centers of inquiry and literacy.* Portsmouth, NH: Heinemann.

Christiansen, P., & Young, M. (1996). *Yesterday, today, and tomorrow: Meeting the challenge of our multicultural America and beyond.* San Francisco: Caddo Gap Press.

Cohen J. (Ed.). (1999). *Educating minds and hearts: Social emotional learning and the passage into adolescence.* New York: Teachers College Press.

Dewey, J. (1997). *Experience and education* (reprint ed.). New York: Free Press.

Duarte, E., & Smith, S. (2000). *Foundational perspectives in multicultural education.* New York: Longman.

Finnan, C., & Swanson, J. (2000). *Accelerating the learning for all students: Cultivating culture change in schools, classrooms, and individuals.* Boulder, CO: Westview Press.

Fritzberg, G. (1999). *In the shadow of "excellence": Recovering a vision of educational opportunity for all.* San Francisco: Caddo Gap Press.

Ginwright, S. (2004). *Black in school: Afrocentric reform, urban youth, and the promise of hip-hop culture.* New York: Teachers College Press.

hooks, b. (1994). *Teaching to transgress: Education as the practice of freedom.* New York: Routledge Falmer.

Huber, T. (2002). *Quality learning experiences for ALL students.* San Francisco: Caddo Gap Press.

Hyde, L. (1983). *The gift: Imagination and the erotic life of property.* New York: Vintage Books.

Jackson, J. (2001). *Harlemworld: Doing race and class in contemporary black America.* Chicago: University of Chicago Press.

Kailin, J. (2002). *Antiracist education: From theory to practice.* Lanham, MD: Rowman and Littlefield.

Kroll, L., Cossey, R., Donahue, D., Galguera, T., Kubler, V., Ershler, A., & Tucher, P. (2004). *Teaching as principled practice: Managing complexity for social justice.* Thousand Oaks, CA: Sage.

Kumashiro, K. (2004). *Against common sense: Teaching and learning toward social justice.* New York: Routledge Falmer.

Mirochnik, E., & Sherman, D. (Eds.). (2003). *Passion and pedagogy: Relation, creation, and transformation in teaching.* New York: Peter Lang.

Nieto, S. (1999). *The light in their eyes: Creating multicultural learning communities.* New York: Teachers College Press.

Nieto, S. (2003). *Affirming diversity: The sociopolitical context of multicultural education* (4th ed.). Boston: Allyn & Bacon.

Portes, P. (2005). *Dismantling educational inequality: A cultural-historical approach to closing the achievement gap.* New York: Peter Lang.

Ramsey, P., Williams, L., & Vold, E. (2002). *Multicultural education: A sourcebook* (2nd ed.). New York: Routledge Falmer.

Sawyer, R. (2001). *Creating conversations: Improvisation in everyday discourse.* Cresskill, NJ: Hampton Press.

Sidorkin, A. (2002). *Learning relations: Impure education, de-schooled schools, and dialogue with evil.* New York: Peter Lang.

Sleeter, C., & Grant, C. (2002). *Making choices for multicultural education: Five approaches to race, class, and gender* (4th ed.). New York: Wiley.

Trifonas, P. (Ed.). (2002). *Pedagogies of difference: Rethinking education for social justice.* New York: Routledge Falmer.

Vincent C. (Ed.), (2004). *Social justice, education and identity.* New York: Falmer Press.

Walling, D. (2005). *Visual knowing: Connecting art and ideas across the curriculum.* Thousand Oaks, CA: Corwin Press/Sage.

Williams, B. (Ed.). (1996). *Closing the achievement gap: A vision for changing beliefs and practices.* Alexandria, VA: Association for Supervision and Curriculum Development.

Wilson, B., & Corbett, H. (2001). *Listening to urban kids: School reform and the teachers they want.* Albany: SUNY Press.

Zins, J., Weissberg, R., Wang, M., & Walberg, H. (Eds.). (2004). *Building academic success on social and emotional learning.* New York: Teachers College Press.

Reflection:

Freire, P. (1970). *Pedagogy of the oppressed* (p. 58). New York: The Seabury Press.

Exploratory Democratic Practice: Cultural Futures Delphi

Cogan, J., & Derricott, R. (Eds.). (1998). *Citizenship for the 21st century: An international perspective in education.* London: Kogan Page.

Cookson, P. (1986). Charting the unknown: Delphi and policy Delphi strategies for international cooperation. *International Journal of Lifelong Education 5*(1), 3–13.

Hill, K., & Fowles, J. (1975). The methodological worth of the Delphi forecasting technique. *Technological Forecasting and Social Change, 7,* 179–192.

Jillson, I. (1975). Developing guidelines for the Delphi method. *Technological Forecasting and Social Change 7,* 221–222.

Kurth-Schai, R. (1991). Educational systems design by children for children. *Educational Foundations, 5*(3), 19–39.

Kurth-Schai, R. (1988). Collecting the thoughts of children: A Delphic approach. *Journal of Research and Development in Education, 21*(3), 53–59.

Kurth-Schai, R., & Green, C. (2000). Conversation, composition, and courage: Re-envisioning technologies for education and democracy. *Educational Studies, 31*(1), 19–32.

Kurth-Schai, R., Poolpatarachewin, C., & Pitiyanuwat, S. (1998). Using the Delphi cross-culturally: Towards the development of policy. In J. Cogan & R. Derricott (Eds.), *Citizenship for the 21st century* (pp. 77–92). London: Kogan Page.

Linstone, H., & Clive, W. (Eds.). (1977). *Futures research: New directions.* Reading, MA: Addison-Wesley.

Linstone, W., & Turoff, M., (Eds.). (1975). *The Delphi method: Techniques and applications.* Reading, MA: Addison-Wesley.

Martorella, P. (1991). Consensus building among social educators: A Delphi study. *Theory and Research in Social Education, 19*(1), 83–94.

Poolpatarachewin, C. (1980). Ethnographic Delphi futures research: Thai university pilot project. *Journal of Cultural and Educational Futures, 2*(4), 11–19.

Rauch, W. (1979). The decision Delphi. *Technological Forecasting and Social Change, 15,* 159–169.

c h a p t e r   6

Advocacy

> *Beyond assumed configurations of power*
> *constrained by immediate concerns and circumstance*
> *beyond practiced stances of solidarity*
> *reliant upon force of argument and strength of opposition*
> *beyond islands of benefit, hard won*
> *for deserving but exclusive constituents*
> *lie paths toward civic liberation.*

*E*arly on the morning before the LEAD Charter School Board was to be officially announced Caine and Althea met again.

"Well, we're going to the meeting at Jim's this afternoon and we're both still uncertain, right?" Caine asked hesitantly.

Althea slowly nodded as Caine continued, "I talked with another university professor about Jim's charter school initiative. He was generally quite encouraging and even offered to consult if we proceed. But he also said that the charter school will need to be "contextually connected"—which he said meant that it needs to be part of a "sustaining community" and not become what he called an "isolated phenomenon." His research indicates that while charter schools often start out with a specialized constituency, they must develop a broader base of support if they are going to be success-

Re-Envisioning Education and Democracy, pages 85–108
Copyright © 2006 by Information Age Publishing
All rights of reproduction in any form reserved.

ful. That's difficult because all of the schools he's studied begin with the ideas of one creative person or a small group of effective advocates. Along with all the other demands of getting up and running a school, coalition building and maintenance is ignored, and in the long run that's lethal. There is also a tendency over time to simplify the mission defensively and to become a "one special feature" site. He worried too about "burn out" and what he called "a staff succession crisis" after the first wave of enthusiasts have left."

"Tell me about it," said Althea. "All of those are clear and present dangers for us at PIP."

"So, do you think Jim has his coalition partners at LEAD fully on board for the long haul?" Caine asked. "And is LEAD still open to adding some new partners to share in moving on this proposal? I don't know how much any of us are truly open to new ideas or directions. I thought about that yesterday after I met with one really tough critic," Caine said quietly.

"What about the critic?" Althea asked.

"Wow! She was almost overwhelming. I've encountered a lot of high intensity people in all my years in court and in politics but, well, wow! The bottom line for her, I think, is that anything short of comprehensive public education reform is futile. More than just futile—unethical! She contends that charter schools, magnet schools, vouchers, home schools, and any other kind of specifically focused programs for specifically selected students not only draw off needed resources but also segregate. They reallocate resources—like money, teachers, equipment, even buildings and for sure public attention—diverting all that from truly needy public schools. As for segregation, she argued that selective schools actually promote racism and class divisions, while providing well-meaning reformers with what she called 'illusions of progressive accomplishment.'"

"Wow, indeed. That's quite an indictment, as you would say," Althea mused.

"What's more, organizations like LEAD, she said, should resist these diversions and go for radical systemic change. LEAD is too important to waste its energies and imagination on superficial educational pseudo-reforms. She knows about Jim's project and concludes that the impact of this type of charter school would be incremental at best, and at worst would play right into the hands of the power elite. It will just further segregate, stratify, and provide false satisfaction. She did agree that public education should continue to be LEAD's core mission, and that the 'E' in LEAD must always stand for 'Education.' But she was adamant about progressives working more directly and creatively to confront the educational injustices structured into current school systems at all levels. We must do more than give a few kids, their well-intentioned parents, and a handful of innovative teachers short-term relief programs—especially ones that get a lot of co-opting publicity. She said we must not give up on broader visions. No, I think she said *deeper visions*."

"Jon, you sound a little intimated by her," Althea said with a smile.

"She did have me squirming both by her analysis and also by her passion. We do need to hear these critical accounts even though it's hard to listen. We mostly try to counter those who we assume are opposed to our ideals. But she is definitely a "friendly critic." I'm wondering now how many there are within the LEAD coalition who could expend that much energy promoting the values we share. I wonder too how many would support her emphasis on LEAD's 'E' word. Jim is really smart, energetic and dedicated to the community organizing approach that has been so important through all his years at LEAD. But I don't think he has her strategic sense of possibility—or, a commitment to, in her words, the "civic responsibility of promoting progressive social change through public education." Anyway, I came away, a little battered and a lot more thoughtful. But then she kindly gave me more reading and another long list of websites."

Althea remained silent.

Caine waited and then asked, "OK Althea, now what about you? Do you think a charter school is the way to go?"

"I'm still not sure, Jon. Charter schools have real flaws, but they can also be incredible opportunities. All the possibilities have not yet been exhausted, as far as I can tell. Do you think that this time we can avoid some of the risks, do something important, and have a broad impact?"

"I honestly don't know. I've been close to the charter school movement, and seen by many as a strong supporter for a long time. I wrote most of the legislation and helped push it through. On balance, I do think that charter schools are one very promising approach," Caine said.

Althea took a moment and then replied, "I agree, and yet I'm torn because I think what I really want is to get involved in something that could make a difference for *all* public school students, not just for a select few. I'm troubled by a sense that we typically do the most for young people at both ends of the spectrum—you know, exciting opportunities for the 'gifted and talented' and impressive programs like Building Visions for kids at the other end of the achievement scale. That's really understandable because sharply focused programs can more quickly show concrete results. But in the long run, across the whole system, only small numbers of specifically targeted kids actually receive what all students deserve: small classes, innovative programs, state-of-the-art technology, and highly dedicated and creative teachers."

Caine remained thoughtfully silent. It was not a moment to lead the witness.

Althea paused again before continuing. "I guess what's bothering me is that the LEAD idea is just as individually-centered as most other public school reform initiatives. Sure, there's a much more explicit social justice agenda. But doesn't Jim want his LEAD charter school to carefully select able students?" She looked down again at the top page of the proposal packet in front of her. "Doesn't he want to attract students who, as it says here, can become "LEADers in the ongoing struggle to organize democratic communities?" That's great stuff, Jon. I mean, I really do like the political ideas in Jim's proposal, but isn't it all focused on preparing a select group of individuals for public leadership?"

"But that leadership is badly needed, Althea. Besides, there's a lot of public resonance for preparing future leaders," Caine stated. "The School Board will be responsive, the media will eat it up, and even the usual critics will confine themselves to attacking the mission statement's progressive rhetoric. Wait a minute . . . maybe I'm starting to glimpse your point."

"Do I have a point?" Althea laughed.

"This LEAD initiative has an abundance of good words. As you say, Jim is excellent at writing inspiring language. The mission statement is quite a piece of work! Yet it is, as you also point out, individually focused. But that's how we usually think about democracy. As we've said to each other before, we talk mostly about an individual rights-based democracy. We think about public education in much the same way—as preparation to assume individually identified societal roles. What Jim wants to do is to model a public school initiative that effectively prepares select individuals to exercise leadership in their critical role as social activists."

"You sure can sum up a case," Althea remarked. "And Jim's dead right. We should focus our reform efforts on public schools. That's why we're here this morning. Education and democracy almost seem to be the same thing. They are always about teaching and learning, and both are about getting better at knowing and doing."

"But how do we know if we're getting better?" Jon asked quietly. "How can we know if LEAD's charter school proposal is moving toward a form of democracy that is deeper in its meaning and broader in its reach?"

"Oh, this is why I hate all the philosophy and theory, Jon. We ought to be able to answer that question, or at least come to agreement on some things that are necessary. Can we identify all that happens in public education that is *not* democratic? That's easy. Can we point to new ideas or strategies in the LEAD proposal that are likely to make learning more democratic, and democratic participation and governance more informed and inclusive? I'm not so sure. How can we break out of being stuck?"

"Hopefully, we'll both gain some new insights this afternoon," Caine mumbled.

Flashes of brilliance scatter in the wind
restless skies move restless minds to wander and wait
seeking collective discernment
among promising though impermanent paths.

Jim MacIver began the meeting with a broad smile. "It's great to see all of you here." He glanced around the table and continued, "We all agree this charter school is LEAD's most important immediate opportunity. We all agree on the goals identified in the draft mission statement. Now that it's no longer a draft, we can put muscles and flesh on this skeleton."

"Wait a second please," Althea interrupted. "Jim, the mission statement is excellent and, as you know, we discussed a few possible revisions and additions when we chatted on the phone last week. I've been doing a lot of thinking and I wonder if anyone else had suggestions they wanted to share before we move on. Jim, I know you said you consulted with each of us individually, but that's not quite enough. I'd like to hear from others."

"Yeah, this is an excellent mission statement, Jim," Jack McClusky spoke briskly. He is the Community Relations Liaison for the public employees union and a member of the State Trades and Labor Council. "So, let's be quick about any lingering afterthoughts. We all know that any mission statement is just boilerplate—yeah OK, we need 'em to head up proposals, but nobody actually takes them seriously. The crucial stuff is the guts of the proposal—so let's get on with it!"

"I'm not so sure no one pays attention to the goals and objectives, Jack," Caine said. "Anyway, I'd also like to hear what others think about Jim's draft. We can get on with the program details in a few minutes."

Jim looked particularly impatient, but remained silent. His LEAD staff colleague, Bobbi Williams, quickly looked around the table and said, "OK people, we've got to manage time on this. There's a lot of heavy lifting to do to meet what the school district and state administrators want. I know the mission statement is important, but it's not the really tough work we have to get done. Besides, I've shown this draft to a couple of staff at the School Board and they didn't see any landmines."

"Well, I see a few explosive possibilities!" June Washington was the President of the Teachers Union local. "First, the language on the failures and inadequacies of public schools seems unnecessarily harsh. Those sections are quite negative—won't that make at least some of the School Board members defensive? And, from the teachers' point of view, we're sensitive about the "school failure" label. We're usually made the scapegoats. And there may not be enough explanation up front about it being a teacher-based program, recognizing teachers' professionalism, their imagination, their commitment, and so on. Jim, I don't think we're talking about any wholesale revisions here."

"Yes, don't look so panicked, Jim," Althea laughed. "My suggestion would be to strengthen our democratic intentions. Like how democratic are we proposing to be? What do we mean when we say "democracy" and how do we enact that in this charter school?"

"Oh come on Althea," grumbled Jack. "This is a straightforward mission statement for a complicated proposal. It's not some kind of big-deal philosophical treatise. We all know what's meant here. We all share a progressive take on politics and public education. I know we all probably have our favorite catch word or feel-good phrase to include, but this opening section is just symbolic."

"Look Jack, I do think we need to be careful," Margaret Rudolph said quietly. She coordinates the federation of consumer cooperatives across the county. "I've seen initiatives hijacked by powerful players, or smart special interests, or skillful adversaries when we well-intentioned folk could not be coherent about what we meant, or what we actually needed, in proposals like this one. I'm referring to words like "community" and "cooperative" and "partnership" that became quicksand for us."

Jim, Bobbi, and Jack exchanged glances and almost in unison leaned back from the table. Bobbi began typing notes on her laptop.

"That's what's happened a couple of times at PIP too, Rudi," Althea said. "What I think we should try for—and we're just about there, Jim—is to signal that we're not aspiring to 'democracy as usual' with a charter school that will turn out to be 'education as usual.' Jon and I have been reading and conversing a lot. Jack, I agree we do need to do most of this in the details, but I'm also sure that we desperately need to be as clear as we can about our central values."

"Jim, can I say something too?" a voice came from a group seated together around the end the conference table.

"Sure, of course," Jim replied quickly. "I'm sorry, let me introduce all of you. These folks are going to be the core of the LEAD school faculty. Some of you have already met Kirk Peterson. He does visual arts over at the Building Visions Workshop and has been astoundingly successful. Mary Mitchell is a great science and math teacher. She was the city's science teacher of the year awhile back. Joy Garcia is awesome in literacy, literature and communications and has been part of a bunch of innovations. She has done amazing work with multicultural programs. And last, but certainly not least, over in the corner is Morrie Bernstein who has pioneered ground-breaking, community connected, social studies curricula all over the metro area."

Joy Garcia looked around the table as she said, "I too think it's worth a little of our time to be careful about what we mean by Jim's fine words, and how they can be played out in our classrooms. Ms. Putnam, just what do you mean that this project might turn out to be 'democracy and education as usual'?"

Althea turned to Caine, "Jon, do you want to begin?"

He began carefully. "Over these last weeks, both Althea and I were struck with how narrowly the concept 'democracy' is understood. Now Jim's statement refers to our interest in "deeper democracy." But most people we read or talked with seem stalled on democracy as if it's limited to campaigns and elections. For some, it meant the "rule of law" and Constitutional rights. Important concerns certainly. But don't we have a shot here at broadening and deepening understandings of what democracy can mean and what we can become? Can't we do more than play into the typical voting and rights expectations?"

Jack erupted, "Jon, Jon, come on! More than any of us here you should know that any talk that can be effectively labeled as "different" or, God forbid, "liberal" by our many opponents is suicide. I for one do not want to be part of another martyr movement! This LEAD project is all about doing what is doable, right here, right now!"

Caine glanced warily at Althea before he continued. "Of course we all want this to work, but I've become aware that most of what we've actually accomplished in the past is incremental change at best. I know that's true for the legislation I had a hand in. That's the way politics works. I don't think that in most of what happens—whether through LEAD's many good programs, or at PIP, or in Rudi's community co-ops, or through the unions—we've actually broadened the base of accountability much in spite of all our impressive rhetoric. All of our valuable efforts are still produced largely top down—from beginning to end. Look, I know we all feel we've made progress. LEAD and its partners are really good at what they do, and what they do is necessary and commendable. But has it been sufficient for the "deeper democracy" we say we aim for? Are we actually aiming for that in this project? I'm not so sure."

Jim glared at a point on the wall above Caine's head as Althea picked up the commentary. "Yes, maybe this time we can design and enact something that is more open and adaptable—you know, with broader participation by many more kinds of people than we usually involve. The people in this room, and I know others are to join us later, are probably more representative than most proposal groups. But maybe this time, even this is not enough."

Jim responded sharply, "Come on. LEAD is just about alone in this town providing both progressive visions and effective programs. We've done it at great sacrifice for many years. We have enough enemies to contend with without having opponents at work inside the tent!"

"Look Jim," Caine responded, "You quote John Dewey in your mission statement. Sure he was a professional philosopher who thought it was his job to work on ideas like these and make them useable. But I think he also argued that it wasn't a philosopher's job to do that alone. It wasn't a top-down division of labor thing. We're all responsible and capable when we interact with others on important civic tasks. Dewey believed that knowledge and values develop as we actually do things together—through social action, social learning, and social imagination that's broadly inclusive and deeply participatory."

"So this "deep democracy" is what?" Morrie asked sarcastically.

Althea paused. "I don't know how to say this yet. I guess I think that all of our talk about "education *and* democracy" or "education *for* democracy" or "democracy *in* education" are, at the core, grasping for the same thing. I think we're trying to say something crucial—and yes, Jack, very political. We're trying to be clearer about how we come to value, and what we value; about how we come to know, to understand, and to act—all in ways that really *are* inclusive and empowering—in ways that deeply affect how we structure teaching and learning, right?" Turning to Joy, Althea concluded, "So, I don't think settling for superficial boilerplate is as pragmatic as it might seem. I don't think rushing past a mission statement this afternoon is our best choice."

"Oh boy, this will take awhile," Bobbi muttered. Her's was the only utterance to break the tense silence.

*   *   *

A week later, spanning four more long meetings including an all-day Saturday marathon, the planning group crowded in around the conference table in LEAD's offices. The room now had poster paper covering three walls with multicolored words and phrases as well as several complicated diagrams.

A newcomer spent several minutes scanning the walls. Melvin Bolton was the Executive Director of the city's Urban League, "Man, you've got a lot of good ideas and tough problems!" he said as he took a seat. "And you're probably not finished yet, right? Am I too far behind the curve already?"

"No way, Mel . . . I came into this on Saturday morning, felt lost for about fifteen minutes and then found myself right in the thick of it," said Elizabeth Johnson, a senior administrator in the State Department of Education.

Jim hurried to steer the direction of the meeting. "We're keeping all that stuff up on the sheets in mind as we move ahead, Mel. But we've got a tight deadline. Today we're going to try to identify and maybe rank order the conflicts—maybe some contradictions—in what we've put up on the wall. But we must get on to the many specific organization and programming alternatives we've raised so far."

"Let's lay off the newsprint sheets today if we can," Jack McClosky implored. "Let's stick to the operational stuff we need to get done. Let's leave all that touchy-feely stuff *on* the wall so we don't appear to be too *off* the wall!"

Althea laughed and said lightly, "I agree with your agenda, Jack—but not with your description of our wall."

"So let's get started," June Washington urged. "Are we going to be a middle school or high school or what?"

Morrie responded quietly, "Middle school is a great point in a kid's development, but there are so many things in their lives that might make it tough to reach many of our objectives. If we do a high school charter, I think we may have a much better shot at some really effective teaching and learning."

"That makes sense. Let's assume for now that it'll be a high school," June said hurriedly. "But I'm not only interested in the age of the students, I'm also concerned about the number we can serve. How can we avoid risking what several of us have warned about before—you know, about becoming just another school with special resources for a limited number of kids. For me, I've been there and done that! We've got do more."

No one spoke for a long moment.

Jim said, "From the beginning, my vision was to establish a distinctive progressive school that will out-perform other versions of public education. I'm sorry June, but this project has to be a well-focused, top notch demonstration if it's going to make a difference."

Althea looked intently at Jim as she said, "But even if we pull it off, Jim, how do we keep it from becoming just another a visible, but isolated model school program? We know, more or less, how to get good ideas up and running. But how do we move beyond a singularly focused project, or an organization, or an agency?" Althea turned to June and nodded as she said, "Been there, done that, too!"

"Now look," Jim said quickly, "LEAD's been working on this charter school idea for several months. We were moving on this long before the big election-day shock set in! As Bobbi told you, we've been in touch with the School District and the State people all along. Now we're facing some daunting deadlines if we want to get *anything* started."

"Yes, can we move back to some program thinking for a minute?" Morrie asked. "I have poured over Jim's LEAD draft and thought about all our long meetings. There are so many good possibilities. But I have nagging questions, maybe reservations."

"What are the main ones, Morrie?" Althea asked.

"Well, what Jim proposes here looks like a senior year in high school for students carefully selected for a range of leadership attributes. You know, the "LEAD leaders" bumper sticker idea we've joked about. But quite seriously, this charter school is being developed as stand-alone training academy for budding community activists with a strong academic core curriculum. Isn't this another overt elite recruitment strategy? As you sketch it in your draft, high school juniors will apply and be selected on academic achievement criteria matched up with a leadership experience profile."

Jim interrupted, "That's not exactly how I'd put it, but yes, we do need to identify, recruit, and train organizers and advocates. We are under attack and we're not winning much of anything, anywhere. LEAD's position on all of our programs over the years, and certainly in this Charter School, is to focus on strong democratic leadership —preparing community-based leaders to spearhead social justice. We've got to get a more diverse "best and brightest" stream of talent into our communities if we are ever to build an effective democracy."

Bobbi broke in, "When we passed this around the School Board staff, they liked the leadership goals and especially the rigorous academic emphasis. We all know that LEAD does not present 'lowest common denominator' proposals!"

"But who will these students turn out to be?" Mel asked. "This opportunity might be too late for a lot of the young people we work with at the Urban League. Even though they're the majority of kids in our public schools, the ones we still call a 'minority' don't have the same opportunities, including chances to get selected for this elite academy."

"That's a good point, Mel," Jack said. "And I'm not sure the blue collar families—where both parents have to work, maybe three or four jobs in each household just to survive—will get their kids across this LEAD selection threshold."

"And from the families I know at PIP," Althea said, "most of their middle and high school kids have to work after school. They may not be able to chalk up enough community service points to look good on their charter school applications."

"And aren't there quite a few leadership programs anyway?" asked Joy.

Elizabeth nodded and said, "I've just reviewed two more promising university proposals at the Department."

The group fell into thoughtful silence. Then Jim said sharply, "What difference does it make what others are up to? We've got to move on *this* project *now.*"

"I know we have to get moving, Jim," Joy said quietly, "but I'm really not clear enough yet on our alternatives."

Looking around the table, Kirk asked, "If not the LEAD Academy, then what? You know, I'm working with kids who are at the other end of the spectrum from Jim's selection criteria. I don't have them for very long, but long enough to know that many of 'em connect or could be connected with most of the goals we have up there on the wall. For sure, the video thing I do doesn't work for everyone—no one thing ever does! But these are 'last chance' kids—not stars, not what Jon called 'poster children.' No, I'm not saying we should somehow duplicate Building Visions in who we recruit. But I don't think concentrating on either end of the food chain is very promising. What can we do?"

"Maybe we should rethink the democratic 'leaders' and 'followers' distinction." Morrie said almost inaudibly.

"Come on," Jim said forcefully, "We've been over this stuff for days and you've had the draft for weeks. A complete proposal is within reach. This project is critical. This school is doable. So let's agree and get on with it!"

No one around the table looked at Jim.

Bobbi looked close to tears.

Jim looked down to inspect his white knuckles.

*   *   *

Two days and three more meetings later, Caine remarked lightly as he sat down in the LEAD conference room, "Isn't it interesting that while we can sit anywhere, we end up taking the same chairs every time? Just like back in college or on commuter trains."

"What amazes me," Althea responded with a laugh, "is that while we do sit in the same places, we don't keep the same positions. I may be more opinionated than anyone here, but I feel my views shifting all the time."

"Well, in what we now have on the table and up on the wall, I see two different paths." Joy glance quickly at the posters that had multiplied on the conference room walls. "First, we have the stand alone, LEAD Leadership Charter School, more or less as Jim originally proposed it."

Jim broke in and said, "But it's way different than the draft we started out with. We've made lots of changes since then."

Joy nodded and continued, "And then we have, what should we call it, a cluster of ideas for a ninth grade democratic education immersion program nested in one of the regular high schools."

"Right," continued June, "We have a sketch for an integrated democratic education program for a high school, and, at this point, a smaller, more fully detailed, leadership-training charter school."

"When Jon, Mary, and I talked with Superintendent Tuscano yesterday about the ninth grade idea," June said, "he suggested two possibilities. Capitol Central, which already has some pretty innovative programs including a school-within-a-school. It is also the largest and maybe the most diverse high school in the district. The other site he mentioned, with, I think it's fair to say, far more enthusiasm, is Grant High."

Caine continued, "I think Tuscano was pushing us to do something major with Grant because it persists in being well below state standards on achievement tests. Truthfully, it's at the bottom of the charts. June says staff morale is in the dumpster, and Grant has a dismal drop out rate."

"What about the original LEAD idea?" Jack asked looking at Jim and Bobbi.

"He was acquainted with it—but rather noncommittal. He said he was worried about sustaining charter schools and was wary about the growing criticism in the media."

"But what did the Superintendent say about the money we may need to begin and support our ideas?" Jim persisted. "As Bobbi noted at our last meeting, if you go the ninth grade route, there won't be any start-up funds like we'd have available to begin a charter school."

June responded, "True, but I think we could make a strong pitch for special funds for a 'low performing school.' I doubt the Feds will come through with anything, but as Jon well knows, the state legislature appropriated some monies to address 'failing schools' and the district has set aside money for 'innovative solutions'."

"I agree we have two options," Jack said. "And I know we don't have time to generate others. These two are different enough to decide between, and work up one formal proposal. We have to move on, and I think Jim's Leadership Charter School is farther along and much easier to understand than all the ideas in that ninth grade project."

Bobbi nodded vigorously.

A long silence followed, eventually broken by Jim speaking in an uncharacteristically quiet voice. "We must keep moving. So now, how about one of our famous LEAD non-binding, straw votes—everybody in the room votes. That's democratic, right?"

"Well, that's one part of it . . . " Caine murmured.

"OK, we vote . . . after all we've been through these last ten days, we don't need secret ballots." Jim barked. "We'll take June's last proposition: the high school ninth grade thing or the LEAD Leadership Charter School—and no abstentions!"

"Ah, I love it . . . democracy at work," Morrie said with a smile.

"Right," Jim said without a smile. "High school? . . . LEAD Charter School?"

"I count three for the Charter School and ten for the ninth grade." said Mel.

"Non-binding, but interesting." June said.

Jim said with determination, "I've seen this coming for days. The LEAD leadership idea may not have the votes in this room, but I still need a compelling case against it. And I'm not convinced by the opposing plan."

Caine said firmly, "We've been over the main points many times. Let me sum up . . ."

As he was shuffling his notes, Althea gestured to him. "Excuse me, Jon," she spoke quietly. "All of you know I voted for the ninth grade idea, but I don't want to oppose the charter school alternative. This moment should not be another occasion to do the devastating critique or craft another assertive persuasion scenario we progressives do so well. We can be pretty divisive and hurtful."

"I've got a thick skin, Althea." Jim said sarcastically.

June broke in, "But this is not about you and your skin, Jim. It's about how we learn to advocate for positions, and take on really tough decisions in ways that move us toward our shared goals. We've come a long way together. Look, I know we all have competitive habits and I am aware that we all share meeting fatigue. But we've got a special opportunity—right here, right now!"

"I agree with June," Rudi said. "If we can't respect and accommodate our differences here, how can we reform institutions to do that?"

"So why not go for both?" Elizabeth said. "I really mean it. Look, I am part of the state's new program assessment process, so I review a lot of proposals. I've seen all kinds of proposals approved and disapproved in the last few years. Both of these could fly! They are emerging coherently and could be well presented. More important than any of that—both are desperately needed."

Mel looked troubled as he said, "But are there enough resources to do both? I don't only mean the money. What about people, places, materials? You know, there's a lot of work to be done right away to get either of these programs in shape."

Bobbi nodded vigorously.

June said, "What if we went forward with the ninth grade idea and thought more about the leadership school as an intensive summer program. Wait Jim—now hear me out. We shouldn't select out all the leadership potential kids from places like Capitol Central or Grant or any of the other high schools. I know those kids are needed right there in those schools. But we should do what the original LEAD proposal intends—develop community leaders. And an imaginative summer program could really work!"

"I agree with Elizabeth that both are necessary," Joy said. "Why can't both be developed? Isn't that possible? Do we really need to decide either/or?"

Morrie said, "I'm interested in both too. My tendency is to make decisions quickly and then never look back. But I was having real trouble choosing one program above the other. I don't know why it didn't occur to us earlier that we might move in both directions at once. Some interesting connections could emerge . . . "

"Maybe so," Jack said quickly, "but I know I need to keep focused and I don't think LEAD should risk overextending its scarce resources or diluting its impact."

One by one the group turned to look at Jim.

"Alright, so here's how it's going to work," Jim said slowly. "If most of you want to do this ninth grade thing, LEAD won't stand in your way. Jack, Bobbi, and I will see about what's possible for a summer program. I know now that there are some good reasons for LEAD not to go the charter school route. You guys may be right—maybe a summer thing could work even better—I don't know—but I am not giving up on leadership development. Use the conference room for as long as you need to," Jim said as he stood up. "We'll stay connected and see if LEAD can be of any strategic help with your ninth grade plan as well."

"I'm with you," Jack said to Jim, and Bobbi nodded.

Given long standing commitments to equity and participation,
what does it mean to share power?

Our educational, political, and governance experiences provide numerous opportunities to learn about gaining and maintaining power. However, despite elegant rhetorical assertions to the contrary current institutional forms and political practices provide few opportunities to experience effective power sharing. Sustaining broad participation, organizing coalitions, and building consensus are the most demanding dynamics of democratic practice at all levels of politics and governance. Yet teaching and learning about these vital processes are submerged in our everyday lives. Mass media, the learning place for most political participants, typically feature individual personalities, sharp conflicts, and seemingly decisive responses to dramatic events. In education policy contexts, public attention is drawn to controversial actions of administrators or to simplified and stylized conflicts over 'core values.'

While fascinated with power, we remain deeply ambivalent. We tend to resolve our attraction and suspicions by relying completely on our partial understanding of power as control, force, and dominance. From our largely spectator perspective, we scan across the presented political landscape. We focus most often on individual intentions and actions, but we also center on institutions and organizations when these are involved in public education politics.

We are drawn to the plight of individuals. Progressive reform initiatives are often prompted by human rights violations or neglect of individual needs. A significant portion of public school policy is motivated by long-standing commitments to equalize educational opportunities. Legislation such as the Individuals with Disabilities Education Act mandating improved physical and programmatic access, or litigation such as *Brown* v. *Board of Education* and related decisions on racial equity, are important rights-based public policies.

Education politics is said to be democratic if individual citizens can vote for tax levies and school bond issues, or elect school board members, state legislators, mayors, and governors. Even candidates for national offices emphasize education issues in their campaigns. Yet throughout these processes, the extent and quality of citizen awareness and participation remain deeply problematic.

Our most prominent values in education, politics, and governance feature images of autonomy and self-sufficiency as power's central objectives. While individual liberty is a crucial part of democratic life, a nearly exclusive emphasis on individual rights and personal autonomy can overshadow other aspects of power necessary for change-centered social thought and action. Gaining, using, and preserving what we claim as personal power becomes far more important than sharing it. Skilled and strategic development of constantly adaptive *interdependence* is difficult to envision and sustain.

Similar to illusions of personal autonomy, the habit of unreflective reliance on established authority is deeply ingrained. Participatory forms of education, politics, and governance exact high costs. Democracy is not resource efficient. Important individual and social resources—knowledge, time, money, and attention—are always limited. The understandable tendency is to delegate responsibility for complex and controversial societal concerns to a small number of official decision-makers, political activists, and specialized experts supported by bureaucratic organizations. Politically appointed officials, such as state commissioners of education, make key decisions. These political actors are almost exclusively informed by lobbyists, consultants, and professional staff. Established hierarchies of knowledge and power, though not regarded as democratic, are widely accepted as realistic and unchangeable. Large, impersonal, political and educational bureaucracies are taken as necessary forms of 'democratic elitism' through which established power elites compete to influence decisions and policy implementation in specialized areas. Knowledgeable, skilled and well-positioned individuals interact within government bureaucracies far removed from the public gaze.

Political processes are said to be democratic if organized groups can advocate positions and present them for elite consideration. Yet access to the processes and resources necessary for such advocacy is strikingly uneven. Established organized interest groups such as unions, professional associations, and instructional materials and testing vendors, have the resources and skills appropriate for bureaucratic politics. Less well-established groups, such as those mobilizing for targeted progressive reforms, find it difficult to penetrate and maintain effective access to the very stable structures of democratic elitism. Those advocating more equitable opportunities for children of poverty, for example, find themselves struggling to push beyond the legacy of compensatory education, an approach that typically arrays fragmented programs to help low income students catch up in a limited number of basic skills. Fundamental injustices related to socioeconomic status are not addressed. The status quo, with respect either to education or to power sharing, is not significantly altered.

Pervasive asymmetry in power sharing results in a *shallow democracy* characterized by elite-dominated discourse and decision-making, low levels of public attention, voter indifference, and growing citizen disengagement.

Shallow democracy reinforces voters as spectators—passive consumers of issues, policies, and candidates that are presented in ways almost indistinguishable from commercial advertising. This kind of politics results in *low intensity citizenship* in which civic responsibility can be discharged by fragmentary complaints, preferred ignorance, and episodic voting.

Predominant approaches to education, politics, and governance maintain stable distributions of power and constrain patterns of participation. By resigning ourselves to the reality of limited involvement in discharging key societal responsibilities—including shaping the future of public education—we restrict important opportunities to express social integrity and ingenuity. We urgently need to develop more inclusive and interactive approaches to social inquiry, deliberation, and advocacy—the essence of democratic life.

> *Empowerment . . .*
> *to establish mutual trust and sustain self-assurance*
> *with openness and humility*
> *engaged in deep sensing*
> *that responsibly receives and respectfully returns*
> *slight shifts in perception*
> *of self and situation,*
> *of challenge and choice,*
> *not protecting, not guiding, not leading*
> *instead attending to, reflecting back, and moving with*
> *always with.*

A deep democracy is *radically social, persistently exploratory,* and *compellingly aesthetic.* The distinguishing criteria of deep democracy as envisioned here are recognizable in many traditional versions of the good society. Aspirations for a social order that supports extension of *justice,* pursuit of *truth,* and experience of *beauty* are widespread and long-standing.

A deep democracy is *radically social* when it is broadly inclusive and authentically collaborative. Politics and education, at all levels and in all venues, involve dominant elites and a limited set of special interest groups. Reliance on these established political processes structures a narrowed public discourse, solidifies established forms of opposition, and reinforces alienation. Developing a deeper set of democratic processes would expand the number of active participants across their life span and through all stages of inquiry, decision-making, and implementation. Such movement requires broad engagement of school age youth, adult citizens, and disadvantaged groups to support 'border crossings' between disparate positions and expectations. In finding such pathways, difficult encounters and negotiations will occur. These are necessary to engage and possibly integrate what may appear to be sharply conflicting goals, values, and approaches. Deep democracy entails going beyond our familiar political postures to broaden and deepen political engagement and confront democratic elitism.

This challenge is approachable when democratic processes are *persistently exploratory.* Shallow democracy offers a sense of certainty with minimal citizen effort. Yet the realities of constant change that flow from the dynamics of our experienced world signal pervasive uncertainty. Amid relentless change, it is necessary to engage individual and collective ingenuity and resourcefulness. Deep democracy requires continuing collaboration in teaching and learning that sustains openness and yields adaptive response. Deep social inquiry requires creativity over caution, inclusiveness over efficiency, and visionary movement over defensive response. It is difficult, but necessary, to encourage and sustain conceptual diversence and multiplicity in adapting both to the turbulent and to the subtle changes in our multilayered lives. We need to invent and reinvent ways to avoid premature closure and superficial response. As engaged citizens, decision-makers, educators, or researchers, multiple modes of inquiry and assessment must be in play. In educating for deep democracy, there are no easy answers.

Deep democracy is *compellingly aesthetic* as it engages the emotions and energies necessary to persevere through the difficult experience of change. Democratic education, politics, and governance can be guided by aesthetic principles. A sense of symmetry can engage both the critique and the re-balancing of complex relationships such as resource distribution and other influential hierarchies. 'Checks and balances' can be more than a metaphor in democratic life. Policy and practice grounded in this constitutionally sanctioned guideline can be refined to more effectively guard against detrimental concentrations of power in government, corporate, and nonprofit venues. The metaphor can also be useful in promoting symmetries among structures of argument and evidence in democratic discourse.

A sense of graceful, intricately patterned movement can inform political perspectives. The metaphor of dance accentuates the importance of collaboratively choreographed intellectual, interpersonal, and civic interaction. In situations of challenge and controversy, unproductive habits of 'standing alone' or 'digging in our heels' can be overcome. The 'dance of democracy' is enriched not only through traditional forms of mutual action, but also through surprising encounters requiring joint improvisation.

The aesthetics of sound can also function as guiding principles for deepening democracy. The metaphor of music amplifies the significance of conceptual possibilities encoded in the emotional undertones of social inquiry and political participation. Attunement to experiences of discord, harmony, and resonance enhances skill in civic orchestration and performance. Achieving systemic reform entails listening to the music, not just to the words.

Democracy is a dynamic, multifaceted social composition. It can be shaped to create sites for the expression of strategic intuition, imaginative policy, and artistic advocacy. A more inclusive, more widely exploratory, and more aesthetically informed political process opens opportunities for deeper experience of democratic learning and life.

> *"If we are ever to move from our inegalitarian social order*
> *to a diverse, egalitarian and democratic one,*
> *we must speak and listen in a way that sustains and extends the possibility*
> *of actively making sense together."*
>
> —Susan Bickford
> *The Dissonance of Democracy: Listening, Conflict, and Citizenship*

Exploratory Democratic Practice: Interactive Website

Internet-based applications can be configured to support imaginative, yet pragmatic, contributions to democratic reform. *Interactive websites* can be structured to promote broader conversations, disseminate public scholarship, and provide a platform for continuing social inquiry. Rather than facilitating social learning, however, most websites developed for instructional purposes treat users as individual consumers. This pattern is strongly reinforced by pressures to extend commercialization of the Internet. Collaboration among users remains technically difficult and is discouraged by prevailing approaches to site design. New emphases and functions are required if we are to realize the potential of the Internet to support democratic imagination, discourse, and action.

In preparing to develop an interactive website, we recommend the following:

- A core design group should be convened to assume responsibility for orchestrating the process. The group should begin by composing a summary of its agreement on general purposes, content, and intended patterns of use.
- The core design group should use technologically specialized help for initial site construction to assure that standard webpage protocols and features are reliably operational.
- The *graphic design* of the site should reflect consensus on focal concepts and central goals, as well as ease of use.
- *Posting rules* (i.e., who can post what, how, and when) for the website should be determined and reviewed regularly by all those participating in the reform initiative.
- Deliberate *strategies* should be developed *to elicit and sustain contributions* from reform participants and from the broader community. Participants should be encouraged to use the website to interact regularly with each other and with community members.
- The core design group should select a *webmaster* to maintain the interactive site.
- Reform participants should regularly *monitor* the website to assess its usefulness and suggest revisions to the core design group.

Active involvement in the construction and evolving use of an interactive website can be an important tool in envisioning and enacting systemic democratic reform. Traditional functions can be coordinated with features designed to sustain collective deliberation on significant reform issues. Conventional features (e.g., posting schedules of events, general information, research resources, and project documents along with links to other relevant websites) provide valuable support. These should be extended through inclusion of collaborative strategies designed to promote on-line dissemination of knowledge that is *socially constructed* (e.g., through *Conversational Reading* [Chapter 1], *Ethnographic Futures Interviews* [Chapter 3], *Cultural Futures Delphi* [Chapter 5], graphic design informed by *Visualization* [Chapter 4], *Strategic Narratives* [Chapter 7], and especially *Public Intellectual Essays* [Chapter 8].

Thematic Bibliographic References

On democratic theory:

Benhabib, S. (Ed.). (1996). *Democracy and difference: Contesting the boundaries of the political.* Princeton, NJ: Princeton University Press.

Berkman, M., & Plutzer, E. (2006). *Ten thousand democracies: Politics and public opinion in America's school districts.* Washington, DC: Georgetown University Press.

Blaug, R. (1999). *Democracy real and ideal: discourse ethics and radical politics.* Albany: SUNY Press.

Bohman, J. (1996). *Public deliberation: Pluralism, complexity, and democracy.* Cambridge, MA: MIT Press.

Bohman, J., & Rehg, W. (Eds.). (1997). *Deliberative democracy.* Cambridge, MA: MIT Press.

Brettschneider, M. (2002). *Democratic theorizing from the margins.* Philadelphia, PA: Temple University Press.

Burch, K. (2000). *Eros as the educational principle of democracy.* New York: Peter Lang.

Connolly, W. (1995). *The ethos of pluralization.* Minneapolis: University of Minnesota Press.

Dahl, R. (1989). *Democracy and its critics.* New Haven, CT: Yale University Press.

Dahl, R. (1998). *On democracy.* New Haven, CT: Yale University Press.

Festenstein, M. (1997). *Pragmatism and political theory: From Dewey to Rorty.* Chicago: University of Chicago Press.

Fisher, F. (2003). *Reframing public policy; discursive politics and deliberative practices.* New York: Oxford University Press.

Fishkin, J., & Lasslett, P. (Eds.). (2003). *Debating deliberative democracy.* New York: Blackwell.

Fullinwider, R. (Ed.). (1999). *Civil society, democracy, and civic renewal.* Lanham, MD: Rowman & Littlefield.

Fung, A. (2006). *Empowered participation: Reinventing urban democracy.* Princeton, NJ: Princeton University Press.

Fung, A., & Wright, E. (2003). *Deepening democracy: Institutional innovations in empowered participatory governance.* New York: Verso Press.

Galston, W. (2002). *Liberal pluralism: The implications of value pluralism for political theory and practice.* Cambridge: Cambridge University Press.

Green, P. (Ed.). (1999). *Democracy: Key concepts in critical theory.* Amherst, NY: Humanity Books.

Guinier, L. (Ed.). (1994). *The tyranny of the majority: Fundamental fairness in representative democracy.* New York: Free Press.

Gutmann, A., & Thompson, D. (1996). *Democracy and disagreement.* Cambridge, MA: Harvard University Press.

Hernandez, A. (1997). *Pedagogy, democracy, and feminism: Rethinking the public sphere.* Albany: SUNY Press.

Hibbing, J., & Morse, E. (2002). *Stealth democracy: Americans' beliefs about how government should work.* Cambridge: Cambridge University Press.

Jacobs, L., & Skocpol, T. (Eds.). (2005). *Inequity and American democracy: What we know and what we need to learn.* New York: Russell Sage.

James, M. (2003). *Deliberative democracy and the plural polity.* Lawrence: University Press of Kansas.

Kahne, J. (1996). *Reframing educational policy: Democracy, community and the individual.* New York: Teachers College Press.

Keenan, A. (2003). *Democracy in question: Democratic openness in a time of political closure.* Stanford, CA: Stanford University Press.

Levine, P. (2006). *The new progressive era: Toward a fair and deliberative democracy.* Lanham, MD: Rowman & Littlefield.

Lukes, S. (1974). *Power: A radical view.* New York: Macmillan.

Macedo, S. (Ed.). (1999). *Deliberative politics: Essays on democracy and disagreement.* Oxford: Oxford University Press.

Mackie, G. (2004). *Democracy defended.* Cambridge: Cambridge University Press.

Mouffe, C. (2000). *The democratic paradox.* New York: Verso.

Shapiro, I. (1996). *Democracy's place.* Ithaca, NY: Cornell University Press.

Skocpol, T., & Fiorina, M. (Eds.). (1999). *Civic engagement in American democracy.* Washington, DC: Brookings Institution Press.

Trend, D. (Ed.). (1996). *Radical democracy: Identity, citizenship, and the state.* New York: Routledge.

Verba, S., & Nie, N. (2002). *Voice and equality: Civic voluntarism in American politics.* Cambridge, MA: Harvard University Press.

West, C. (2004). *Democracy matters: Winning the fight against imperialism.* New York: Penguin Press.

Whittman, D. (1995). *The myth of democratic failure: Why political institutions are efficient.* Chicago: University of Illinois Press.

Young, I. (2000). *Inclusion and democracy.* Oxford: Oxford University Press.

On education for democracy:

Arnot, M., & Dillabough, J. (Eds.). (2001). *Challenging democracy: International perspectives on gender, education and citizenship.* New York: Routledge Falmer.

Arnstine, D. (1995). *Democracy and the arts of schooling.* New York: State University of New York.

Axelrod, R. (1985). *The evolution of cooperation.* New York: Basic Books.

Banks, J. (Ed.). (2004). *Diversity and citizenship education: Global perspectives.* San Francisco: Jossey-Bass.

Banks, J., McGee, C., Cortes, C., Hahn, C., Merryfield, M., & Moodley, K. (2005). *Democracy and diversity: Principles and concepts for educating citizens in a global age.* Seattle: University of Washington, Center for Multicultural Education.

Bigelow, B., & Peterson, B. (Eds.). (2002). *Rethinking globalization: Teaching for justice in an unjust world.* Milwaukee, WI: Rethinking Schools Ltd.

Boler M. (Ed.). (2004). *Democratic dialogue in education: Troubling speech, disturbing silence.* New York: Peter Lang.

Brosio, R. (2000). *Philosophical scaffolding for the construction of critical education.* New York: Peter Lang.

Cogan, J., & Derricott, R. (Eds.). (1998/2000). *Citizenship for the 21st century: An international perspective on education.* London: Kogan-Page.

Crittenden, J. (2002). *Democracy's midwife: An education in deliberation.* Lanham, MA: Lexington Books.

Dewey, J. (1916/1984). *Democracy and education.* New York: Macmillan.

Dimitriadis, G., & Carlson, D. (Eds.). (2003). *Promises to keep: Cultural studies, democratic education, and public life.* New York: Routledge Falmer.

Elkin, S., & Soltan, K. (Eds.). (1999). *Citizen competence and democratic institutions.* State College: Pennsylvania State University Press.

Gimpel, J. et. al. (2003). *Cultivating democracy: Civic environments and political socialization.* Washington DC: Brookings Institution Press.

Goodlad, J., Mantle-Bromley, C., & Goodlad, S. (2004). *Education for everyone: Agenda for education in a democracy.* San Francisco: Jossey-Bass.

Limage, L. (2001). *Democratization, education and educating democratic citizens.* New York: Routledge Falmer.

MacBeath, J., & Moos, L. (Eds.). (2003). *Democratic learning: The challenge to school effectiveness.* New York: Routledge Falmer.

Macedo, S. (2000). *Diversity and distrust: Civic education in a multicultural democracy.* Cambridge, MA: Harvard University Press.

Martin, J. (2002). *Cultural miseducation: In search of a democratic solution.* New York: Teachers College Press.

McDonough, K., & Feinberg, W. (2006). *Citizenship and education in liberal-democratic societies: Teaching for cosmopolitan values and collective identities.* New York: Oxford University Press.

Milner, H. (2002). *Civic literacy: How informed citizens make democracy work.* Hanover, NH: University Press of New England.

Niemi, R., & Junn, J. (1998). *Civic education: What makes students learn.* New Haven, CT: Yale University Press.

Olssen, M., Codd, J., & O'Neill, A. (2004). *Education policy: Globalization, citizenship, and democracy.* San Francisco: Sage Publications.

Parker, W. (Ed.). (1996). *Educating the democratic mind.* Albany: State University of New York Press.

Parker, W. (Ed.). (2002). *Education for democracy: Contexts, curricula, assessments.* Greenwich, CT: Information Age Publishing.

Parker, W. (2003). *Teaching democracy: Unity and diversity in public life.* New York: Teachers College Press.

Potter, J. (2002). *Active citizenship in schools: A good practice guide to developing a whole school policy.* New York: Routledge Falmer.

Smith, S. (2000). Morality, civics, and citizenship: Values and virtues in modern democracies. *Educational Theory, 50*(3), 405–418.

Soder, R. (Ed.). (1996). *Education, democracy, and the schools.* San Francisco: Jossey-Bass.

Thayer-Bacon, B. (1997). *Philosophy applied to education: Nurturing a democratic community in the classroom.* New York: Prentice-Hall.

Walling, D. (Ed.). (2004). *Public education, democracy, and the common good.* Bloomington, IN: Phi Delta Kappa Foundation.

Wolf, P. (Ed.). (2004). *Educating citizens: International perspectives on civic values and school choice.* Washington, DC: Brookings Institution.

Reflection:

Bickford, S. (1996). *The dissonance of democracy: Listening, conflict, and citizenship* (p. 173). Ithaca, NY: Cornell University Press.

chapter   7

Imagination

Understanding the costs of continuity
we challenge each other to dream
the need is so great, there must be a way
to see differently, to move differently, to move on
purposive, practical, playful, prophetic
striving to realize hopes not yet fully conceived
we seek new horizons.

During a dinner break two days later, energetic conversations scattered across the tough choices facing the planning group. Some of the exchanges were lengthy and intense. Troubled looks outnumbered smiles and laughter.

"So, what do we know about the Grant High building? Do we know anything more than that it's *supposed* to be up to code?" Morrie asked sarcastically. No one answered.

"Since we're throwing out worries," Mary said, "what about the laboratory and computer equipment we'll need to do first rate science and math. Will the District provide all the equipment and materials we'll need help move Grant out of its hole?"

Re-Envisioning Education and Democracy, pages 109–133
Copyright © 2006 by Information Age Publishing
All rights of reproduction in any form reserved.

"They have done that for some new programs in the past," June said reassuringly. "Several Board members and District staff have shown real interest in our ideas."

Elizabeth said, "And there may be some state money available for technology."

"And we have a number of partnership possibilities," Bobbi interjected. "Kirk got most of his Building Visions video set-up from a couple of local businesses and we're talking with several interested computer and software vendors."

"Wait!" Joy said. "Let's not let technology drive this project. We should be clear about our curricular directions. Then we can go out and negotiate with potential partners."

"Yeah, almost all of my co-ops have gotten stuck with used computers and obsolete systems happily donated as tax write-offs from those publicly generous local business types," Rudi said with a heavy sigh.

"And partnerships always come with strings," Melvin said. "Whatever we do, we don't want our kids exploited for corporate photo-ops. We should look at the politics and all the strings attached."

"All politics come with strings, right Mel?" Caine said quietly. "Even our well-intentioned progressive brand of democratic education comes with strings."

Shortly after reassembling in the littered conference room, the members turned to Jim who was standing in the doorway.

"What is all this going to mean for LEAD?" Althea asked

"I'm not sure," Jim began. "I agree that my original charter school concept as such isn't timed right. I did learn a whole lot from our discussions here, even when we disagreed. We did disagree a lot, didn't we? But it's also pretty clear, even to me, that the school administration is under the gun. They've got to show results big time and of course they're more interested in this ninth grade program. And we all know the School Board has become really skeptical about any new charter schools, especially since all the publicity about 'irregularities' and 'school failures.'"

"Why not go ahead and propose funding the other idea we've talked about, Jim?" Mary asked. "You know, a summer leadership academy for high school juniors. LEAD could recruit the kind of kids you want over this school year. I bet one of the colleges or universities in town would have facilities and maybe the District could even give some summer school credit."

June and Elizabeth nodded.

"Jim, if we can get this Grant High thing rolling, you should be able to recruit promising LEAD leaders from there in a couple of years." Caine said reassuringly. "The academy idea is, as you have claimed all along, also desperately needed."

After a brief pause, Bobbi made one of her infrequent extended comments. "We have put tons of work into the LEAD charter school proposal. I really hate giving up on that. But now I think we have two doable projects. I think a lot of our earlier work can actually be used in each. The mission statements will not turn out to be all that different, right? Really only how, where, and when we try to reach those goals will be different. I agree with Jim that we're really pushing the schedule, the imaginations, and the politics of all those we need to get on board to have the Grant program up and running by September. It'll be tough enough to revamp a ninth grade in an existing and very troubled high school. While I do like the idea of a summer leadership program, right now, we'll need to focus on the Grant proposal. And I want to be clear as one LEAD staffer, that I want to be involved in both of these projects. I think others here at LEAD can help with some of the Grant paper work, too. Right Jim? You have convinced me on the possibilities of the ninth grade project. Let's move it, people!"

"Thanks Bobbi," Caine said. "I hope all of us can stay connected to both projects. We do need to keep LEAD involved and we need to push hard now on the Grant High option."

Heads nodded and smiles circulated around the table. Jim smiled tightly as he turned and left the room.

"June, why don't you facilitate this session," Caine suggested. "It's always important to have teachers prominent in any education reform effort."

"Always the politician, Jon. All right, I'll sit at the head of the table tonight. It's true that some Board members and the media, especially around election time, tend to dump on teachers. But the Board and the administration have been somewhat more responsive to teacher-based initiatives on curriculum, even if they've not always been so great on our conditions of work."

"Let's figure out what has to be done and keep moving," Rudi said nodding toward Bobbi. "What Althea has dubbed the "deep democracy year" needs to get fleshed out. This is exciting!"

"Well, 'exciting' is one word for it—'daunting' is another," Joy said. "Remember, the School Board sees Grant High as arguably its biggest problem. We've already reviewed parts of the situation. Grant has a shockingly high turnover rate for students and staff. The current principal said this is his last year. The staff has serious morale problems. Grant has way more than the average number of students at or below the poverty line, more new immigrants, more dropouts, and more serious truancy. And, of course, it also has gangs, drugs, and in-school violence. And the Superintendent visibly shudders at Grant's ongoing low test scores. He also gets a little pale when he refers to the actual graduation rate, even for five years."

"No place to move but up!" Morrie sighed. "At least Grant's building is said to be up to code."

"Yeah, all those kids at Grant deserve some big changes," Kirk said, "not just something a little different this time, or something new for just a few. I hear the school has been promised many things in the past. Our ninth grade must make obvious differences in kids' lives. Look, I'm new to all this organizational design talk, but I've been working on the margins all my life and this year with really marginal kids over at Building Visions. We need to get the kids at Grant to care about learning, about each other. And we've got to do it so it shows!"

"Yes, and we need to do that for *all* students, across the full range of backgrounds and abilities." June said. "It's really hard for public schools to remain focused broadly on improving education for all kids."

"So we've packed all these complex ambitions into Grant's mission statement," Joy said, "but maybe on paper they sound too much like platitudes—just more lofty but naïve ambitions."

"Sure, we do have ambitious language. But before we shy away from words that may seem too familiar to us or too fuzzy for others . . . like "learning" "responsibility," "community" or "democracy" . . . let's take charge of them. Let's make them work!" Mary said forcefully. "We can show the School Board what we mean by these ideas and how we're going to put them into practice in spite of the daunting conditions Joy just listed."

"Right!" Morrie said. "I have been through several so-called 'curricular reforms' before and so have Joy, June, and Mary. All of us here are aware of the many traps that await us. But I'm excited too . . . even though at my age, maybe I should know better. What I do know better at my age, is that there are things we can do in the classroom and with the community to move toward the "deep learning" and "deep democracy" promises we make."

June nodded as she said, "And I know there are many other teachers and staff in the District that agree with our general objectives and have the experience, ideas, and energy to do this."

"And we know that even though they have doubts and other expectations," Melvin said, "Tuscano and the Board are at least interested and sympathetic to trying something different at Grant. Even they don't want 'more of the same'."

"But there is only so much one school, any school can do," Joy said. "Aren't we asking for an awful lot?"

Elizabeth nodded and said, "Well, we do want a lot. There are good reasons why the charter school route is so attractive. Narrower objectives, focused resources, and a self-selected student body can mean far fewer risks and usually good publicity, at least at first."

"So people, let's get some more specifics on what next year's ninth grade at Grant should look like." Bobbi urged. "The School Board will need more than our good looks, our boundless enthusiasm, and our very well stated intentions!"

Warm wind and filtered light
the dance of shadows before the dawn
disparate dreams coalesce
new energy to rise with the sun.

Early the next week, Althea met with her longtime colleague May Haun-Crawford in Althea's office. May ended an intensely expressed description of her frustration with her job at County Human Services, now made more acute by the political tensions following the recent election. "Althea, Partners in Participation **is** the most satisfying part of my life after my family. Being Board Chair and working with you and all these cooperating agencies is such a contrast to downtown. I know it's stressful around here too; but it's a different kind of stress...a good kind."

"May, why don't you move over here and become PIP's Director," Althea said. "You're perfect for this job and it's the right time for you to do it."

"No, oh no. Althea, you *are* PIP." May said sharply. "You're our first and only Director. This is all about your ideas, your contacts, your creativity and your incredible energy. PIP is you!"

"Thanks, May, but we both know PIP is a whole lot more than me." She paused and then continued quietly, "I've been pretty unsettled for a while. We've had many conversations that touched on what's next for PIP and maybe indirectly about what's in store for you and me. I love this place and I love you May. But I think this is about the right time for me to move on. And I think it's exactly the time for you to take PIP onto its next stage. There are new possibilities here. You know I wouldn't leave PIP hanging, or leave this job to anyone other than someone like you."

After a moment, May continued, "OK, Althea—we've been friends a long time and we've always been honest with each other. So, yes, I've actually thought about this too. It's so hard to think about PIP without you, but I have imagined myself here in this office, even in that chair. I feel it's possible. I think I could do some good work. But look, if it does work out that way, what about you? What would you do?"

"May, I've been asked to apply to be the Principal at Grant High to help launch a new program."

"What? Oh Althea, I never could have seen this coming! You—a high school principal? OK, so you are a visionary *and* a topnotch administrator, but you're not a schoolteacher. Well, I guess you did do that early-childhood stuff in college and then something more in grad school. But don't they have all kinds of regulations and requirements for public school principals? I mean, there must be a million hoops to jump through. I'm really floored by this, Althea."

"Well, I am too. So I've got a doctorate in educational policy and administration, and I think that'll get my foot in the door. Although my masters degree was in child development, at one point I actually did complete a secondary teacher's license. Unfortunately, my only secondary school experience was ten weeks of practice teaching. I think I only survived that because I matched up one of my classes with the five-year-olds at a nearby daycare. That worked! Anyway, I was certified, did the preschool project, and then later received the fellowship and headed off to grad school."

"And then a little later you came here to build PIP," May paused a moment. "Are you sure you want to do this?"

"I think so, May. I'm a little scared . . . well, truthfully more than a little. It's another world out there in public education land. But I've learned a whole lot since Jon Caine and I first started working on the LEAD proposals last November. This group I'm working with on the Grant High project is really creative, but also very realistic. Almost all the people we've been consulting with around the community have been encouraging. I believe we can pull off some good things at Grant. I'd like to be there to try. Still I know there are many tough hurdles ahead."

"How long do we have to sort this out—here at PIP, for me with the County, for you at Grant?" May asked.

"Not long. I have my first interview at the District Office next Monday."

*   *   *

Later that day, the planning group met in LEAD's conference room. Bobbi had assembled their working drafts and piled them high in front of each person at the table. They had agreed to rotate conveners and Caine was conducting this meeting. They had also agreed to avoid specialization so that everyone could actively participate in drafting and reconciling each detailed section of what had become a long and complex proposal.

"Let's see if we can get a sense of the thrust of this thing without getting too bogged down in the specifics," Caine began. "Althea has her first interview for principal on Monday and we should at least have our story straight."

"She'll do just fine," June said looking at Althea. "I've talked with the entire Teachers' Union Executive Committee and with several key members of the Principal's Union Board. They think Althea could be a very good candidate. There may be some others applying, but honestly, few principals want to get stuck with Grant. Besides, I don't think any of them are conceptually ready for this proposal. Being a principal does tax the imagination and Grant is a very risky prospect."

"It was a struggle but I like the way we've worded our concerns about of the trend toward re-segregation in public schools," Melvin said patting the stack of folders in front of him. "We must raise the serious issues—like class, race, and what is taken to be academic achievement—in a manner that is strong and direct, but also constructive. We don't want to 'beat people over the head', but we must be sure that our social justice objectives don't get lost in all the operational details that follow."

Rudi nodded vigorously and said, "Yes, I also like how we've handled our comprehensive reform ambitions. We state them quietly, but emphatically. They do reflect our commitment to extend this 'pilot program' beyond Grant to open new opportunities for students throughout the District. Of course, we shouldn't shock the School Board or the State Education Department too much. We should not come off as naively overambitious. But we don't want them to normalize our intention to work toward deep changes."

"It does read well so far, Rudi," said Elizabeth, "and I believe we can make it understandable for the decision-makers."

"But this proposal as it's evolving is not exactly like the ones the Board usually gets," June said. "I know we'll be able to hit all their formal inclusion requirements. But can we collapse our important objectives and complicated program details into a package with the bold headed sections and elaborate planning and evaluation grids they've come to expect?"

Kirk followed immediately: "I know that the papers Bobbi put in front of us are almost phone book thick. But we don't have only one version of all this, do we? I mean, look at the kind of episodic, nonlinear development of bits and pieces we've connected and reconnected at various times. It's a lot like the video things I do with my students . . . it all depends on why and for whom we set up a shot . . . on how we take advantage of software opportunities that just come up. We revise and edit together as we go along. Just like what we've done here. We didn't frame proposal sections like we were deducing them from logical propositions, you know like some geometry thing, right Mary? It's been, well, more like spontaneous when we work together. I'm not sure how we can condense all we've been through, all we've learned so far, and all we've still *got* to learn, into some written document that will be convincing to the Board and all the state and district bureaucrats."

Bobbi interrupted, "And doing all this has been, and will continue to be, very time intensive. People, we are not an efficient bunch!"

"Democracy is not efficient!" Morrie stated. "Messy is closer. . . . "

"Right," Joy said abruptly. "This sure isn't an 'education as usual' proposal. This is about what public education should be. They'll see some of that right away. I want to believe Elizabeth is right about this . . . that they will begin to understand. We know they may never fully agree with us . . . but maybe we can help them to see where we're headed."

"We do have good language about our objectives in the rationale," Althea said. "But they're going to want to know *how* we will actually move toward these goals over the ninth grade year. I'll need an effective 'how to' summary in my head for Monday."

"Hey, we don't have to lay out everything in massive detail. We can't do that and anyway that's not how schools work—like everything flows neatly from some fixed blueprint," Joy said. "Much of it just happens."

Caine tried to focus his colleagues' comments. "So first we're proposing no special recruiting or selecting or creaming off special students. This program is for any and all of the kids who show up ready to start ninth grade at Grant next September. It's not one of the district magnets, right?"

"No, it's an open enrollment site with preference given to neighborhood kids. It's a big building and it hasn't over-enrolled in years," Mary said.

"I think the distinguishing features of our ninth grade homeroom plan," Joy continued looking at Althea, "are the 'integrated civic engagement core curriculum' and substantial prep time for teachers. What we promise is that if we get to do this for four years, Grant will be transformed into a place where kids will stay in school, the test scores will go up, and the graduation rate will become acceptable."

"That's a lot and, of course, we're expecting even more than that," Morrie said.

"Although we're excited about these opportunities, we don't want to hype this too much. We need to be measured in our promises," June said.

"And the story we tell the School Board doesn't have to be the story of all of our individual and collective discoveries in this process," Joy said. "This proposal is kind of a collective autobiography, but it shouldn't read that way."

"Yes, if we're trying to brief Althea for her interview we ought to concentrate on what would make the most sense to the District people," Rudi suggested.

"Right," Morrie said. "Now let's get to those glimpses we want Althea to deliver on Monday—the 'bullets' we want Bobbi to load into that high caliber executive summary Althea will fire at the interview."

Bobbi groaned and looked to Caine.

"First and foremost," Caine began, "we've got to make the case that this "deep democracy immersion experience" can really meet the needs of Grant's "under-served students." The Board knows they're sitting on a high stakes policy move. If they can't show that placing a school on probation results in genuine support for teachers, stronger programs, and improved student performance, then it's all just a political ploy. Beyond the usual risks, they now have to answer directly to the Feds. Most important, however, if this doesn't work they will have visibly failed these students and violated the public trust."

"Yes," Mary joined in. "And we've got to show that what we're proposing is likely to help these kids stay in school, pass the standardized exams and meet all other state requirements, and then, graduate with solid plans for continuing their education after high school. Althea can focus on our proposed homeroom structure as the key to meeting these objectives."

Looking at her notes, June read, "The homeroom's major responsibilities are to develop community among the students, assess student needs, develop support for students individually and collectively, and provide for continuing reflection and connection."

"What some of that means is grouped under "learning to learn," Joy continued glancing at a document in front of her. "There will be continuing diagnostic testing, preparation for the standardized tests, attention to individual and social development, academic and early career planning, and involvement of other school staff such as social workers and counselors."

"Yes, but Grant High, as we now see it, is about more than *individual* academic achievement as measured in grades, test scores, and promotion. It is also centrally about constructing and maintaining an ongoing *democratic learning community*," Morrie stated firmly. "The community building pieces have to do with establishing responsibility for each others' learning . . . for each other's attendance, behavior, and academic performance. It's about developing skills and responsibilities regarding Grant High as a larger learning community, and making connections to other communities in the neighborhood and all around the city."

"The ninth grade immersion year pivots around the homeroom component and continues throughout students' high school careers featuring the many dimensions and possibilities for citizenship," Mary read from her draft. "Each homeroom is a full period that starts each school day. The ninth grade homeroom teachers have summer development time and two preparation periods daily. In addition to the one prep hour that all teachers are provided to cover individual teaching responsibilities, the second period is added to make it possible for all ninth grade faculty to meet together regularly. After their stint with the ninth grade immersion year, these teachers return to their regular mixed grade teaching assignments, but continue to teach the one hour homeroom block, hopefully following their initial ninth grade advisory group all the way through to graduation."

"That's a proposal the Board will definitely cost-out," Bobbi interjected.

Kirk continued the summary: "So we'll have sixteen teachers specially assigned and prepared for the homerooms and for the core curriculum and instruction. And the kids will be assigned to balance race, gender, and economic background . . . and they'll not be tracked by ability."

"Let's stick with the teachers for a moment," Althea suggested. "Who will they be? Teachers from the current Grant High faculty?"

June responded: "The Superintendent intends to reassign many of the Grant teachers. Some of them have requested that. As with any "troubled school," Tuscano has both the discretion and incentive to recruit new staff.

We already have four of the 16 we need right here. Morrie in Social Studies, Mary in Science and Math, Joy in Communication Arts and Literature, and Kirk in Visual Arts. Those of us who have been talking with other teachers about this proposal have encountered quite a few with real motivation to become part of this program. You certainly wouldn't find many willing to be at Grant next year without changes."

Mary said, "We do have an interesting curriculum proposal for science-math for citizens. We can meet almost all of the graduation standards and easily become more connected to what goes on in communication arts and social studies. And I like the Board's supportive talk about technology improvements throughout Grant next year. In addition to some more science equipment, they promise to equip all classrooms with computers ... not only in a computer lab. And Kirk thinks that some of those who helped him out at Building Visions will come through with some video gear."

"I'll believe the equipment promises when the stuff actually gets there," Morrie muttered. "I've been through all this before. Promises in the spring are not necessarily met in September!"

"Do you have enough yet, Althea?" Caine asked.

"Can we really do all this with just the sixteen teachers per year we're asking for?" asked Elizabeth.

Bobbi responded promptly pointing to her laptop. "It'll work. I've crunched our numbers against the proposed budget, required periods, Grant's classrooms, program costs, and the expected enrollment. The District says the teacher roster is somewhat flexible in our case. Well, we end up with class sizes that are smaller than the District average but larger than what would be optimal."

"Always!" Morrie complained. "More of the same, again and again! I really am worried about whether the Board will come through at all on this. And we *need* that month of teacher prep time at the end of each summer—for team building, for strategizing the homeroom, and to coordinate what is a very complicated core curriculum. The Board will want to do less, but we can't compromise very much."

"And we really need that four-year commitment," added Joy. "We can't show results in one year, maybe not even in two."

"We all know we have some hard work ahead, including some tough bargaining with the District." Caine said. "While they do have other priorities to meet and they don't fully understand what we're up to, we do know this proposal interests them."

Elizabeth agreed. "Boards all around the state are looking for something better."

"Yeah, they've said right along they're committed to turning Grant around." Melvin said: "They must address any school they've identified as failing. But still, from their point of view, we're asking for a lot. From our point of view, we need a lot."

Caine continued, "You folks with education experience know better than I do—but I sensed openness in our conversations with the Superintendent, some of his staff, and with several Board members. My political instincts are strongly positive on this. Now let's get back to giving Althea something to deliver in her interview next Monday."

Bobbi looked down at her laptop and read: "Grant will have sixteen ninth-grade homerooms with a "*democratic immersion experience*" that has a "community building" and "learning to learn" emphasis. The proposal is to keep those homerooms at a full period throughout the four years. We'll have four communications arts and literature teachers, four social studies teachers, four science-math teachers and four visual and performing arts teachers. The way it looks is that the homerooms will have around 25 students each to accommodate the projected 400 ninth graders."

"How about all the graduation standards and guidelines?" Elizabeth asked.

"Yes, along with the money and the test scores they worry about, we do have to show that we can meet or exceed everything on the books," June stated.

"Our integrated core curriculum can really work," Morrie said strongly. "Through a community-oriented social studies curriculum we can provide real-world exposure to complex issues and hands-on experience with democratic strategies and practices that are essential for active citizenship. And we can address all the relevant grad standards in a manner that is both developmentally appropriate and deeply challenging for ninth grade students. This curriculum can be clearly connected to what Joy and her colleagues can do in communication arts, and there are great opportunities for developing nontrivial links into science-math for citizens."

Joy continued: "Of course a wide range of 'literacies' and modes of expression are necessary to support full civic participation. Our proposed communication arts curriculum will focus on 'reading/writing/speaking/listening' as paths toward personal and social empowerment. In addition we'll emphasize multicultural literature and media studies. All of this can be bridged to the other core classes, for instance working on oral reports or creative writing assignments that include visuals and maybe computer graphics. We'll also need to work on creative ways to support ninth graders in preparing for the standardized reading comprehension and composition tests."

"I'm glad you raised the testing issue again," Mary interjected. "We've got to find ways to use testing to actually *promote learning*, rather than letting it continue to drive and diminish the curriculum. It's becoming more and more clear that performance on standardized math exams is a primary factor not only in limiting students' access to more advanced work in math and science. It also limits access to post-secondary education broadly, and to technology related careers. "High stakes testing" is high stakes for the students far more than it is for administrators or teachers. For this and other reasons, our ninth grade science-math for citizens program is something a number of us have been hoping to try for a long time. It's going to be a mix of real world science and math applications relevant to citizens as contributing members of a complex society... not only as intelligent consumers and employable workers. And there is still the elective schedule slot that individual students could use to do a more conventional math or science course. Anyway, the regular tenth, eleventh, and twelfth grade offerings at Grant include elective opportunities."

"You know, Mary, your example of the childhood asthma problem is dynamite." Caine commented. "It's a lot like scientific detective work... that's what epidemiology is primarily, isn't it? And lots of environmental science, and math that goes with all that. It has the social studies students doing community context and institutional analysis... it touches on really tough issues like local history, personal ethics, poverty, racism, and even 'ageism'. And you also link it up with popular culture. The visual arts instruction is both critical and possibly creative. Very impressive!"

"Yeah, lets not forget the arts." Kirk added. "Visual literacy has become crucial in the social action arena, not to mention web art, the video stuff we do at the Workshop, 'street theatre' and of course, hip-hop, rap and alternative music. I know we can produce some spectacular artistic and performance pieces that connect the classes and push the skills of all the kids. Remember, Althea, all these will be group processes along the lines of what we do at Building Visions."

"Hey Althea," Bobbi said with a wide grin, "do you have all this down for your job interview?"

"Oh yes. I've got everything everyone said on the tip of my tongue!" she replied. "Now let's see. On Monday morning I have to convince the District people that a person with, if you stretch it, acceptable credentials; but whose actual school administration experience was with four and five year olds in a well funded program; that a person who hasn't set foot recently in a secondary school except for community meetings; a person who has never actually taught a high school class; and a person who's allied with *this* collection of reformers who are proposing an ambitious ninth grade "democratic immersion experience"... is a viable candidate. So, I'll be asking them to take a big risk with our sketchy ideas for Grant High, and then to take an even bigger risk with me."

June broke in quickly. "Don't underestimate yourself, Althea. You truly are an impressive candidate. We have a very interesting proposal, even at this early point. Look, I've been through a lot of these processes. This has been different and our ninth grade project is intriguing. It *can* be convincing, even in scattered glimpses."

"Count on it, Althea" Elizabeth said encouragingly.

"Hey," said Kirk. "Have we settled on a name for this Grant program?"

"I thought we agreed on 'Deep Learning for Deep Democracy,'" June said. "It seems to capture both the pedagogy and the civic engagement goals we're trying for."

"Well I suppose I can remember that at least," Althea said with a sigh.

"You'll do just fine," Rudi added.

"Come on, Althea," Melvin said, "you have the support of all LEAD's coalition members around town, the enthusiastic support of the Grant neighborhood organization, and an almost official endorsement from the teachers, staff, and even the principals' unions. You've got momentum!"

"I hope so," Althea said with a sigh. "Look, I'm really worried. I can't possibly answer all the questions they'll have."

"You won't have to," Bobbi stated emphatically. "I'll fax them the executive summary and our full proposal is not due at the District for almost three weeks. You'll do just great on Monday. We'll have the rest of our act together soon and the paperwork out the door by the deadline." Bobbi began shifting another tall stack of draft documents and supporting materials across the table toward Althea, "But you'll want to browse these over the weekend."

"And who's going to tell my kids that their mom will be out of action for another weekend?" Althea asked.

Given commitments to deeper democracy in schools and society,
how can we develop feasible collective visions?

Hopes for experiences of deep democracy in schools and society are not easily sustained as significant barriers continue to exclude the majority of citizens from effective self-representation and social advocacy. The controversies and challenges imposed necessitate responses that are not only systemic in scope and democratic in process, but also innovative in principle and practice. Yet *social imagination,* even in the face of seemingly irresolvable social problems, is rarely well developed as a public policy response. Instead we return to familiar approaches, regardless of whether or not they have proven to be effective in the past. A common strategy, and one of particular importance to school age youth, is that of retreat from intractable societal challenges by deferring action and shifting responsibility from one generation on to the next.

Consider, for example, the level of difficulty entailed in attempts to address the environmental and human costs of a consumer driven economy. Although patterns of human suffering linked to environmental degradation are persistent and compelling, far more influential in shaping social policy are the economic ambitions of those most highly rewarded by free market activity. Both private and corporate interests are further reinforced by widespread public concerns for economic security as measured by rates of employment and consumption. Innovative reform proposals, even exploratory public discourse, aimed at rethinking and restructuring global capitalism remain undeveloped or hopelessly mired in controversy.

Daunted by the patterns of destruction and injustice so deeply entrenched within the structure of our society, we turn to K–12 education. We educate for intelligent consumption and environmental protection to establish a basis for informed individual choice. We support advanced opportunities in science and mathematics to further the quest for technological solutions. We encourage participation in relevant forms of service such as school-based recycling. All this we do in hopes that the cumulative efforts of well-educated young people, who behave responsibly upon reaching adulthood, will yield positive results.

Although educating for individual responsibility is an important and appropriate strategy, unless we acknowledge the social conditions and political structures shaping the lives of children and youth, there is little reason to assume such efforts will result in transformative change. In a deeply stratified, age-segregated society, today's youth—whether in homes, schools, or communities—face increasingly limited opportunities to develop mutually affirming relationships with each other or with caring adults. In an adult-centered society, young people grow up as members of an under-represented and under-served political constituency with limited opportunities for meaningful civic participation and contribution. Failing to mobilize the collective imagination and resolve necessary to confront these realities, we focus our energies on instructional initiatives aimed at improving individual young people. In effect, we impose on youth the heightened personal responsibility that comes with enhanced awareness, while restricting or delaying indefinitely their capacity to join with others in taking effective social action. Policies and practices intended to promote a strong sense of self-worth and social efficacy contribute instead to feelings of demoralization, apathy, and alienation.

But public schools can offer more promising responses to pressing social concerns. Engagement of a broader set of communal interests in environmental education, for example, means first strengthening connections between each young student and a diverse set of adults. More extensive cross-age relationships can enrich processes of teaching and learning and support the development of educational strategies that move principled action beyond the classroom and into our homes, businesses, and civic and government organizations. Projects designed to affect substantive change—such as conserving non-renewable resources or advocating for legislation to counteract environmental racism—are most effectively accomplished through ongoing interaction among persons across generations, neighborhoods, and cultural affiliations.

Public schools can also facilitate broad-based student involvement in the development of youth-centered political perspectives, organizations, and initiatives. While promising new directions do emerge from the interplay of adult/youth perceptions, school age youth—by virtue of their distinctive developmental status and social position—are capable of *original* insights. If provided opportunities to deliberate and to act together—independent from intensive adult intervention—imaginative responses, not readily expressed in mixed-age settings, could be more fully developed. Acknowledging, for example, the importance of peer culture in shaping patterns of consumption, students might begin by working together to develop 'environmental impact statements' regarding the environmental consequences of their personal lifestyles. Such considerations, and related possibilities for visionary response, might be further augmented through participation in technologically mediated conversations (e.g., e-mail, chat rooms, blogs, etc.) with young people across the country and around the world. As resource consumption by U.S. citizens continues to dominate the global scene, it is crucial for American youth (adults also) to be cognizant of, and diligent in response to, the magnified impact of our actions on those whose lives are most significantly threatened by environmental degradation (e.g., women, children, the poor, persons of color, and citizens of developing nations).

Overall, the requirements for a politics of age-based inclusion feature *trust* as the platform for creative problem solving. Trust in persons and in processes is developed over time and through mutually supportive experiences and interactions. We cannot defer civic engagement until adulthood. Social inquiry linked to political participation is a lifelong practice that must begin early. Public schools can offer opportunities to envision and to experience new relational patterns that deepen and extend roles and responsibilities across generations.

Compassion . . .
to honor the aspirations of others
while remaining true to one's own
empathy and affiliation
creativity and hope
resonance across distinct yet parallel visions
emerge through shared struggle for the common good.

Caring attention and creative response to each other and to our natural and social ecologies cannot be accomplished in the abstract, at a distance, or based on illusions of stratified worth. While aspirations toward "the greatest good for the greatest number" are of central importance to democratic life, and paths toward collective well-being are to be determined "of, by, and for the people," our political and social systems are actively exclusionary. Rhetoric encountered in public discourse signaling the primacy of broad-based consensus and concern—"the American people think" or "the public demands"—is not matched by programmatic efforts to become more responsive to the majority of citizens. Through public policy aimed at specific constituencies, we continue to stratify and segregate not only on the basis of age, race, and gender, but also on the basis of achievement and ability—both attributes narrowly defined and closely linked to socioeconomic status.

In all aspects of public life, the exceptionally able and accomplished— often indicated by material affluence and political influence—are generally well served (e.g., through individual and corporate tax codes). The deeply disadvantaged—citizens below the poverty line and those assigned to categories of serious need—receive limited and uncertain support (e.g., through fragile public assistance programs). Attention and resources are apportioned in a congratulatory way to those selected into the 'top' (e.g., justifications of tax cuts that disproportionately favor the most affluent). When public policy attends to those assigned to the 'bottom', it is often with reluctance and condescension (e.g., rationales for diminishing support for those impoverished and dependent).

The majority of citizens—those occupying the large and diverse 'middle'—are programmatically overlooked while being called upon to support both ends of the socioeconomic spectrum. Middle-income citizens are taxed on a higher proportion of their earnings than their more affluent counterparts. They also experience curtailed public services (e.g., police and fire protection, recreation, and mass transit), increased government fees (e.g., rises in higher education tuition, licenses, and public transportation fares) and rising taxes (e.g., sales and property taxes).

Our educational systems reflect a similar stratified structure—a stable hierarchy with limited mobility between levels and substantive indifference toward advancement of the 'whole.' The affluent have always benefitted from opportunities to enroll their children in high property value school districts or private schools. While in recent years the redistribution of state revenues has yielded some progress toward fiscal equalization, current trends feature movement back toward greater reliance on local property taxes coupled with sharply curtailed state assistance. In response to these changes, well-resourced school districts are somewhat more resilient while poorer districts face draconian cuts.

The less visible injustice is the draining of resources from the 'middle' in public education. The majority of schools as well as students are neither affluent and academically advantaged, nor deep in poverty and struggling with special learning needs. The current pattern of *disinvestment* in public schooling reduces the quality of education available to the majority of all students. The most visible rationale for drastic reductions is budgetary crises attributed to sluggish global, national, and local economies. Seldom mentioned are the pervasive effects of tax cuts and the consequences of politically attractive pledges of "no new taxes." The impact of sharply reduced public school revenues is significantly, yet almost silently, experienced by students and families in the middle.

Any attempt at public education reform will confront this multilayered system that is highly resistant to change. Student experience and performance is similarly shaped by placement within a three-tiered hierarchy of expectation and opportunity. 'Gifted and talented' programs exemplify the top tier. These range across K–12 public schools and are supported by a well-organized body of skillful advocates including education specialists, parents, and teachers. Even during times of severe budget shortages and resource reallocations, school districts are reluctant to cut back on programs for high achieving students.

The bottom tier consists of programs mandated for students with special needs as defined by federal and state statutes (e.g., programs to support English language learners or students grappling with legally defined cognitive, emotional, or physical challenges). Reforms seeking equity and democracy have traditionally focused on the least advantaged students, usually identified by economic and racial/ethnic attributes. These students *are* disadvantaged and should remain an essential concern. Public schools are rightfully required to maintain these programs even in the face of serious resource shortages.

The mid-level is occupied by the majority of students who sit in more crowded and less well-equipped classrooms, to be taught by teachers with less preparation time and little assistance. At the policy level, they are treated with indifference and condescension in non-crisis periods as well as during times of painful constraint. Their fate as learners and citizens may be brushed by well-meaning rhetoric from time to time, but their problematic condition deepens. Students in the majority, the very large and diverse middle, are chronically underserved.

To attend more fully to the needs of the majority of American students is to take seriously the assertion that democracy is "for the people." This is not a call for reducing performance standards or leveling student opportunity to a lowest common denominator. Instead, it is a challenge to extend empathy and principled response beyond familiar reactions to the pressing demands posed by special interest advocates—a call to devote imaginative attention to the varied and dynamic concerns of a large and complex whole.

Creative openness to others' conditions, interests, and ideas—radically social imagination—is required to sustain a deep and dynamic democracy. The majority of U.S. citizens are educated in public schools. Public schooling is seen across the spectrum of political perspectives as a significant social responsibility. Public schools remain as one of the few social institutions capable of supporting continued, purposeful, and egalitarian interaction among diverse constituents. As a primary site for social learning and civic action, a vibrant system of public education offers invaluable opportunities to nurture the development and expression of collective political imagination.

"Love and imagination may be the most revolutionary ideas available to us."
—Robin D.G. Kelley
Freedom Dreams: The Black Radical Imagination

Exploratory Democratic Practice: Strategic Narratives

Narrative is a basic component of thinking, conversation, deliberation, and decision-making. Strategic narratives can connect realistic contexts, resources, and even personalities with broad reform ambitions and opportunities. When socially composed, they can be used to play out design and implementation scenarios.

Building on the experiences and insights gained through interaction among a broad range of participants during the early phases of a reform process, small groups (usually 3–5 members) can develop complex story lines interpreting challenges and possibilities to be confronted in their particular reform context. For example:

- One group might consider two or three crucial ideas or concerns in a specific reform initiative, and then compose a narrative that illustrates tensions likely to arise during implementation.
- Another group might anticipate problems, even crises, in the future of their project and construct narratives that provide early warnings.
- For a third group, the narrative might focus less on dramatizing tough challenges, and more on playing out plausible story lines that resolve some of the conflicts or develop directions useful in moving toward substantive reform.

Completed narratives can then be utilized to guide reflective conversations, first among the authoring group and then more broadly with others involved in the reform. 'Lessons learned' through this social practice can be incorporated directly into design, analysis, and planning.

These collaborative compositions—from problem portrayals, to change scenarios, to end state depictions—can extend imagination and engage emotions. Both the authoring group and the other members with whom the narratives are shared, interpret the web of events, the situations described, and the scripted dialogue in light of their own experiences and possibilities to be explored collectively. They usually broaden understanding of important issues and elicit alternative approaches to the task of democratic reform.

Thematic Bibliographic References

On curricular reform:

Appleman, D. (2000). *Critical encounters in high school English: Teaching literary theory to adolescents.* New York: Teachers College Press.

Audet, R., & Jordan, L. (Eds.). (2005). *Integrating inquiry across the curriculum.* Thousand Oaks, CA: Corwin Press/Sage.

Barton, A., Ermer, J., Burkett, T., & Osborne, M. (2003). *Teaching science for social justice.* New York: Teachers College Press.

Beach, R., & Myers, J. (2001). *Inquiry-based English instruction: Engaging students in life and literature.* New York: Teachers College Press.

Boostrom, R. (2005). *Thinking: The foundation of critical and creative learning in the classroom.* New York: Teachers College Press.

Caine, R., & Caine, G. (1997). *Education on the edge of possibility.* Alexandria, VA: Association for Supervision and Curriculum Development.

Clark, J.V. (1996). *Redirecting science education: Reform for a culturally diverse classroom.* Thousand Oaks, CA: Corwin Press.

Cress, C., Collier, P., & Reitenauer, V. (2005). *Learning through serving: A student guidebook for service-learning across the disciplines.* Sterling, VA: Stylus Publishing.

Doll, W., & Gough, N. (Eds.). (2002). *Curriculum visions.* New York: Peter Lang.

Egan, K. (1997). *The educated mind: How cognitive tools shape our understanding.* Chicago: University of Chicago Press.

Freedman, K. (2003). *Teaching visual culture: Curriculum, aesthetics, and the social life of art.* New York: Teachers College Press.

Gallego, M., & Hollingsworth, S. (2001). *What counts as literacy: Challenging the school standard.* New York: Teachers College Press.

Gamoran, A. et al. (2004). *Transforming teaching in math and science.* New York: Teachers College Press.

Gardner, R., Cairns, J., & Lawton, D. (Eds.). (2003). *Education for values: Morals, ethics and citizenship in contemporary teaching.* New York: Routledge Falmer.

Gay, G. (2000). *Culturally responsive teaching: Theory, research, and practice.* New York: Teachers College Press.

Goodman, S. (2003). *Teaching youth media: A critical guide to literacy, video production, and social change.* New York: Teachers College Press.

Gutstein, E., & Peterson, S. (Eds.). (2005). *Rethinking mathematics: Teaching social justice by the numbers.* Milwaukee, WI: Rethinking Schools, Ltd.

Halstead, J., & Taylor, M. (2002). *Moral and citizenship education: Learning through action and reflection* (1st ed.). New York: Routledge.

Henson, K. (2004). *Curriculum planning: Integrating multiculturalism, constructivism, and education.* Long Grove, IL: Waveland Press.

Hutchison, D. (1998). *Growing up green: Education for ecological renewal.* New York: Teachers College Press.

Kessler, R. (2000). *The soul of education: Helping students find connection, compassion, and character at school.* Alexandria, VA: Association for Supervision & Curriculum Development.

Kist, W. (2004). *New literacies in action: Teaching and learning in multiple media.* New York: Teachers College Press.

Kliebard, H. (2002). *Changing course: American curriculum reform in the 20th century.* New York: Teachers College Press.

Kuhn, D. (2005). *Education for thinking.* Cambridge, MA: Harvard University Press.

Lapsley, D., & Power, C. (Eds.). (2005). *Character psychology and character education.* Notre Dame, IN: University of Notre Dame Press.

Lowenberg, D. (2003). *Mathematical proficiency for all students: Toward a strategic research and development program in mathematics education.* Santa Monica, CA: Rand.

Macedo, S., & Yael, T. (Eds.). (2001). *Morals and political education (Nomos XLIII).* New York: New York University Press.

Monroe, B. (2004). *Crossing the digital divide: Race, writing, and technology in the classroom.* New York: Teachers College Press.

Moses, R. & Cobb, C. (2001). *Radical equations: Math literacy and civil rights.* Boston: Beacon Press.

Nieto, S. (2004). *Affirming diversity: An alternative approach to education.* New York: Teachers College Press.

Noddings, N. (2002). *Educating moral people: A caring alternative to character education.* New York: Teachers College Press.

Noddings N. (Ed.) (2005) *Educating citizens for global awareness.* New York: Teachers College Press.

Ponzio, R., & Fisher, C. (Eds.). (1998). *The JOY of sciencing: A hands-on approach to developing science literacy and teen leadership through cross-age teaching and community action.* San Francisco: Caddo Gap Press.

Reich, R. (2002). *Bridging liberalism and multiculturalism in American education.* Chicago: University of Chicago Press.

Scapp, R. (2002). *Teaching values: Critical perspectives on education, politics, and culture.* New York: Routledge Falmer.

Selman, R. L. (2003). *The promotion of social awareness: Powerful lessons from the partnership of developmental theory and classroom practice.* New York: Russell Sage Foundation.

Sizer, T., & Sizer, N. (1999). *The students are watching: Schools and the moral contract.* Boston: Beacon Press.

Smith, R., Karbek, D., & Hurst, J. (Eds.). (2005). *The passion of teaching: Dispositions in the schools.* lanham, MD: Scarecrow Education Press.

Stanton, T., Giles, D., & Cruz, N. (1999). *Service learning: A movement's pioneers reflect on its origins, practice, and future.* San Francisco: Jossey-Bass.

Stavy, R. & Tirosh, D. (2000). *How students (mis-)understand science and mathematics: Intuitive rules.* New York: Teachers College Press.

Thayer-Bacon, B. (2000). *Transforming critical thinking: Thinking constructively.* New York: Teachers College Press.

Thornton, S. (2004). *Teaching social studies that matters: Curriculum for active learning.* New York: Teachers College Press.

Tobin K., Elemsky, R., & Seiler, G. (Eds.). (2005). *Improving urban science education: New roles for teachers, students, and researchers.* Lanham, MD: Rowman & Littlefield.

Vaughn, S., & Bos, C. (2002). *Teaching exceptional, diverse, and at-risk students in the general education classroom* (3rd ed.). Boston: Allyn & Bacon.

Wade, R., & Woods, G. (Eds.). (1997). *Community service learning: A guide to including service in the public school curriculum.* Albany: State University of New York Press.

Warren, D. & Patrick, J. (Eds.). (2006). *Civic and moral learning in America.* New York: Plagrave Macmillan.

On structural reform:

Abbs, P. (2003). *Against the flow: The arts, postmodern culture and education* (1st ed.). London: Falmer Press.

Ayers, W. (Ed.). (2000). *A simple justice: The challenge of small schools.* New York: Teachers College Press.

Bodilly, S. (2001). *New American schools' concept of the break the mold designs: How design evolved and why.* Santa Monica, CA: Rand.

Boyer, W.H. (2002). *Education for the twenty-first century.* San Francisco: Caddo Gap Press.

Carlson, D. (1997). *Making progress: Education and culture in new times.* New York: Teachers College Press.

Christensen, L., & Karp, S. (Eds.). (2003). *Rethinking school reform: Views from the classroom.* Milwaukee, WI: Rethinking School Ltd.

Chubb J.E. (Ed.). (2005). *Within our reach: How America can educate every child.* New York: Rowman & Littlefield.

Clinchy, E. (2000). *Creating new schools: How small schools are changing American education.* New York: Teachers College Press.

Cohen, D., & Hill H. (2001). *Learning policy: When state education reform works.* New Haven, CT: Yale University Press.

Darling-Hammond L. (2001). *The right to learn: A blueprint for schools that work.* San Francisco: Jossey-Bass.

Datnow, A., Hubbard, L., & Mehan, H. (2002). *Extending educational reform.* New York: Routledge Falmer.

Fletcher, S. (2000). *Education and emancipation: Theory and practice in a new constellation.* New York: Teachers College Press.

Fullan, M. (2003). *Change forces with a vengeance* (1st ed.). London: Falmer Press.

Ginsberg, M., & Wlodkowski, R. (2000). *Creating highly motivating classrooms for all students: A school wide approach to powerful teaching with diverse learners.* San Francisco: Jossey-Bass.

Goldenberg, C. (2004). *Successful school change: Creating settings to improve teaching and learning.* New York: Teachers College Press.

Harris, A. (2002). *School improvement.* New York: Routledge Falmer.

Johnson, L. et al. (Eds.). (2005). *Urban education with an attitude.* Albany: SUNY Press.

Kahlenberg, R. (2001). *All together now: Creating middle-class schools through public school choice.* Washington, DC: Brookings Institution Press.

Kinsler, K., & Gamble, M. (2001). *Reforming schools.* New York: Continuum.

Kugelmass, J. (2004). *The inclusive school: Sustaining equity and standards.* New York: Teachers College Press.

Legters , N., Balfanz, R., Jordan, W., & McPartland, J. (Eds.). (2004). *Comprehensive reform for urban high schools: A talent development approach.* New York: Teachers College Press.

Senge, P., Nelda, H., Lucas, T., Kleiner, A., Dutton, J., & Smith, B. (2002). *Schools that learn: A fifth discipline fieldbook for educators, parents, and everyone who cares about education.* New York: Currency-Doubleday.

Simons, J. (2005). *Breaking through: Transforming urban school districts.* New York: Teachers College Press.

On perceptions, conditions, roles, and responsibilities of youth in society:

Bracey, G. (2003). *On the death of childhood and the destruction of public schools: The folly of today's education policies and practices.* Portsmouth, NH: Heinemann.

Cannella, G., & Viruru, R. (2004). *Childhood and postcolonization: Power, education, and contemporary practice.* New York: Routledge Falmer.

Comer, J. (2004). *Leave no child behind: Preparing today's youth for tomorrow's world.* New Haven, CT: Yale University Press.

Day, C., & Van Veen, D. (Eds.). (1997). *Children & youth at risk & urban education: Research, policy & practice.* Antwerpen: Garant Uitgevers NV.

Dwyer, P., & Wyn, J. (2001). *Youth, education and risk: Facing the future.* New York: Falmer Press.

Engle, S. (2005). *Real kids: Creating meaning in everyday life.* Cambridge, MA: Harvard University Press.

Entwistle, D., & Alexander K. (1997). *Children, schools and inequality.* Boulder, CO: Westview Press.

Fine, M., & Weis, L. (2003). *Silenced voices and extraordinary conversations: Re-imagining schools.* New York: Teachers College Press.

Furlong, A., & Cartmel, F. (1997). *Young people and social change: Individualization and risk in late modernity.* Berkshire, UK: Open University Press.

Giroux, H. (2003). *The abandoned generation: Democracy beyond the culture of fear.* New York: Palgrave Macmillan.

Glaser R. (Ed.). (2000). *Educational design and cognitive science.* Mahwah, NJ: Lawrence Erlbaum Associates Inc.

Hacsi, T. (2002). *Children as pawns: The politics of educational reform.* Cambridge, MA: Harvard University Press.

Hallett C. & Prout A. (Eds.). (2003). *Hearing the voices of children.* Basingstroke, UK: Taylor & Francis.

Hirsch, B. (2005). *A place to call home: After school programs for urban youth.* New York: Teachers College Press.

Lareau, A. (2003). *Unequal childhoods: Class, race, and family life.* Berkeley: University of California Press.

Lesko, N. (2002). *Act your age: A cultural construction of adolescence.* New York: Routledge Falmer.

Polakow, V. (2000). *The public assault on America's children: Poverty, violence, and juvenile injustice.* New York: Teachers College Press.

Rubin, B., & Silva, E. (Eds.). (2003). *Critical voices in school reform: Students living through change.* New York: Routledge Falmer.

Sadowski, M. (Ed.). (2003). *Adolescents at school: Perspectives on youth, identity, and education.* Cambridge, MA: Harvard Education Publishing Group.

White, R., & Wyn, J. (2004). *Youth and society: Exploring the social dynamics of youth experience.* Oxford: Oxford University Press.

On social and political imagination:

Egan, K. (2005). *An imaginative approach to teaching.* San Francisco: Jossey-Bass.

Greene, M. (1995). *Releasing the imagination: Essays on education, the arts, and social change.* San Francisco: Jossey-Bass.

Simpson, D. et al. (2005). *John Dewey and the art of teaching: Toward reflective and imaginative practice.* Thousand Oaks, CA: Sage.

Slaughter, R. (2004). *Futures beyond dystopia: Creating social foresight.* New York: Routledge Falmer.

Sloan, D. (1983). *Insight-imagination: The emancipation of thought and the modern world.* Westport, CT: Greenwood Press.

Reflection:

Kelley, R. (2002). *Freedom dreams: The black radical imagination* (p. 12). Boston: Beacon Press.

Exploratory Democratic Practice: Strategic Narrative

See Prelude

c h a p t e r   8

Risk

Dreaming is dangerous
aspiring to advance the greater good
we face possibilities for even larger loss
failure rightfully feared
expectations, when heightened then denied
can only deepen disillusionment among those who have already lost too much
social venturing, daring with and for each other
brings complexity beyond individual command or control
wary of moving on, we know we cannot turn back.

"*C*an you believe it's been nearly a year since we began g on these deep democracy projects last November?" Althea asked as they walked briskly down the main Grant High corridor.

"Well, I remember the election all too vividly," Caine said soberly. "Candidly, I still miss being up at the capitol. Yet, I'm not so sure I would trade this past year with the LEAD project or here with the ninth grade program even for being back in the Senate."

"Oh? You're still the politician aren't you, Jon." Althea said with a smile.

"Maybe not quite the same politician now. What should I expect at today's meeting?" Caine asked.

Re-Envisioning Education and Democracy, pages 135–159
Copyright © 2006 by Information Age Publishing
All rights of reproduction in any form reserved.

He was referring to the joint meeting of the ninth grade faculty with most of the members of the Ninth Grade Advisory Council. The Advisory Council was made up of community members and ninth grader's parents who had volunteered after some coaxing from Althea and the teachers. Representing the LEAD proposal group were Margaret Rudolph from the Federation of Cooperatives, Melvin Bolton from the Urban League, Bobbi Williams from the LEAD staff, and Jonathan Caine. They were joined today by three parents and two members from the Grant neighborhood—the community association organizer and the president of the local Small Business Association. The meeting was scheduled during the regular late morning prep hour.

Althea had not answered Caine as they entered the classroom already buzzing with conversation. Looking for a chair, Caine overheard one of the teachers saying, "You know what's hard? I don't mean just that all this is taking tons more time than any of us ever imagined. I suppose we should have been more realistic. But what's really awful for me is that the things that bugged us or blocked us before—last year or even before that—they're all still in play, big time, here and now."

"I hear you, but this is a little different too," Joy Garcia replied. "We're not so isolated as most teachers are. We see a lot of each other every day and our curriculum is pretty interesting, right? OK so it is really challenging, but I think we actually like that."

Tuning into another nearby exchange, Caine overheard, "...so maybe there's just too much...the needs and demands just go on and on and on...."

Kirk Peterson replied, "Yeah, there are days when it *is* all too much. But then we are seeing some progress with the student projects—that means a lot!"

It was Morrie Bernstein's turn to convene the Advisory Council's biweekly meeting and he began by saying, "OK, let's get rolling! Today can we please stick to the agenda and leave some time, if we can, for new concerns. Mary?"

"Yes, a quick announcement that installation of the computers for all the classrooms will be done by next week. As you all know, the science-math rooms got their networks early in October and we've been on them heavily ever since. We've had to share some computer time with the other classes until they got hooked-up. Everyone should be up and running by next Monday. We've got several tech-smart volunteers to help us this weekend. And remember, some of the kids are ready to be 'computer tutors' in the writing and social studies classes. There are several who are quite proficient."

"So much for the good news," Morrie said with a frown. "As today's agenda indicates, we have some more "new program gets slammed by reality" items. Let me summarize: The usual ninth grade slump has long since arrived. We all know that sets in when the novelty of any new program wears off. All the hype we gave in those early weeks is over, and everybody has to face up to all the hard academic work and all the rules. No more halo effects for morale building. The kids complain that our homeroom strategies have separated them from their friends and now they're with a bunch of people they mostly don't like, and a few say they really hate. What's more, we're asking them to be responsible for each other and to make community-regarding decisions. They have little experience with that kind of responsibility. A few sharp observers have pointed out that this Council doesn't even include student representatives. That's "undemocratic," they claim."

After an extended pause, Joy said, "The first agenda item comes as part our struggle to compose a ninth grade student governance and judicial process that fits with our deep democracy objectives. The older kids from the upper grades are expressively cynical about any kind of student government. They're pretty cynical about learning too . . . they say stuff like "Get real! Everybody knows Grant is the dumb school." And they let our ninth graders know that any judicial set up is just a front for the principal and the teachers. Older kids are very persuasive. And I think I pushed the *"democratic immersion experience"* line just once too often. They immediately saw an acronym and came up with a T-shirt design featuring: **WE'RE GOING TO D.I.E. AT GRANT HIGH!**"

There were groans and perhaps a hint of possible agreement with the slogan.

Morrie smirked and continued, "Along with that, we're trying to keep the absentee rate down through homeroom peer pressure. The group project emphasis seemed to work back in September, but since then the truancy rate is inching up. Still, it's well below last year's level, thank you. But those debatable health excuses are on the rise. It's a trend, for sure, and if we're committed to keeping these kids in school, we need to find some new angles."

"You're right," Althea said. "Attendance is highly correlated with community-building, improved test scores, and good graduation rates. It must be an important concern for us."

"So, now that we've finished with the first two waves of diagnostic testing, we have more individual student development to manage as well as keeping the groups rolling along." The speaker was the communications teacher Caine had overheard earlier. "Yes, I admit it. I'm swamped! I've got massive catch up to do in writing and now that we're finally getting computers, I've got to get up to speed on keyboarding and the new writing software as well. Writing in groups is great, but it takes lots of preparation, care, and feeding. For more than a third of my kids, English is not their first language. I've got two kids who just started with us last week—I've got four more with diagnosed learning disabilities and two with major physical limitations." He paused and then sighed, "and half of my classes hate school and half of those probably hate me."

A parent broke in. "I know it's rough for you, but my son has never liked school and now at least he leaves in the morning without a struggle. He's my fourth child at Grant, and as Mr. Bernstein just said, things always get difficult this time of year."

Morrie nodded, "Yup, it's November . . . the leaves drop, it gets grayer, it turns colder, and school morale dives into the dumpster!"

There was nervous laughter and as it subsided Althea said, "There certainly are rhythms in all of life—here too. For now, we know that the heavy battery of recent diagnostic tests have identified more widespread challenges than we expected. What are we doing about that?"

"Our daily staff sessions give us more opportunities to plan and coordinate for each student—not only the ones below the threshold. We can do both individual and group things. It's hard, but I can see a few gains already," Joy said.

One of the social studies teachers added, "Look, it's OK for us to get a little discouraged. The 'Learning to Learn' components will take at least this full year to set in, and we'll need to stay on it through the next three. I find the 'community building' and 'exploratory democratic practices' more difficult than the teaching I'm used to. Few of these students have had positive experiences with cooperation in school before, and maybe nowhere else. Even those students on sports teams and in music or dramatic groups have focused on individual performance and individual achievement. There's plenty of individual learning here, but 'community accountability' is hard to get going and keep moving. But then I know we've only been at it a little more than two months."

Again heads nodded around the room.

"Well, I hate to bring up more good news," Morrie said with a sarcastic grin. "But our out-of-the-building community projects do seem to be taking hold. We now have far more than half of the ninth graders involved in well organized service learning slots—mostly here in the neighborhood. All of the placements are team assignments. We'll have everybody in service learning by the end of the month. Most of the ones not yet assigned are our new kids (yeah, I know . . . several more each week) or those who have special schedule conflicts, and as usual a few placements didn't work out."

Melvin said, "I hear some good things about the kids out in the community, Morrie. How about you folks?" He looked at the community members.

"Well, no complaints from any of my people yet," the Small Business Association representative offered. "I'm a little skeptical, though, about them being out of school a couple of times a week. But let's see how it goes."

The community organizer said, "It seems to be working. And I think it's a little too soon to know if they can come through on the ambitious environmental and housing projects they've started."

"The teams in the two neighborhood co-ops are terrific," Margaret said enthusiastically. "They're fun to be around. They're working hard and have already made good suggestions. They've even generated a few changes and are very responsible."

Althea waited to see if there was any more to be said on that point and then asked, "What about the curriculum? Are we doing "learning to learn" and "community building" as we proposed? And what about everything else the ninth graders are supposed to be learning—including the things they'll be tested on?"

"Isn't it a little early for that?" Caine asked quietly.

"Definitely not," Althea responded. "At the meetings with the other high school principals and with the district staff, this appears to be the main question about Grant. They're interested in our learning and community goals—even in the democratic citizenship perspective we have—but there are 'bottom lines.' The budget has a set of bottom lines that are both frightening and unavoidable for us. For the School District, the "critical indicators" are attendance rates and test scores. We can tell them all we want to about our good intentions, smother them with the skewed demographics we serve, or the distribution of special learning challenges among our students—but they'll always look at our budget, attendance, and test scores."

"Hey Althea," Kirk interjected, "Grant's demographics aren't so skewed—our students represent this neighborhood right-on, and they're not far off the whole city's distribution. Remember, we're deliberately not 'selecting' or 'magnetizing' or whatever it's called, and so we're not going to draw specially talented or interested students away from other schools—if we did that, *then* our demographics would be skewed."

With some intensity, Melvin said: "It's the usual race, and yes, class divide too. I've been saying right along that the District has got to get serious about "equal opportunity." Public schools—this public school especially—is just about the only ticket for poor kids and kids-of-color. For a change, we've got to make sure our neighborhood kids aren't getting the bottom of the barrel in their school as they get in most of the rest of their lives. We've have to make sure they're getting a fair shot with really good teachers, like you guys here—and with class work that is challenging and relevant to their lives, and up-to-date textbooks as well as computers."

Morrie looked around the room and said. "Ah, equity and diversity..."

Mary spoke first. "Another critical diversity issue, at least in Science-Math for Citizens, isn't just student ability and background—that's always there—but they're all over the place on what it means to learn both individually and collectively."

"Are you losing confidence in this new program?" a parent asked.

"No!" several teachers said almost in unison.

Kirk added, "I feel we're on the right track—but man, we're just getting started and there's so much to do! And there's still so much to learn—at least I have a lot to learn."

"Remember, it's November." Morrie said. "There are rhythms at work!"

Swirling water, sharp cliff and jagged rock
degree of danger cannot be anticipated until it descends
drawn over the edge and into the depths
falling, crashing, changing
with no assurance of flowing on.

Althea had been taping conversations she considered essential to Grant's ninth grade program. All the teachers and most students and their parents had given her written permission. Still she asked each time before she punched the record button. At her desk late one December afternoon, she played snippets of recent recordings as she prepared to tackle another pile of required paperwork.

[From an exchange with a teacher:] "Then what are we going to do about all the huge individual differences that the diagnostic tests documented? I'm trying to minimize ability grouping as much as possible. These kids are suspicious of the tracking they've been part of before, and we promised them "no tracking" here at Grant. Yet some of them just don't need the remedial attention that so many of the others do. I'm not sure how we're going to work this out."

*   *   *

[A discussion between two teachers:] "We still have too many disruptive students here. No matter what, they won't listen; they won't follow instructions. And there are a few who actually menace the other kids right here, in my classroom, so my classes are way off schedule."

"I know, I know! Even a couple of suspensions by you, Althea, didn't seem to help that much. Our early version of the student judicial system isn't working so well either. When they do pass judgment, the students are really punitive. I share much of their anger and frustration with each other. Our draft rules are pretty clear and some kids knowingly violate them. They're used to pushing limits. But we want our new system and the regular Grant disciplinary procedures to work together and not end up like some kind of harsh 'double jeopardy' for the ninth graders."

"Of course we want our ninth graders to help build a workable system. We don't want to give up on these kids and put them in the old Grant process with the detention holding pens and all that. I agree we don't have many promising strategies as yet. These kids are used to acting out and being suspended or even expelled. Some just don't want to be in school— not even in our spunky little democratic community. I think I'm at a loss."

* * *

Althea stopped the tape and looked at the 'must do' stack on her desk. She found herself nodding as her thoughts drifted across the challenges in each pile. She remembered there was a conversation with Kirk Peterson she needed to think hard about. She found it on her recorder and punched 'play.'

[Althea's voice:] "Kirk, I do hear your 'why me?' plea, but all of us need to be involved in this. You have the deep respect of your fellow teachers and the ninth-graders. You've got the Building Visions experience to fall back on. All kids, and clearly ours here at Grant, love the technology. But it's not only the video and digital cameras that are important to them, Kirk. It's you too."

[After a long pause, she continued:] "You know we all must be involved across the board on this. Usually teachers have handed off these kinds of things to counselors or social workers, and especially to assistant principals for disciplinary action. And you know "these kinds of things" refer to a series of incidents involving mostly our ninth graders—gang-related activities in and near the school; very unacceptable language; threats to students and in one case to a staff member; racial, ethnic, and sexual harassment of various kinds; and most immediately several fights on the school grounds. While these are hardly new events for Grant or any urban high school, they are big challenges for us and dramatically so for our evolving student governance and judicial system."

[Kirk's voice:] "I know, I know—but I still ask you, why me? I'm not a cop. I'm not a lawyer. I'm not a judge. I am a video artist."

[Althea's voice in a sharper tone than she had remembered:] "Kirk, you're a teacher! In the ninth grade program proposal we submitted last spring, we all committed ourselves to finding new ways of achieving justice. Justice in a democratic learning setting can't be accomplished either by doing school discipline 'as usual' or by backing off and refusing to confront tough problems head on. Some of these events are pretty awful. Look, first we have to protect our students and prevent as many of these things from happening as possible. And we need to address the damage done to people—and to the facilities. In all, we're trying to work out what 'justice' means as we go along. We're trying to make some terrible experiences into 'teachable moments' so we can find deeper ways of holding each other accountable, and learn more about what it means to move together as a community."

[Kirk's voice:] "Very eloquent, Althea! Great speech! Yeah... OK. I do think there are some new openings with most of these kids. I know some of them pretty well. OK... OK! So I didn't know what I was getting into and I sure don't know how it's going to turn out. Maybe none of us knew—maybe none of us can know. All right, but I'll need everyone's help. I mean, I'll need lots of support. And we're going to need you, Althea, to run interference with the authorities, the parents, the community groups, the rest of the students, and the rest of the faculty too."

[Althea's voice:] "That's my job. And the 'authorities' you mention are my bosses. I'm not thrilled about this part of my life at Grant either... and, Kirk, thank you."

*   *   *

[Althea's voice at a teachers' meeting:] "We're getting tough questions and a few formal complaints about all of the group work we have going. Some students don't like working on projects and assignments with others who, of course, they neither like nor respect. They are concerned that the group component of their own grades will drag them down. Some parents don't think their kids are advancing at an appropriate pace. The grading period is ending now and they're worried and very insistent about their own child's achievement. As a mom, I can understand their concerns."

[Mary's voice:] "Yes, the individual-community split did come up during our first round of parent conferences. It's really difficult to explain especially in science and math. We had so little time with the parents who actually showed up, and we wanted to emphasize our attention to their particular child. I'm not sure how we can get our strategy across in the short run. Grades will still be reported on individual report cards and there will always be lots of reinforcement for competition and individual achievement as the only things that matter."

[Morrie's voice:] "We have to find new ways to communicate with students and their parents about the social aspects of learning, as well as the individual parts. I've also gotten a few complaints about community service. One couple thought it was a waste of time and wondered if students were really learning anything. To another parent, the community connections seemed more like a luxury when so many basic learning needs were starkly evident. Another pointed out that her son has a job just so the family can make ends meet. The service learning seemed, well, almost redundant."

[Mary's voice:] "Maybe we need to do something to help our students talk about *all* the aspects of what's going on here, with their families and even with each other."

[Althea's voice:] "But we wrote about all this back in the first newsletter that went to parents and to others in the neighborhood. And we do have all of the information on the ninth grade webpage."

[Joy's voice:] "I think the newsletter is at best a necessary ritual—it's just one of the many notices the kids stuff in their backpacks. And how many hits are we getting on the webpage from outside this building? Can we say "digital divide?" So, how *do* we get them to understand? To trust us?"

*   *   *

[A conversation with one of the ninth grade teachers:] "Some of the other Grant teachers, you know, the ones in the tenth, eleventh, and twelfth grades, are getting more vocal and more skeptical about our ninth grade program. Sure, they're probably a little envious of our two prep hours. Yet several have also expressed concerns about whether or not the ninth graders will be ready to move on. They say we're leaving the "real teaching" for them next year. I mean, their cynicism could undermine what we're trying to do."

[Althea's voice:] "That's part of my job—to have everyone at Grant supporting everything we do—especially the ninth grade. I'll keep working on it . . . really; I promise."

*   *   *

[Althea's voice:] "These videos are wonderful, Kirk. Jim was right about you, I'm glad you're part of all this at Grant."

[Kirk's voice:] "Thanks, do I get a raise? Look, I'm sure that some of these kids didn't show up expecting to learn anything in my class, and certainly nothing really connected to their other classes. Weaving classroom assignments and activities, their service learning, and their own life experience is not what any of them have done in school before. But more than that, it's the linking up with what's important in their real world—issues in their own neighborhoods—like violence, drugs, gangs, and several kinds of discrimination. You know, what's important to them personally turns out to be really energizing. This group project, for instance, focuses on the homeless families in the neighborhood. Some of the students do their service learning in a nearby family shelter and some others at the local food bank. They're out collecting stories for their voice-over. They're also trying to find a good way to convey the terrible crunch on affordable housing they've been researching in Social Studies. One team is lobbying their

Communication Arts teacher to assign some poetry and fiction about homelessness. But . . . I . . . "

[After a long pause, Althea's voice:] "But what?"

[Kirk's voice] "But . . . even though I know there are hazards in any of these projects, something really hard has come up. A pair of students interviewing at the family shelter discovered that one of their Grant classmates lives there. Well, first, there's the overall confidentiality concern we've talked a lot about. These two haven't told anyone but me, as far as I know. I'm not sure what else I should do. I think they have a good sense of their responsibility and I want to trust them on this. Second, the school social worker told us in September that we had to report students who don't have a permanent address and who might have special counseling needs. I know the kid and she doesn't appear like a needy type to me. She's been absent a couple of times but so have a lot of others. I just don't like this 'mandatory reporting' thing. There's her privacy to respect, but then there may be good reasons to go up to the social worker's office. What should I do?"

* * *

[Althea's voice from a conversation with Jonathan Caine:] "Of course, I read Karla Morgan's column regularly. I know about some of her feature reporting too; she did a nice piece on PIP a couple of years ago. Why does she want to interview me about Grant now?"

[Caine's voice:] "I think you can put her off for a while. She may have actually picked up on what's going on here from me. I talked with her on the phone last week and you know how enthusiastic I can get about Grant."

[Althea's voice:] "Hold on, Jon. I doubt Grant is going to be a great platform for either of us to run on just yet. We have a slew of things that the papers would just love to report on. We are moving, and in a couple of years, in four for sure, we could be golden. But *this* winter we've got more problems than solutions. Maybe in the spring, when the budget axes get their annual sharpening, a big feature could do us some good. I'll return her call and see if I can get a rain check."

* * *

[Althea's voice in a conversation with a School Board member who had visited Grant and spent most of his time with the ninth grade:] "I'm relieved you counseled patience. I know there's a lot of pressure for a quick turn around and instant results. But as you wisely said—'all this takes time.'"

[The Board member's voice:] "Yes it does. In all the years I've been on the Board, I think the hardest thing after our relentless budget wars is finding an appropriate time frame for evaluating programs—and evaluating people. The Board did make a formal four-year commitment to you at Grant. But candidly, we may have to change our minds before then. Things keep shifting. We've got a mountain of priorities to juggle and the worst budget pressures I've ever seen. And half of us on the Board are up for re-election in the next round, and you know what can happen during campaigns."

*   *   *

[Althea moved the tape ahead to capture two student voices:] "Yes it is *too* freedom of the press, Dr. Putnam. We know our rights, and you have imposed "prior censorship" on *The Citizen.*"

[Althea's voice:] "We only want your faculty advisor to see the copy before it's put on-line. The regular Grant High student newspaper has the same rules."

[Another student voice:] "But this *isn't* the regular school paper—it's just for us democratic immersion ninth graders. Everyone keeps telling us to "take responsibility for our learning and for each other"...but you won't even trust us with being responsible for our own webpage."

*   *   *

[Althea frowned as she forwarded the tape to listen to other students at an extremely tense meeting:] "Like we've done this work in our classes already about African American history and about scientists and poets and even politicians. We talked with our parents and other people all over the community back from when school started in September...you know, like oral history. So why do we have to do all this Black History Month stuff anyway? We don't want to be, well, like this book here says, "simplified and categorized in a color-coded month." And February is the shortest month, anyway!"

[A lightly accented voice interrupted:] "But Dr. Putnam, those of us from Africa have stories to tell too...and maybe we're even more African, and they're more American. Can't we at least be a part of what the school does about Africa?"

[First student voice:] "And all the white kids and maybe the teachers too think all of us students-of-color are the same—you know we're not—that's just not true, and..."

[The recent immigrant voice:] "And we're not going to let what's African and what that means be *told* to us. Several of us were born there and our families are important too."

*   *   *

Althea ejected the cassette and sighed about the many plans for Febru-ary. The School District had mandated a Black History Month. There were going to be tough negotiations ahead on many levels. As she searched her desk drawer for another cassette, she wondered about the way Grant would handle the upcoming holidays. Would the new ninth grade pro-gram have an impact on the way the many religious traditions were repre-sented and respected, as well as doing justice to all the racial and ethnic concerns? Handling spiritual learning directly in a public school setting has always been risky. She snapped the cassette she wanted into her mini-recorder. She reflected on how uncertain she was about whether the ninth grade staff's commitment to "fresh approaches" to the cultural and reli-gious holidays would balance out positively. Several veteran Grant teach-ers had already expressed reservations about any new programs and had counseled a "low profile." It was, she had agreed with them, a very compli-cated matter.

She started the new tape intending just to catch the drift of the recorded conversations. She knew she should be rushing to finish the draft memo flickering on her computer screen. Perhaps out of avoidance, she ignored her computer and listened to another conversation at a recent teacher's meeting.

* * *

[A science-math teacher's voice:] "Some of the things we're trying do make big waves. But it's also pretty clear that teaching health and PE at Grant the old way wasn't doing much good."

[Mary's voice:] "Look, we're going to take heavy flak from several direc-tions and I agree we have to be careful. But we've got to try to do what we think is responsible. May I change the subject from sex education? I'm get-ting real uneasy about our math curriculum. The things we're doing in "math for citizens" aren't just the old 'consumer-readiness with the check-book' and credit card exercises. It kicks numeracy into critical thinking and problem-solving in neat ways. But..."

[A teacher's voice:] "So, what's your problem, Mary?"

[Mary's voice:] "The standardized tests expect things that we aren't teaching directly. As we begin to prepare our students for the wave of tests that are coming next spring, it's going to be apparent that except for the few kids taking other elective math classes, most won't have a clue on a sig-nificant number of questions."

[A science teacher's voice:] "Without some of those things, chemistry and physics classes are going to be either out of bounds for our ninth grad-ers, or at least a major struggle for them. That'll be true for A. P. Biology also. We already use some algebra-based biometrics and that's confusing for most of our kids."

[Mary's voice:] "What are we going to do? What can we do?"

*   *   *

[Joy's voice:] "Doing writing across the curriculum is, of course, an amazing opportunity. But doing writing, editing, and instruction is really tough on our teachers who aren't trained in communication arts. I mean, we can forestall some things with spell check and grammar monitoring on the computers. But helping with effective composition and the specific assignments in whatever class is involved is, at the very least, time consuming. It means spending time in class on writing and a lot of time on the papers. OK, Althea, we get some efficiency by doing it on-line, but still it's very demanding. I sense some of the other teachers are, well, maybe starting to resent it. After all, as one science-math colleague reminded me kindly, 'Hey, we don't ask you to correct students' miscalculations or measurement errors on our assignments.'"

*   *   *

[The Community Association organizer's voice at a recent meeting in her office:] "Althea, you know it's almost impossible getting the parents involved. They're just too busy, some with two jobs...and it's really tough to get neighborhood people to attend meetings. I'm trying but..."

*   *   *

She was about to eject the tape and get back to her unfinished memo on school discipline. But the tape ran on to an Assistant School Superintendent saying to her: "You know I don't want to nag you, Althea. We do understand at the District Office that all this does takes time. But you do have to be able to assure us that those tests next May will turn out better for Grant—at least for the ninth graders. Can you do that?"

The tape ran out and the machine clicked off.

Given the costs and consequences of failure, how can we responsibly risk innovation in an increasingly dangerous world?

In perilous times, during the most challenging moments of change, activists experience a heightened awareness of risk. Although initially understood as a neutral concept signaling possibilities for gain or loss, risk has come to connote danger, and is intrinsically linked to accountability. All social systems have struggled to respond to world events perceived as ever more threatening. Highly specialized economic and technological sectors have developed to manage risk (e.g., the insurance industry, technological forecasting). Ethical systems posit general principles (e.g., utilitarianism) and decision rules (e.g., prudence) to apply in perilous situations. Legal systems have evolved elaborate concepts (e.g., liability) and procedures (e.g., injury and damage assessment) for resolving disputes over accountability for risk-taking. In all these interdependent activities, 'risk' has come to refer almost exclusively to negative outcomes and the assignment of responsibility for them.

During times of societal stress, public schools are subjected to intense scrutiny and obliged to respond to a formidable array of accountability demands. Public attention is riveted on a series of cascading fears—declining academic performance will reduce economic competitiveness and eventually threaten the 'American way of life.' Access to material affluence, individual freedom, and representative democracy appear to hang in the balance. With so much at stake, those concerned with the fate of public education struggle to limit risk. They redouble efforts to demonstrate performance, fiscal, and political accountability.

Performance accountability for public education is always a central concern. Public faith in the system's ability to transmit knowledge, skills, and dispositions essential to the nation's economic and civic well-being must be sustained. Assessments of student performance—grades, graduation rates, and well-publicized test scores—are intended to inform students, parents, schools, districts, and the general public. Students receive messages about their current situation and future prospects. Parents use the information to make wise selections among specific schools and programs for their children. Standardized assessments are utilized to inform evaluations of teacher and administrative performance. Test scores are also used comparatively to shape public perceptions, and are connected to sanctions and incentives.

Fiscal accountability is required by all sources of school funding. Without doubt, fiscal accountability has become the most important 'bottom line' in public education policy. Substantial tax contributions are required of all citizens whether or not direct benefit is received. Public confidence in the system's ability to effectively distribute private earnings for public purposes can never be taken for granted. In response, public fiscal accounting has become increasingly complicated, highly specialized, and expert-driven. As with most areas of technical expertise, professional accounting personnel are largely concentrated in central bureaucracies that are experientially distant from programs and classrooms. Although largely hidden from public view, the processes of financial management, accounting, and auditing directly impact all aspects of public education.

Political accountability is enmeshed in fiscal and performance assessments and entails all levels and branches of government. Public trust in the system's ability to respond with sensitivity and fairness to a wide range of public interests and concerns must be sustained. Local, state, and national education bureaucracies impose diverse accountability demands on public schools as directed by elected officials, boards, and legislatures. Political accountability inevitably extends to the judicial branch where in any given year, cases involving almost all aspects of public school life are brought before the courts. Numerous non-governmental constituents of public education (e.g., corporations, civic organizations, labor unions, commercial vendors, charitable foundations, religious organizations, athletic boosters, etc.) also make strong accountability claims appropriate to the special interests they represent.

In each of these interrelated areas of accountability—performance, fiscal, and political—there is an understandable tendency to defend against negative outcomes. Public education risks are predominantly managed by documenting accountability in relation to non-controversial and achievable goals that can be assessed through familiar methods. But even these 'tried and true' accountability strategies involve risk.

In times of perceived crisis, aspects of student performance are scrutinized in detail, expressed almost exclusively in quantitative terms, and interpreted within elaborate statistical frameworks, even though such techniques are themselves methodologically controversial. Policy directives aimed at improving test performance are imposed even though more extensive testing further strains school budgets already stressed to the breaking point. Although intended to reduce the perils associated with chronic low performance in some schools, expensive unfunded mandates may actually heighten risks of broader system demise. Legislating laudable high standards without allocating financial resources is ultimately counterproductive. The situation is rendered even more hazardous as punitive measures are deployed in response to poor test results. Authorization to publicly identify and then move to disband 'failed' schools is widely sanctioned. Yet these actions risk undermining the long-term efforts of dedicated school personnel and further the erosion of public confidence in public education. Although 'failed' schools are correlated with large populations of low-income students, test-driven accountability undermines public involvement even in the most affluent districts. Along with good intentions and closer program assessment, prevailing standardized testing policies can reinforce regressive stratification, generate distrust, diminish opportunities for broader collaboration, and make educating for the public good far more difficult.

Under conditions of fiscal constraint, innovations are generally avoided. But crisis-driven 'survival' and 'preservation' budget strategies can also result in unintended negative outcomes. Equitable public school financing is a significant policy challenge even in times of relative affluence. It has always been difficult to sustain public interest in supporting low-resource school systems in central cities, inner-ring suburbs, and rural communities.

As state budget shortages deepen, increased reliance on property tax-based funding becomes politically attractive, even though it is understood that less affluent schools and districts will be most strongly and negatively affected. Reluctant acceptance of increased financial inequities in the name of budget necessity risks strengthening isolation, ignorance, and structural segregation.

In current public education politics, fears concerning potential loss of opportunities or services are mitigated by special interest group advocacy. Influential advocacy groups focus on the specific concerns of selected populations rather than broad shared interests. Beyond the lobbying and other political activities of these groups, it is expected that parents will attend to their own children's development and negotiate beneficial exceptions if problems arise. It is expected that teachers and administrators will bargain for the conditions of their work through professional associations and unions. While most educational interest groups' stated purposes and public rhetoric feature much needed reform, their political behavior is defensive—generally reinforcing 'education policy as usual' with all of its risky consequences. Even the combined efforts of well-organized interests simply do not result in broadened and strengthened support for public schools. Education politics remain mostly fragmented, individualized, and fear-driven as widespread disenchantment with public schooling deepens.

In the absence of more meaningful, authentic, and comprehensive approaches to accountability, the erosion of public trust and the decline of public investment in education will continue. We can no longer responsibly assume the risks of maintaining a 'public' for public education comprised of individuals treated as passive consumers in a free market of educational opportunity. Neither can we continue to jeopardize the lives of so many young people and their families by calling for equity, but failing to demand equitable outcomes. Deeper learning and broader participation are necessary for the development of more inclusive and intelligent forms of assessment. Without more widely shared power, more deeply shared responsibility, and more complex understanding of the costs and consequences of established education policies, the 'public' will not support necessary transformations of public schooling.

Attention to risk is of course necessary. But difficult times require more than activists' caution, more than innovators' visions diluted by prudence, and more than constant fear of personal liability. Daring dreams require deeper learning. Democratic aspirations require taking chances.

> *Integrity . . .*
> *to respond with sincerity, sensitivity and strength*
> *refusing to abandon others*
> *to persistent and predictable tragedy—*
> *public purposes unfulfilled*
> *dissonance between voiced intent and lived experience*
> *diminishes communal resolve—*
> *expression of civic virtue*
> *is the wellspring of democratic spirit.*

While risking innovation in public education is necessary, it must occur within the context of ethical scrutiny and civic responsibility. At the very least, risk taking with integrity requires honest explanation and assessment of school-related expenditures, activities, and accomplishments. Intelligible interpretations of critical issues and their implications must be made accessible to diverse constituents. Carefully validated research findings must be made available to policy makers who are then obliged to respond accordingly.

Integrity requires steadfast coherence between expressed intent, principled action, and desired outcome. We cannot allow efforts to realize eloquently stated civic goals for public education to be thwarted by pressures of political expediency, or crippled by repeated failure to allocate sufficient resources. We must not continue to betray the aspirations of young citizens. We must not continue to promise enhanced educational opportunity only later to deem such goals unattainable, or to treat such hopes as desirable but dispensable luxuries. Our sanctioned accountability practices must address issues of significance to individuals and society by means that are transparent, authentic, and demonstrably effective.

Risk taking with integrity further demands that not only specific components be held accountable, but that the venture of *public education as a whole* adheres to criteria that are widely shared and highly valued. Integrity requires comprehensive response that effectively integrates the concerns of diverse constituents, along multiple dimensions, and through varied approaches.

Although challenging and not without risk, it is possible to develop innovative accountability practices. When implemented with integrity, such practices hold promise for deepening public support for public education. We can begin by envisioning and enacting approaches to *performance accountability* that not only support added dimensions of individual development, but also advance the common good.

Assuming continued emphasis on standardized testing as a primary performance measure, we might advocate for more inclusive and multifaceted participation in test design and interpretation. Conversations should be encouraged between test designers and providers, elected officials, and educational research professionals, as well as those active in schools and classrooms. More intensive and broad-based deliberation, while time consuming, can yield clarification of testing goals, improve test content, and develop more sensitive diagnostic approaches.

Even more important, motivating increased public support for public schooling rests on efforts to extend the range and authenticity of performance expectations. Community forums can be convened to identify and explore the many dimensions of civic learning not well appraised through standardized assessments. For example, preparing all students for *lifelong involvement in processes of teaching and learning* might be accepted as an appropriate civic goal to be advanced through public education. Widespread and continuing social inquiry is the essence of both individual development and a vibrant democratic polity. Public schools could further be assisted in developing performance objectives and related assessments through which students demonstrate increasing *responsibility for their own learning*. This might be accomplished by requiring substantive experience with choice and self-evaluation on the elementary level, followed by negotiated design of personal development plans upon reaching high school. Such plans could implicate course selection and identify meaningful directions for post-secondary education. Student development in relation to this goal could be complemented by requirements for worthwhile *contributions to other students' learning* (e.g., through mentoring, tutoring, group projects) and *contributions to the school and broader community* (e.g., through school and community service, public scholarship, and civic action). Such performance objectives will challenge conventional assessment procedures, but can be coordinated with standardized testing to broaden and deepen performance accountability.

We can envision and enact more accessible approaches to *fiscal accountability* that better include and inform all of public education's many constituents. School administrators can enter into continuing negotiations with diverse public education stakeholders to ensure that fiscal accountability is driven by clearly defined and collectively held priorities. Fiscal specialists can share their expertise through direct communication with other actors in the educational enterprise. New information technologies can be employed to extend opportunities for 'participatory budgeting and management.' Competing views of fiscal 'realities' and 'possibilities' can be shared with the concerned public—not only during times of budgetary crisis. This is not to suggest that teachers act as accountants or school principals behave like auditors. It is a recommendation to incorporate both real-time budgetary information and decision-making influence on community, classroom, and school building levels. Overall, increasingly open and accessible public deliberations can clarify important relationships between core objectives of schooling and principles of sound accounting.

We can envision and enact more inclusive forms of *political accountability* that utilize participatory public strategies. We can begin by engaging political visions that recenter progressive aspirations for democracy and reemphasize the responsibility of all citizens to attend to the common good. Such reconceptualizations will feature active citizen involvement in the purposes and politics of public education.

A deepened political accountability requires the evolving engagement of a much broader cast of political actors. Many perspectives on public schooling are necessary to inform civic deliberations. More inclusive political processes can be developed that work with, but also move beyond, current patterns emphasizing individual initiative, centralized leadership, and interest group advocacy. There are opportunities to elicit perspectives and proposals from now largely 'silent' sectors of the public. It is possible to engage these viewpoints in ways that are neither reflexively defensive nor pre-emptively dismissive. Purposeful conversations can be initiated across prior barriers.

This is a long-term project centered on the politics of power sharing that is understood as continuous teaching and learning. We need to envision and evolve *exploratory democratic practices*—techniques that provide opportunities to socially construct and apply knowledge in a systemic, consensual, and purposeful manner. Drawing from the rich literature on democratic theory and pedagogy, are practices that have been shown to:

- expand possibilities for thought and action beyond those initially brought by individuals,
- enrich relationships by increasing the number and variety of meaningful connections among diverse participants, and
- enhance capacities for continued engagement in civic learning and public life that narrow the gap between democratic aspirations and real-world accomplishments.

In light of these criteria, many existing pedagogies (e.g., cooperative learning, critical and feminist pedagogies) and research methodologies (e.g., action research, focus groups) might be adapted first for use in schools, and then extended to social, political, philanthropic, and research settings. In doing so, we engage the energies of grassroots activism. As with all components of deeper democratic practice, grassroots tactics are time and resource intensive. But there is no substitute for the chaotic and surprising interplay of diverse ideas and actions.

Public education is at risk. Principled venturing is required if we are to become more meaningfully accountable to each other, for what really matters.

Deep learning and deep democracy are innovative processes—social practices that work amid shifting constraints, indeterminate resources, and incalculable probabilities of success. Reforms that broaden and deepen fiscal, performance, and political responsibility can be envisioned by centering on concepts of integrity, inclusiveness, and imagination. Despite heavily reinforced fear responses, beyond protective accountability strategies, and in the face of strong pressures to diminish vision, we must continue to seek systemic reform.

> *"There is only one road to democracy: education . . .*
> *Let schools sink further into poverty and privatization*
> *and we will not only put our children at risk*
> *but are likely to imperil the very foundation*
> *of their liberties and our own."*
>
> —Benjamin R. Barber
> *A Passion for Democracy*

Exploratory Democratic Practice: Public Intellectual Essays

Closely related to the Exploratory Essay written for each chapter, is the Public Intellectual Essay. We understand a Public Intellectual Essay to be an exploratory, informative, and broadly accessible composition. It is derived from theory and research and presents analyses, interpretations, and recommendations in ways that engage public attention, reflection, and participation. Such essays range from short Op-Ed pieces for mass media, to concise statements best suited for webpage presentations, to feature length articles and position papers developed for specific policy campaigns. In both campus and community settings, it is useful to encourage the sharing of multiple drafts among participants prior to submission.

Suggested criteria for peer review of Public Intellectual Essays include:

- Engages public attention;
- Is accessible to a broad and diverse audience with careful attention devoted to intended readers and publication venue;
- Integrates professional and public discourse avoiding use of unnecessary jargon or overly technical language;
- Connects conceptual abstractions to readers' lived experience;
- Articulates accessible analyses of contemporary theory and research;
- Identifies resources appropriate for documentation and further consideration (print sources, websites, etc.);
- Offers new insight, distinctive interpretation;
- Incorporates images, graphics, and aesthetic resources as appropriate;

- Identifies feasible opportunities or solution paths; and
- Moves readers to act.

Collaboratively composed essays are useful in extending inquiry and thoughtful expression beyond designated experts, pundits, and officials. Most participants in reform movements can compose Public Intellectual Essays; and many who do provide important perspectives, distinctive arguments, and valuable recommendations.

Thematic Bibliographic References

On the nature of risk:

Beck, U. (1992). *Risk society: Toward a new modernity.* New York: Sage Publications.

Bernstein, P. (1998). *Against the gods: The remarkable story of risk.* New York: John Wiley & Sons.

Burger, E. (Ed.). (1993). *Risk.* Ann Arbor: University of Michigan Press.

Johnson, B., & Covello, V. (Eds.). (1987). *The social and cultural construction of risk.* New York: Reidel.

Stern, P., & Fineberg, H. (Eds.). (1996) *Understanding risk: Informing decisions in a democratic society.* Washington, DC: National Academy Press.

On integrity in public policy:

Braithwaite, V., & Levi, M. (Eds.). (2003). *Trust and governance.* New York: Russell Sage Foundation.

Engvall, R. (1998). *All that appears isn't necessarily so: Morality, virtue, politics, and education.* San Francisco: Caddo Gap Press.

Skrla, L., & Scheurich, J. (2003). *Educational equity and accountability:paradigms, policies, and politics.* New York: Routledge Falmer.

Tyack, D. (2003). *Seeking common ground: Public schools in a diverse society.* Cambridge, MA: Harvard University Press.

On erosion of public support for public education:

Littky, D., & Grabelle, S. (2004). *Big picture: Education is everyone's business.* Alexandria, VA: Association for Supervision & Curriculum Development.

Matthews, D. (1996). *Is there a public for public schools?* Dayton, OH: Kettering Foundation.

On challenges faced by urban schools:

Anyon, J., & Wilson, W. (1997). *Ghetto schooling: A political economy of urban educational reform.* New York: Teachers College Press.

Ayers, W., Dohrn, B., & Ayers, R. (2001). *Zero tolerance: Resisting the drive for punishment in our schools.* New York: The New Press.

Beatty, A. et al. (Ed.). (2001). *Understanding dropouts.* Washington, DC: National Academy Press.

Biddle, B. (Ed.). (2001). *Social class, poverty, and education: Policy and practice.* New York: Routledge Falmer.

Caldas, S., & Bankston, C. (2005). *Forced to fail: The paradox of school desegregation.* New York: Praeger Publishing.

Dance, L. (2002). *Tough fronts: The impact of street culture on schooling.* New York: Routledge Falmer.

Henig, J. et al. (1999). *The color of school reform: Race, politics, and the challenge of urban education.* Princeton, NJ: Princeton University Press.

Hill, P. (2000). *It takes a city: Getting serious about urban school reform.* Washington, DC: Brookings Institution.

Kozol, J. (2005). *The shame of the nation: The restoration of apartheid schooling in America.* New York: Corwin.

Lipman, P. (2004). *High stakes education: Inequality, globalization, and urban school reform.* New York: Routledge Falmer.

Lipsky, D., & Gartner, A. (1997). *Inclusion and school reform.* New York: Paul Brookes.

Lopez, N. (2002). *Hopeful girls, troubled boys: Race and gender disparity in urban education.* New York: Routledge Falmer.

Lucas, S. (1999). *Tracking inequality: Stratification and mobility in American high schools.* New York: Teachers College Press.

Miron, L., & St. John, E. (Eds.). (2003). *Reinterpreting urban school reform: Have urban schools failed or has the reform movement failed urban schools.* Albany: SUNY Press.

Morgan, S. (2005). *On the edge of commitment: Educational attainment and race in the United States.* Stanford, CA: Stanford University Press.

Noguera, P. (2003). *City schools and the American dream: Reclaiming the promise of public education.* New York: Teachers College Press.

Orfield, G., & Gordon, N. (2001). *Schools more separate: Consequences of a decade of resegregation.* Cambridge, MA: Harvard University Civil Rights Project.

Orfield G. (Ed.). (2004). *Dropouts in America: Confronting the graduation rate crisis.* Cambridge, MA: Harvard Graduate School of Education.

Pitman, M., & Zorn, D. (Eds.). (2000). *Caring as tenacity: Stories of urban school survival.* Cresskill, NJ: Hampton Press.

Sanders, M. (Ed.). (2000). *Schooling students placed at risk: Research, policy, and practice in the education of poor and minority adolescents.* Mahwah, NJ: Lawrence Erlbaum Associates.

Simmons, J. (2006). *Breaking through: Transforming urban school districts.* New York: Teachers College Press.

Steinberg, S., & Kincheloe, J. (Eds.). *19 urban questions: Teaching in the city.* New York: Peter Lang Publishing.

Stone, C. (Ed.). (1998). *Changing urban education.* Lawrence: University of Kansas Press.

Street, P. (2005). *Segregated schools: Educational apartheid in post-civil rights America.* Oxford: Routledge.

Weiner, L. (1999). *Urban teaching: The essentials.* New York: Teachers College Press.

On performance, fiscal, and political accountability for public education:

Brimley, V., & Garfield, R. (2004). *Financing education in a climate of change.* Boston: Allyn & Bacon.

Carnoy, M., Elmore, R., & Siskin, L. (Eds.). (2003). *The new accountability: High schools and high-stakes testing.* New York: Routledge Falmer.

Elmore, R. (2002). *Bridging the gap between standards and achievement.* New York: Albert Shanker Institute.

Fuhrman, S. (Ed.). (1999). *The new accountability.* Philadelphia: University of Pennsylvania Press.

Fuhrman, S., & Elmore, R. (Eds.). (2004). *Redesigning accountability systems for education.* New York: Teachers College Press.

Kordsalewski, J. (2000). *Standards in the classroom: How teachers and students negotiate learning.* New York: Teachers College Press.

Ladd, H. (Ed.). (1996). *Holding schools accountable.* Washington, DC: Brookings Institution Press.

Leyden, D. (2005). *Adequacy, accountability, and the future of public education funding.* New York: Springer-Verlag.

Matthews, D. (1996). *Is there a public for public schools?* Dayton, OH: Kettering Foundation.

McDonnell, L. (2004). *Politics, persuasion, and educational testing.* Cambridge, MA: Harvard University Press.

McNeil, L. (2000). *Contradictions of school reform: The educational costs of standardized testing.* New York: Routledge.

Mediratta, K., & Fruchter, N. (2003). *From governance to accountability: Building relationships that make schools work.* New York: New York University Institute for Education and Social Policy.

Mintrop, H. (2004). *Schools on probation: How accountability works (and doesn't work).* New York: Teachers College Press.

Peterson, P., & West, M. (Eds.). (2003). *No child left behind?: The politics and practice of school accountability.* Washington, DC: Brookings Institution Press.

Radin, B. (2006). *Challenging the performance movement: Accountability, complexity, and democratic values.* Washington, DC: Georgetown University Press.

Schrag, P. (2003). *Final test: The battle for adequacy in American schools.* New York: New Press.

Sirotnik, K. (Ed.). (2004). *Holding accountability accountable: What ought to matter in public education.* New York: Teachers College Press.

Stecher, B. et al. (2004). *Organizational improvement and accountability: Lessons for education from other sources.* Santa Monica, CA: Rand.

Wilson, M. (2004). *Towards coherence between classroom assessment and accountability.* Washington, DC: The National Society for the Study of Education.

Wong, K. (1999). *Funding public schools: Politics and policies.* Lawrence, KA: University Press of Kansas.

On 'exploratory democratic practice':

Dewey, J. (1916/1984). *Democracy and education.* New York: Macmillan.

Matthews, D. (1996). *Is there a public for public schools?.* Dayton, OH: Kettering Foundation.

Parker, W. (2002). *Teaching democracy: Unity and diversity in public life.* New York: Teachers College Press.

Paulus, P., & Nijstad, B. A. (Eds.). (2003). *Group creativity: Innovation through collaboration.* New York: Oxford University Press.

Reflection:

Barber, B. (1998). *A passion for democracy* (pp. 232–233). Princeton, NJ: Princeton University Press.

c h a p t e r   9

Inspiration

Dedication
to social causes and consequent relationships
evolving meaning and deepening value
progressive interdependence, source of resonant spirit
spiraling yet steadfast
communal clarity and resolve sustained
beyond fate, beyond reason, beyond despair.

*C*aine was drawn to the political rhythms that he had been part of for so many years. Now that it was early March, the buzz had begun about candidates, the upcoming primaries, and who was raising what kind of money from whom. People regularly asked him about his plans. His name was mentioned among candidate possibilities for several local and statewide offices. But he remained indefinite and said his law practice, his community activities, and his commitment to Grant High kept him busy enough.

He was not at ease when he met with Karla Morgan, the political columnist, for an interview. The gloomy weather didn't help his attitude. They bantered a little. He referred to some of her recent columns. She spoke lightly of current politics and commented on his op-ed pieces that ran regularly in her paper and several others around the state. Then she moved

Re-Envisioning Education and Democracy, pages 161–188
Copyright © 2006 by Information Age Publishing
All rights of reproduction in any form reserved.

into the interview by asking, "I can understand you're being satisfied as a part-time lawyer and becoming sort of a public intellectual, but tell me what is involving you so deeply over at that troubled high school? Why is Althea Putnam putting me off about a story? And are you really out of politics for good?"

Caine responded. "Ah, the multiple question approach we know and love. First, about politics: Yes, I'm still in touch with party people. I go to fund raisers. I get included on panels. A lot of folks who are running, or are thinking about running, have been polite enough to ask for my advice and support."

Karla waited.

After a long pause Caine continued in a quietly serious tone: "You astutely brought up Grant High and politics together. They have become closely linked for me. Karla, I know that given the way we usually pay attention to education and democracy in campaigns, or even in the op-ed pieces you mentioned, is to treat them separately. Yet, without being naïve, I think both education and democracy are, at the core, really the same. They're both about teaching and learning. Participatory, deliberative democracy means generating and sharing ideas and possibilities that lead to action. That's what we should expect in our public schools too. But instead we treat our schools and our politics as if they both are only about economic objectives. While "it's the economy stupid" is usually good campaign advice, it's not so useful for shaping public education in a democracy."

"I know you wrote something like that at least a couple of times on our editorial page," Karla said. "But I thought you were referring to the Grant project. You seem now to be saying something else—maybe something more?"

"I realize that I'm not being clear. But I've come to this understanding slowly—much too slowly I'm afraid considering how long education was at the top of my policy agenda. Getting involved with Jim MacIver's ideas for a charter school last year, and now with his summer academy for youth leadership, but mainly through my work with Grant, I've learned a lot. I've also been reading and talking mostly about education and politics."

Karla remained quiet, tilted her head expectantly, and poised her pen over her note pad.

Caine continued with uncharacteristic hesitancy. "I know we complain a lot about both education and our democratic institutions and practices. I gripe and you write about their failures and shortcomings all the time. Grant had been declared a 'failed school.' It's only one of far too many in the state and around the country. In recent memory, we've had unsatisfactory elections with plenty of criticism about procedures and basic fairness. We've heard a lot about campaign finance and the poor quality of the campaigns themselves. Look, I've been in many campaigns and won them all until this last one. But I've slowly come to realize that I was neither contributing much to the improvement of democratic deliberation, nor to deepening political participation. You pointed out the nasty tone and shallow cliché level discourse of that last campaign and wrote about miserable voter turnout rates. Our political process is on the edge of failure, Karla, just like too many schools. At Grant, kids were frequently absent—just like most eligible voters, maybe. Kids at Grant had trouble getting into learning as it was presented—just as few voters really get involved in campaigns. At best, they pay attention when politics is entertaining, but usually just turn it off as boring and irrelevant. Teenagers first skip, and then drop out of school—just as adults mostly skip or drop out politics. Or even if they do stay in school and politics, they cruise along on the surface or at the margins—you know, occasionally having bumper-sticker conversations about some event or alleged scandal or about personality quirks of a candidate or a teacher. At best they're learning sound bites—like answers for the test or name recognition in the voting booth. Politics and public education cannot just be about going through the motions. That's not good enough, Karla. It's really dangerous!" He took a deep breath and reached for his coffee.

"You've obviously been thinking a lot about this. Didn't you know all that before you lost the election and got pulled into this public school initiative?" Karla asked skeptically.

"Only glimpses. A lot of preferred ignorance with a touch of denial. After all I was touted as "Mr. Education" in the Senate—even you called me that a couple of times. I knew the issues that resonated during campaigns and worked in Senate politics. I did push what I saw as reforms. And I lost the last election—but that wasn't the tragedy."

Karla waited again until he continued. "The tragedy was the compromise—the incompleteness of what we did manage to get passed. Sure, our reform was well intended, but it got eaten alive by incremental politics—and then by the budget black hole we've gotten ourselves into in on state, national, and local levels. I was really good at keeping that kind of low impact politics going, even while I was talking about deeper needs and more comprehensive reform."

"But Senator Caine," Karla interrupted, "comprehensive reform of anything almost *never* happens—and if and when it has, it's only after some big crisis. American politics has never been about radical change. I bet American public education hasn't either—but I guess you know more about that than I do."

"Karla, I don't know as much as I thought I did when I was in the Senate—and not nearly as much as I need to know right now." Caine said firmly. "I don't know enough to satisfy your quite legitimate questions. I simply don't know enough to help sustain the Grant High program either."

He paused and then said quietly, "I no longer prefer ignorance. I need and want to learn—and in trying to do that, I've come to understand that I need and want to teach."

"Teach? Teach? You want to become a school teacher?" Karla asked incredulously.

"No, no, I don't think so. Still, I've been thinking for almost a year about ways of doing politics differently. I've seen wonderful things over at Grant, as well as some mistakes and chronic problems. I have seen a whole lot of inspired teaching, and know that alone is not enough. I have seen candidates, groups, and parties with great ideas, inspired ideas. We both know that's not enough. Even emphatically declaring "crises"—not just in public education but for other important issues too—is mostly instrumental rhetoric. It's not about real reform. We don't work very hard at understanding or doing anything very much beyond what's most politically expedient and least costly. We end up doing pretty much what we've done before, even as we try to sound very critical or call for bold innovations. We're so locked into the next competitive victory . . . "

Karla was jotting notes furiously as she asked, "So you're announcing that you're going to run for something? For what? Your old Senate seat isn't up next year."

"Give me some more time please. I don't know yet. It probably won't be next year—I just don't know enough now to make the next move. But I've been reading, thinking, and talking a lot about these possibilities for the last few months. And I'm not only talking with political people. I'm talking with people I've never really listened to before. And here, today, I am talking with you on the record. Maybe I just made a non-incremental move . . . "

Full moon rising
blue lily unfolds on a dark emerald pond
fragile, rare; it should not have survived
in this forsaken part of the city
surprising, ephemeral, resilient.

Althea knew better. To walk down the corridor, hoping that for even one hour she could focus on just one challenge, was an impossible wish. She knew that each demand pressing in on her deserved her undivided attention. But that wasn't realistic. Maybe that luxury had been available back in September, but now, in March, the intertwining problems and possibilities were snarled in her mind. "Where to begin?" she said to herself. That was the wrong question—she was always in the middle of things. 'Fresh starts,' 'clean slates,' had been illusions even as the ninth grade project began. Grant was a school with a tough history. To dream of ideal conditions now, at the end of the winter trimester, Althea knew was a dangerous diversion.

An administrative voice in her head chanted, "Prioritize! Prioritize!" Her change agent voice advised, "Don't settle for small victories." Her non-profit activist voice told her, "Don't confuse friendly co-optation with systemic reform." Her organizational leadership voice said, "Listen, learn, and support!" Her public school principal voice directed, "Concentrate on raising test scores, cutting the drop out rate, and staying within budget!" Her voice as a mother called out, "Spend more time with your kids!"

She laughed as she entered the room, assuming that everyone else had similar conversations going on in their heads. As her ninth grade teachers looked up at her intently, she worried whether she had actually been thinking out loud.

The whiteboard in the classroom was filled to the edges with agenda items. The teachers had adopted the practice of putting their concerns and needs on the board throughout the day and then committing themselves to discuss each one within the next two sessions. That commitment was not always met.

She glanced away from her colleagues' expectant glances and considered the agenda possibilities. She took in only the items that had been underlined in red—those that at least two of the faculty members thought were 'urgent.' No other rank order was indicated for this morning's session. The underlined concerns were:

- *Preparing for the standardized tests in April!* The word '*Preparing*' had been lightly crossed out and '*Teaching to*' written above it.
- *What are we trading off to do test prep?* '*Plenty*' was scrawled below.
- *Recruiting candidates for next year's ninth grade faculty.*
- *Continued development and implementation of school governance and disciplinary procedures.* In Kirk's distinctive script, '*Help!*' had been added.
- *Program Evaluation of the ninth grade curriculum [due in June!].*
- *Next year's program budgets [due next month!]*
- *Faculty Performance Evaluations.*
- *The Superintendent's site visit.* '*When*' and '*Why*' followed, each in different hands.
- *Requests by local media—do we need P.R.?* '*Be careful!*' in another script.
- *Relations with the rest of Grant's faculty and staff.* Several specifics followed.
- *Finding ways for mutual closure on community-based student projects.*
- *SUSTAINING STUDENT REPONSIBILITY FOR EACH OTHER*—the capital letters were underlined three times.
- *Planning student transitions into the tenth grade.* Someone had followed that in red: '*They're not going to be ready!*'
- *Recognizing and rewarding leadership among students and staff.*
- *Subject areas to worry about: science and math, especially MATH.* The list was longer but only math was underlined—four times.

- *Parents' concerns: progress of their child, special unmet individual needs.* That list was longer too, but only those two were underlined.
- *Student mobility and class turnover. 'I just got two new kids in my homeroom today,'* was scrawled in under this item.
- *'Mission Creep!'* underlined four times.
- And one more entry, a Zen poem scripted diagonally across one corner of the white board:

> *A single blossom and it is spring*
> *although there are ten thousand miles of snow*
> *south of the river . . .*

Althea turned from the board and said, "Another easy agenda, I see. I think we should hide all the red markers. Who's convening today?"

"You are," Morrie said. "You're the only one in the room who's smiling. We're in need of some optimistic leadership!"

With a deep breath, Althea responded, "I *am* optimistic even if we have at least all these problems underlined on the board, and there are probably several of others we haven't even noticed yet. OK, let's do five minutes on 'Mission Creep!'"

"I'm spending more and more time on basic literacy rather than on working on our democracy-building goals." Joy began. "I'm being squeezed by what's immediately needed. I'm not feeling the connections we have hoped for, and I feel like I have to compromise too often."

"But Joy," Mary said quickly, "the connections are our job together. I mean, none of us can do this deep democracy teaching by ourselves. It has to be a collective effort as well as a collective experience. We're not alone."

"Yeah," said another teacher, "but we, or at least me, seem to be ending up rushing to meet all the immediate classroom demands—all those little things individual students really need to be ready for the tests that are coming."

"And the not so little ones too," Mary continued. "We do risk falling into the 'teach to the test' trap we promised ourselves we'd avoid. And yet we've got to improve those scores."

Althea waited, but no one else spoke. "As usual, we have to do many things at the same time. Some conflict and that's the way I'm sure it's always been in education—not only in this program now at Grant. Yes, we're part of the larger district organization and also have to play by the state's rules and regulations. At the same time, we have to prepare our students for the tenth grade. And all of us, students too, need to continue building community."

"OK, OK," Mary sighed. "I'll work with the other sci-math teachers on this. I know we've got to help each other keep a sense of perspective, and help each other with priorities. But it's easy to feel frustrated and alone."

"Many more high priority items still up there on the board," grumbled Morrie, impatience in his voice. "What's next?"

Kirk replied immediately, "A lot of this is related, but we need to take on the student responsibility thing and get our governance and disciplinary systems installed school-wide. We have a long way to go and we don't have much time!"

"So how, then, do we get students to be responsible for each other?" Joy asked. "Sure, they agreed to work at keeping absenteeism and drop-out down. And I think we're a little ahead of last year on those, aren't we?"

Althea nodded as Joy continued, "Most students have already done enough group or team projects to get a little better at sharing the load and improving their interpersonal skills. But I'm not sure they're very happy with all this. A few of the better students, better academically, have gotten really angry with what Morrie calls "free riders" and the persistent indifference or non-cooperation from other project teams."

Nods and murmurs swept the room.

"And sadly," Joy said quietly, "we know that for many kids, cooperative learning is scary. For some of our average ability students, and maybe even more so for those performing below average, group projects are experienced as just another occasion to look stupid. We know that for ninth graders, what others think about them really matters. I suspect that some of our absenteeism is related to this. I'm not sure what we can do to help."

No one spoke until Althea said as she jotted down a note, "That's important! Let's devote prime time on that during tomorrow's prep hour."

After a brief pause a social studies teacher said, "And most of the rest of the Grant faculty and a bunch of folks down at the District Office have expressed strong reservations about our Student Governance and Justice Program. We've been consulting Jim MacIver on how we can handle external perceptions. He says all innovations, all initiatives, have a kind of life cycle. Reforms start out with at least indifference from the establishment—like for us, the District bureaucrats tolerated what we first tried out. But now, they say they have serious problems with possible student involvement in curricular planning. I heard that some of our union people don't like that much either. Even worse, there is big time resistance to our student justice system. They're worried we can't meet the District's liability concerns."

"What's the most pressing issue here?" Althea asked in search of a focus.

Morrie jumped in. "No one likes to share power. We teachers don't. Most parents don't. The students don't, in the end, like it either! The Assistant Principals who deal with our toughest disciplinary cases don't want their jobs complicated. The bureaucrats downtown don't think the rules and regulations they worked out over the years should be interpreted differently in each building, much less implemented by a gang of ninth graders. I think the School Board will end up resisting us on this too."

Althea responded, "I've heard some of this from District people. There is a lot of trial and error going on here. We've got what Mary called "troublesome early learning" for all of us—teachers and students as well as the folks downtown. Most of the rest of the faculty at Grant think 'democracy' means voting on everything all the time. We know that's not what we're doing. But we're still not very articulate about what we're trying to accomplish."

"Right. I don't know what to say when I'm asked to talk about Grant," Kirk said thoughtfully. "I end up mumbling *something* when parents or neighborhood people who attend our evening open houses ask how things are going. I think, maybe I should show them some of our video stuff—but then the videos don't really portray how we got there. I mean, we don't document all the processes involved, all the preparation, all the time, all the creativity, or all the attempts to cooperate and collaborate. I don't think we can show how it actually works."

"But Kirk, take that video project on the homeless—everyone responds to it." Joy said intently. "It's more than a good script and all those striking images. It's, well, really moving. There's something there…maybe an unexpected quality that gets noticed. I think it may be that students do *see* things differently. It's not just individual differences—it's who they are at this point in their lives. I've noticed different perspectives on social issues in their writing projects too."

"What does gets noticed," a teacher broke in rather sharply, "is when something doesn't work—when some kid screws up, or when one of us does."

"Right, right, that's just life in the trenches," another teacher commented. "There are plenty of set backs and tough cases. But look, I've also noticed some important changes in our students—in their work individually as well as their group work. I mean, some of the time they really get cranked up about what they're doing. They *are* doing good work. That goes for regular activities, including some of what will be on the tests next month. And also for the group projects that cross between our classes and out into the community."

"Yes, I've felt some of that too," Mary said, "but it's hard to describe it without sounding sort of sappy or self-serving."

"I know, and we have to write a credible, balanced, annual report soon," Althea said with a sigh.

"Some of our most involved students are already asking about next year," a teacher said. "They got their first pitch from the counselors about the tenth grade, and all the requirements, and scheduling their electives. They're apprehensive. They're asking what it will be like. Was this ninth grade year just a one-shot deal?"

"Now there's a very good question," Morrie grumbled.

"And a couple of students have wondered whether this democratic immersion experience is going to carry over—not only into the tenth grade, and to the rest of Grant, but to other schools too." Kirk said.

After a long silence Althea spoke in an administrative tone, "We have task forces working on sections for the annual report. We talked last time about what we wanted to do during the Superintendent's visit, remember? It's on for next Wednesday. We're in good shape on that. But we do need to explain ourselves more effectively. Look, we can show that the student governance system is more inclusive and widely participatory than the old Student Council. We need to be able to show that we're building trust among students, between students and teachers, and, I hope, between teachers, students and Grant's principal. I know we can show some success with our student community approach to justice at Grant, but we need to continue to be candid about the limitations and the mistakes we've made. And we have to continue to talk to our colleagues at other schools about what we're doing and why." She glanced back the board and asked, "Now, what's this leadership item about? Is it about me?"

After a pause, Joy said, "Oh it's about several things, I think. We teachers still get evaluated as individuals. You, Althea, have to visit our classrooms and write reports on each of us...as individuals. We all get our salary increases based on those evaluations, and for two of us, tenure decisions are riding on them."

"I know," Althea said. "Evaluations are always difficult and the procedures I have to follow are all about individual performance. There's nothing really significant on the District forms about collaboration. I was planning to write a detailed letter to go with each teacher evaluation, but I've been told that if I do, I have to do it for the entire Grant High faculty, not just you in the ninth grade program. So now I'm not so sure. On top of that, there are some new personnel evaluation guidelines coming from the Business Community Advisory Board the Superintendent appointed last fall."

"And over on the student side," Morrie said, "grades are individually recorded on transcripts and report cards. Maybe our students are more or less clear about how those grades blended their individual performance and their group work, but to the rest of the world the record is the record. And, Althea, they sure won't be taking those tests next month as cooperative groups!"

"Also troubling to many of our students is the whole Grant High competition and recognition thing," Mary said. "I know, Althea, you have tried to emphasize a lot of group collaboration and team recognition at the monthly awards assemblies. But the overall focus is still on individuals."

Another teacher followed on quickly, "And of course we push individual responsibility in our framework. We emphasize community, but even that leads to expectations for individual effort, recognition, and reward. What matters outside of Grant is individual competitive success. We're bucking some strong cultural tides."

Althea said, "So, as usual, we've got too much to work on. But we have some impressive accomplishments. Yes, I am still optimistic, even in the face of all this up on the board and what has been discussed so far this morning. Maybe the best use of the rest of our time is to break into the task forces and work on reporting and planning for the Superintendent's site visit next Wednesday. OK?"

She wasn't sure they agreed, but the ninth grade faculty slowly assembled in their working groups. She was sure that she was still optimistic, but she wasn't quite sure why.

*   *   *

Superintendent Tuscano brought the Assistant Superintendent for Secondary Education and two Board members along with him on his visit to Grant. The students were used to having adult visitors in their classes and even joining them at lunch. The teachers were a little tense, but made sure that they displayed testing related activities along with other aspects of their ninth grade curriculum. The visitors stayed through much of the day and one Board member joined a group of students at their community service site.

At the ninth grade faculty meeting the next morning there was general agreement that the visit had gone well. They shared the questions they had been asked and reported on conversations they had with their visitors.

"Well, yesterday was at least interesting," Morrie said to begin the meeting. "We deliberately didn't erase our crisis list up on the board, and they all sure looked at it closely. But I didn't sense any of us posturing when they met with us."

"No, I think they were more than just politely curious." Joy said. "They really dug into some of the things we were trying to do. Probing questions for sure, but they listened—they really listened. That hasn't always been my experience with people from the District."

Kirk said, "They were very curious and I was impressed that they spent all day here. I mean, there was at least one of them hanging around the video workshop almost all the time. But do you think they understand us?"

Joy said, "I think they talked a little more to students than I thought they would. They listened closely to the small group sessions in all of my classes. I don't know what they came away with."

"Several of my students said they'd been asked to describe what they were doing and how they liked school," a teacher added. "I don't think the students acted much differently than they usually do. But I agree with Joy, I have no idea what those District people learned."

The ninth grade faculty looked to Althea. "I think over the whole year we've made more than a little dent in District understanding. I agree with you that yesterday went pretty well. Superintendent Tuscano didn't tell me he was bringing anyone else along. So when they showed up, I just told them to go wherever they wanted and talk with whomever they wanted. They already had our Wednesday schedule and seemed to have agreed in advance on what each of them would do. You saw more of them than I did—I was only with the group at our prep meeting yesterday. They had lunch with the students."

"I'm certain they had prepared," Mary said. "I agree with Joy. I had three different people with me yesterday and they didn't repeat questions that the others had asked. Come to think of it, they each did talk about job-readiness and discipline. But overall I think we got a serious site visit."

"We sure did," Morrie said firmly. "I'm just sorry we didn't have a Community Advisory Council meeting for them to observe."

"But some District people did attend council meetings this winter," another teacher said. "They mostly just sat and listened. It wasn't like yes-terday."

"They know our drop out rates are lower," Althea said. "They know our daily attendance rates are better than last year and they have heard fewer gripes from Grant staff—none, I think, from you people. Neighborhood complaints are way down and I think they're cutting me some slack as a new principal."

"You told us last week," Morrie continued, "they've been getting all the required paper work on time. That's what *really* matters down at the District."

"So are we saying that everything is riding on the tests next month?" Mary asked with a little sarcasm.

"No!" Althea responded emphatically. "They do have a sense of our spirit, our commitment, and some of the new things we've been able to do. I don't know about yesterday, but from past visits by the District staff and all the Board members, there is some understanding of the intensity of our collaboration—that we do actively rely on each other. I've seen an appreci-ation that our classrooms function a bit differently. I've heard from parents and school neighbors that the community involvement projects are actu-ally working. Sure, I hear things about the screw-ups, and most I talk with know full well that we still have big problems. Yet so far, at least, almost everyone thinks we're doing about as well as expected."

"Certainly, more than I expected!" Morrie said looking around the room. "OK, I'm supposed to be the grouchy realist. What's more, it's almost the Ides of March and we all know what that means. But, colleagues, I want to tell you that no matter what happens to us on the tests, or what the Superintendent or the Board ends up thinking, this has been just about the best year of teaching I've ever had—and I've been around longer than any of you. This ninth grade project is starting to work, and I'm grateful to all of you. You have struggled to make improbable things possible. We all have—together! I just wanted to say that. Now, let's get back to this redlined list on the board."

Given the relentless demands of democratic learning and life, where can we find sources of renewal?

Sustaining the spirit of democracy in public education faces formidable challenges. The dominating influence of capitalist culture intensifies social stratification and inequity through public policy aimed at concentrating wealth, power, and opportunity. The subtle tyranny of bureaucratic culture's seemingly urgent details draws attention away from broader reform aspirations. Ongoing participation in a culture of opposition accentuates difference, amplifies fear, fragments initiative, and increases isolation. Taken together these cultures of constraint suppress the quality and complexity of our identities and interactions as students, teachers, and citizens, and diminish collective dreams for a deeper democracy.

The cultural values of *capitalism* shape the identities, status, and behaviors of all public school participants. Concentrations of wealth and power pervade all of society. These disparities, however, have especially pernicious effects on public education's central role in building an effective democracy. Political theorists have uniformly contended that a vibrant democracy depends on a large, diverse, and politically engaged middle class. Most Americans still claim middle-class identity, yet their functional role in sustaining democracy has diminished. Concurrently, the most affluent lead lives increasingly separate from middle and lower income groups while remaining disproportionately politically active and influential.

This de-politicizing of the middle has developed through the convergence of several forces. Dominant messages conveyed through mass media, popular culture, and even public schooling suggest that the primary social responsibility of the individual is economic—to be employed and support oneself and one's family. These realities play into a public narrative featuring the individual as a consumer, not as a citizen, whose success is measured by material acquisition, not by civic engagement.

But market forces may require two-incomes, often multiple jobs, and longer hours for the majority of middle class families. Time for democratic participation is significantly restricted. While the core message emphasizes education as the "great equalizer," the reality experienced by most middle class Americans is a struggle just to keep pace. The promise of upward mobility persists, but the prospects for most are dim.

The experienced gap between promise and actual opportunity, the escalating economic demands on individuals as workers and consumers, the constraints on time and information, combine to reduce possibilities for a participatory middle class. Increasingly isolated and apathetic individuals are made fearful by persistent stereotyping of threatening "others." Cynicism overwhelms civic vision and democratic prospects. Widespread feelings of skepticism and doubt are accompanied by a growing sense of helplessness. There is little confidence in major social, economic, and political institutions. Individuals are left alone, to cope as best they can in all aspects of life, including education.

In a word, the middle class has been demoralized. Demoralization is manifest in at least two senses. Core social values—the moral center of civic life—are radically diminished. As important, the capacity to act with political principle and courage is substantially weakened. *Capitalist culture renders the spirit of democracy insignificant.*

Enfolded in our capitalist material culture is the predominant form of all social organization—*bureaucracy.* Some of the most powerful obstacles facing progressive reformers come not from direct opposition to ideals and programs, but from the pressing realities of everyday life. The organizational demands of implementing effective public education policy under conditions of scrutiny and scarcity consume energy and narrow focus. A "more with less" managerial attitude overrides promised reductions in class size, curtails teachers' professional development, and limit their discretion. Teachers are increasingly confined to less creative, deskilled roles. Their work is directed by political and corporate agendas, rather than by professional judgment and quality research. The industrial assembly line model of public education prevails with "production efficiency" pressures ever increasing.

The burdens of bureaucratic culture accumulate to deplete even the most dedicated reform enthusiasts. Co-opted by routine, isolated by indifference, and tyrannized by others' urgencies, systemic reform fades from view. *Bureaucratic culture renders the spirit of democracy distant.*

Possibilities for systemic reform are also constrained by a culture of *opposition*. While conflict and competition are inevitable and in some ways productive, there are problematic consequences for participants at all levels. Vision and opportunity are compromised, as continued immersion in oppositional culture challenges personal and civic integrity.

Potential allies become antagonists as broad organizational purposes and complex issues are simplified in mass media treatments. Politicians learn to present their positions in slogans and sound bites that are easier to grasp than the details of complex analyses. These simplifications ground policy in high moral statements, phrasing advocacy in terms of values and virtues. Political slogans, such as "No Child Left Behind," "We must provide an even playing field," or "Results-based Accountability," are crafted to hint at widely shared moral justifications for controversial policies. They also enable the portrayal of critics as those who would affirm inequality, resist accountability, and advocate for the abandonment of children in need.

Oppositional culture further reinforces political players for seeking and securing power. There is momentum toward authoritarian politics. Power is concentrated at the top, and strategic conflict is carried out predominantly among established elites. Broad social purposes become fused with sustaining leadership ascendancy, and public resources are committed to protect prior victories.

Power, once gained, is further secured through efforts to dominate conceptions of 'what is possible.' The range of acceptability in education reform politics is shaped by definitions of 'what is feasible' as determined by those commanding substantial resources. Policy alternatives are interpreted as betrayals when they originate within an organization, and taken as attacks when they come from outside. Strategies and tactics both within and between groups are primed for sharply polarized conflict. Significant policy positions, potential candidates, and the vast majority of citizens are effectively removed from democratic deliberation.

Non-elite groups face formidable obstacles. Those who do not possess required resources, and continue to struggle nonetheless, are dismissed as just another 'special interest' or 'identity' group. Their positions are misrepresented as demands for specific entitlements. These are characterized not only as unrealistic, but also as unjustifiably targeted and expensive. These tactics marginalize opponents and then pit them against each other—new immigrant families against an established ethnic or racial community, or arts-in-the-schools advocates against parents of athletes. A single stereotyping characteristic is repeatedly imposed and may come to be accepted even by those advocating change. Opportunities for coalitions and broader forms of mobilization are reduced.

Connections to higher purposes are further obscured as co-optation becomes a frequent strategy. The education power elite (e.g., state and federal elected officials, top administrators, corporate lobbyists) maintain their positions, at least in part, by defusing or absorbing their adversaries. By adopting some of their opponents' language or showcasing a small number of exemplary programs, egalitarian rhetoric and innovative practice is appropriated to perpetuate, rather than to change, the status quo. Just below the elite, system functionaries (e.g., school administrators and mid-level bureaucrats, tenured teachers and their unions) reluctantly use co-optation to maintain legitimacy and material resources. Those on the institutional margins (e.g., non-tenured teachers and paraprofessionals, non-essential curricular programs, soft money projects, struggling students and their families) accept diminished identities and expectations in exchange for even minimal levels of inclusion and symbolic support. Education reform advocates, working at all levels are compelled to back away from principled positions and silently endure institutional hypocrisy while reluctantly cooperating with attempts to contain or neutralize the defining features of their progressive designs.

As adversarial interactions intensify, integrity may be compromised by resorting to an 'ends justifies the means' mentality. Given limited experience and imagination regarding non-oppositional social and political processes, reform advocates may find no option other than to adopt the coercive and confrontational strategies they have passionately criticized. Opponents' positions are then oversimplified, at times misrepresented, to serve as rallying cries for negative mobilization. Anger and resentment, while understandable and often energizing, amplify feelings of hopelessness and victimization. Advocates of systemic democratic reform find themselves trapped in a cycle of resistance and protest that offers opportunity for heated expression, but no path toward principled agency.

As social interactions are represented and experienced as predominantly oppositional, fear grows pervasive. Reluctantly then, altruistic ideals are surrendered and a defensive acquiescence to authority emerges. Parents who in most cases express preference for active, humanistic, and interdisciplinary approaches to teaching and learning become convinced that test-driven curricula are necessary for life in a harshly competitive global economy. Citizens who support freedom and diversity accept imposition of increased surveillance, conformity in the practice of patriotism, and de facto segregation by race, religion, and immigrant status. Severe intergroup tensions, exacerbated by ignorance and fear, remain as troubling realities in public schools and community settings, casting doubt on the feasibility of crafting more deeply democratic process and policy. *Oppositional culture renders the spirit of democracy naïve.*

Immersed within the harsh realities of capitalist, bureaucratic, and oppositional cultures, collective awareness of democratic purpose remains illusive, a shared sense of meaningful accomplishment exceedingly difficult to sustain. Unrelenting experience of compromise and constraint leads to feelings of alienation, inadequacy, and despair. We retreat from systemic aspirations to mourn defeat, or settle for small victories. Under these daunting conditions, deeper resources are needed to move beyond the enervation of defensive struggle.

Beauty . . .
to move in concert to affect
the fundamental quality of existence
in small ways, or in large
insights unexpected
compel openness, preparation, and diligent effort
perceptions shift, new patterns emerge, acts of grace
transformative, enduring, sacred.

The cultures that constrain social inquiry and civic participation can neither be put aside nor should they be ignored. It is essential, however, that even within these challenging contexts, the spirit of deep learning and deep democracy is intensely experienced and continually renewed. With a reconceptualized sense of self and others as dynamic complexities, more mature identities can evolve. With a revitalized sense of shared purpose, social movements that are emotionally resonant and strategically feasible can develop. These deepening senses can open opportunities for *inspiration*. Shared with others, experiences of arresting insight and heightened commitment can form social compositions of *beauty*—collective aesthetic experiences that reinterpret constraints and re-energize action. Heightened social sensitivity can lead to more effective relational patterns through which even small shifts in routine can have important consequences. Shared experiences of compelling quality are possible within the specific contexts and events of our daily lives.

Our lives will continue to be shaped by capitalism. The pervasiveness of consumer culture is felt in terms of exaggerated competition, constant insecurity, and a sense that the quality of life is determined by the quantity of material acquisitions. As personal identities and social interactions are centered on consumption, opportunities to engage in non-instrumental pursuits are restricted, especially for those possessing limited material resources. Individual and social experience is deprived of creative depth and vibrancy.

Similarly, processes of teaching and learning throughout our nation's public schools are impoverished as knowledge and skills linked to material productivity are privileged over interpretive and expressive forms. An instrumental imperative is ingrained within the system and expressed through organizational structures and dominant policy directions. In the name of enhanced educational productivity, inquiry is reduced to the development of test-taking strategies, as valued knowledge is collapsed to information that can be framed in response to multiple-choice questions. Under such circumstances, little of what is required of students and teachers is experienced as meaningful, affirming, or generative. Regardless of the level of effort or achievement, a sense of cynicism prevails.

But there is more to life than intellectual and economic productivity. Opportunities for creative inquiry, interpretation, and expression cannot remain luxuries available only to a small few. The aesthetic dimensions of education and democracy must be made significant and accessible to all public school students and their teachers.

Even within test-driven, resource-constrained classrooms, teachers are moved by the struggles and triumphs of their students. For many, it is the disposition to find beauty in the development of each challenging and distinctive young person that called them to the profession. Each teacher's capacity to sense, sustain, and reflect back impressions of the very best in each student should be developed and acknowledged as an essential professional contribution. While smaller class sizes and increased student contact time are not likely prospects in most public schools, there are real possibilities to nurture the complexity of students as learners and social selves. Teachers can be supported in their efforts to understand and respond to their students across more numerous and varied dimensions of human development. Educators can be encouraged to shape learning experiences and environments to effectively enhance social, emotional, intuitive, aesthetic, and visionary capacities. Such efforts are crucial if future citizens are to look to a wide range of personal attributes and creative pursuits in seeking inspiration that sustains meaning and hope beyond ambitions for material gain.

Teachers must also be supported in their continuing efforts to teach not only for, but also beyond, the test. School districts might begin by involving teachers, students, and parents in appropriately contextualizing the role of test-taking within the learning process. While rigorous, comparative assessment is important, quality education involves much more than ensuring adequate test performance.

It is also conceivable that more intensive engagement with varied forms of interpretation and creative expression might enhance the development of knowledge and skills routinely assessed in standardized formats. Research designed to explore ways in which aesthetic and exploratory learning might affect standardized test performance should be solicited and supported.

Our lives will continue to be structured by bureaucracies. Bureaucratic culture evolved as a dominant form of social organization in large part to limit individual and subjective discretion. Appropriate action is determined by hierarchically layered, complexly detailed regulations. Civil obedience is required to promote common goals and to protect the common good. And yet, our identities and intentions can be trivialized as social interactions are centered on maintaining compliance and control.

Many, for example, who accept regulatory positions within public school systems do so on the basis of heartfelt commitments to 'getting things done' in relation to high academic and civic aspirations. They assume their roles ready to use their expertise to shape standards and then to act as facilitators, assisting school-based colleagues in moving toward adaptive forms of compliance that make a positive difference in children's lives. Too often their professional agency is diminished as creative endeavors (research, planning, professional development) are overtaken by obligations to enforce politicized mandates and to respond in a timely manner to extensive reporting demands. Faced with conflicting pressures to 'hold to the letter of the law' in some cases; to lower expectations, look the other way, or grant exemptions in others—they watch as their expertise is squandered, their efforts to promote systemic reform fragmented. Meanwhile, teachers and administrators beleaguered with the 'mountains of paperwork' required to document compliance express frustration at the amount of time stolen away from already limited opportunities for instruction and innovation.

But collective dreams for deep learning and deep democracy require movement beyond conformity and submission to authority. Integrity cannot be reduced to efficient execution of arduous accountability tasks, or to 'just following orders.' Opportunities to reconnect with the passions of deep meaning must be shaped amid the restrictive routines of bureaucratic life.

Even within intensely scrutinized, centrally controlled public school systems, beauty can be found in working together to sustain unwavering focus on the fulfillment of high purpose. Through internal memos and meetings, public presentations and forums, legislative testimony, interactions with the media, and in everyday conversations, we can persistently raise our sights, ask provocative questions, and offer principled rationale for much needed change. Shared inspirational experience can be kept within reach through collaborative efforts to sustain attention on affirming the breadth and depth of what's truly important. Broad-based civic participation in determining high standards, demanding comprehensive and meaningful assessments, and centering education policy and practice on its democratic purpose can better ensure access to the highest quality of learning and life for *all* participants. Especially when confronted with frustrating bureaucratic trials and trivia, we must support each other in keeping our 'eyes on the prize.'

Our lives will continue to be stressed by opposition. In a culture of opposition, the world becomes a dangerous place. Suspicion, defensiveness, and aggression are required in response. As social interactions are centered on confrontation, each person's evolving sense of self-worth and social efficacy is threatened with violation, coercion, and at times severe damage. Persuasion is attempted with strategies and tactics framed in military metaphors. In staged conflicts, collective understanding of pivotal issues is obscured, while acts of compassion are obstructed.

For far too many, daily life in public schools is characterized by anxiety, humiliation, and loneliness. Students, parents, administrators, and teachers are besieged by poverty; racial, religious, and ethnic tensions; gang violence; stereotyping, discrimination and exclusion; bullying; school shootings; and multiple opportunities to experience disapproval, disappointment, and failure. Under conditions such as these, half-hearted or impractical recommendations to advance 'community' and 'democracy' offer only cruel illusions. Even for those who are able to maintain competitive advantage, personal gain is eventually tempered by civic loss.

But there is more to life than performance in battle. Worth, success, and fulfillment cannot be measured solely in terms of culturally sanctioned 'wins' and 'losses.' We cannot allow the active and intentional development of *non-oppositional* identities, social practices, and relationships to remain a hollow utopian task.

Even within harshly stratified, segregated and embattled public schools, possibilities exist to move beyond confrontation and resistance toward self-realization and social harmony. Both the concept and the experience of 'self' are radically social. As humans, we come to understand, to value, and to challenge ourselves in communion with others. We evolve as unique and empathetic individuals as close, multidimensional, and affirming relationships are sustained over time. These qualities of social interaction are required, not only to balance conflict and competition, but also to move beyond passive and isolating forms of non-opposition such as mutual non-interference or shallow tolerance.

Sources of inspiration necessary to develop mature selves and to support principled civic participation are found in the complex harmonies of purpose, performance, and growth. Harmony—beauty expressed as dynamic and resonant balance—is not only aesthetically significant but also functionally effective. The blend of concerted vision and action is a motivating achievement. Social harmony is powerfully resonant in experiences of deep learning and deep democracy.

Maintaining a sense of personal and social harmony despite the pervasive influence of oppositional culture requires focused intent, mutual effort, and openness to surprise—all factors intrinsic to the experience of beauty. These are also complex skills that can be more fully developed, and made more widely accessible, through active instruction and persistent practice. As public schools continue to serve as primary sites for sustained and purposeful interaction among diverse participants, they offer increasingly rare and valuable opportunities to share responsibility for each other's personal welfare, continuing growth, social experience, and aesthetic enrichment.

Taking full advantage of such opportunities within contemporary school contexts requires pragmatic ingenuity. For example, although segregation and stratification of students based on variations in academic performance is likely to continue, this need not be the case across all subject matter areas. School districts might actively choose *not* to track social studies offerings. These might be recast as focal sites for emphasizing non-oppositional approaches to self-development through civic engagement. Gaining experience in active listening, balancing critical thinking with ethical reflection, conducting research that is both academically sound and relevant to real-world concerns, developing discourse and decision-making skills—all leverage possibilities for deeper learning and deeper democracy.

Opportunities to experience mutually supportive forms of social interaction within schools could also be enriched through advising systems that connect individual students with caring adults, and assist peers in responding constructively to each other (e.g., peer teaching, mentoring, and mediation). Broad-based and consequential student participation in school governance is also necessary. Incorporating student voice in curriculum planning and evaluation, in determining disciplinary procedures, and in design and implementation of service initiatives can strengthen emerging civic commitment and competence.

Such competencies could be further developed through meaningful participation in community-based political processes. Public support for intensive school/community collaborations is justified when these efforts address significant societal concerns. The rising incidence of school and community violence, conflicts between economic development and environmental protection, the dynamics of racial discrimination and religious fundamentalism, and tendencies toward reflexive militarism all require sustained attention. Working together across established power differentials and beyond restrictive conceptual boundaries is necessary to improve the quality of civic interaction and to promote imaginative solutions.

In each of these challenging settings—untracked social studies classrooms, school advisory and governance programs, community involvement projects—relational patterns centered on competition and conflict can be balanced with collective efforts to compose more resourceful and fulfilling approaches to learning and life.

Social inquiry and social responsibility can either be enhanced or constrained by cultural and institutional contexts. Civic integrity and imagination are heightened in settings of diverse participation where attention is creatively maintained on the "commonwealth"—a concept that has both material and spiritual meaning. More complex, interdependent and contributory personal and political identities develop as schools and communities are strengthened through broader conversations, coalitions, and commitments. Political processes that connect shared social purpose with the spirit of joint action are necessary for building a deeper democracy. Public education reform that engages inevitable conflicts with intelligent emotion, patient reason, and acts of grace and beauty, is necessary to support that deepening.

> *"This willingness to continually revise one's own location*
> *in order to place oneself in the path of beauty*
> *is the basic impulse underlying education.*
> *One submits oneself to other minds . . . in order to increase the chance*
> *that one will be looking in the right direction*
> *when a comet makes its sweep through a certain patch of sky."*
>
> —Elaine Scarry
> *On Beauty and Being Just*

Exploratory Democratic Practice: Social Poetry

If we are to evolve more deeply democratic approaches to social inquiry and civic participation, our reform efforts must become *compellingly aesthetic*. Human design and decision-making processes are not exclusively intellectual. Tendencies toward narrow rationality and dispassionate expression prevent full integration of emotion, aesthetics, intuition, and spirit. Visions of social reform thereby loose their capacity to inspire and sustain principled action. Initiatives can be shaped to serve as sites for dynamic expression of social intuition, imagination, and artistry. Social poetry—as an *exploratory democratic practice*—is one technique that can be used to direct our attention to the emotions and energies always at play throughout the challenging process of change.

- Participants are organized into small working groups (3–5 members).
- Group members are encouraged to reflect individually on the reform initiative. They are asked to center on its most important aspirations and significant challenges.
- They are then asked to express these aspirations or challenges using either **haiku** (3 lines: 5–7–5 syllables) or **tanka** (5 lines: 5–7–5–7–7 syllables)—both non-rhyming, unpunctuated, Japanese poetic forms.

    e.g., **haiku** form

    > *inequality of*
    > *opportunity limits*
    > *deep democracy*

    e.g., **tanka** form

    > *aesthetic insight*
    > *deepens informed commitment*
    > *connective passions*
    > *sustain radical reform*
    > *beauty awakens wisdom*

- Small groups convene to consider each member's poem and then to collaboratively compose a piece of *social poetry* that incorporates possibilities drawn from each draft.
- As a final step, the full collective is reconvened. Each small group reads their composition aloud and responses are encouraged.

As noted by Gregory Cajete, "In this sharing of poetic experience, both giver and receiver become involved in a dance of meaning in which complex images, symbols, and meanings are explored in direct and personal ways...affecting and engaging individuals deeply and multi-dimensionally."

Thematic Bibliographic References

On the culture and consequences of capitalism for public education:

Crenson, M., & Ginsberg, B. (2004). *Downsizing democracy: How America sidelined its citizens and privatized its public.* Baltimore, MD: Johns Hopkins University Press.

Cuban, L. (2004). *The blackboard and the bottomline: Why schools can't be businesses.* Cambridge, MA: Harvard University Press.

Emery, K., & Ohanian, S.. (2004). *Why is corporate America bashing our public schools?* Portsmouth, NH: Heineman.

Gabbard, D. (Ed.). (2000). *Knowledge and power in the global economy: Politics and the rhetoric of school reform.* Mahwah, NJ: Lawrence Erlbaum Associates.

Giroux, H. (2000). *Stealing innocence: Youth, corporate power and the politics of culture.* New York: Palgrave Macmillan.

Giroux, H. (2002). *Public spaces, private lives: Democracy beyond 9/11.* New York: Rowman & Littlefield.

Grubb, W., & Lazerson, M. (2005). *The education gospel: The economic power of schooling.* Cambridge, MA: Harvard University Press.

McLaren, P. (2005). *Capitalists and conquerors: A critical pedagogy against empire.* Lanham, MD: Rowman & Littlefield.

Milner, M. (2004). *Freaks, geeks, and cool kids: Teenagers, schools, and the culture of consumption.* New York: Routledge Falmer.

Putman, R. (2000). *Bowling alone: The collapse and revival of American community.* New York: Simon & Schuster.

Saltman, K., & Gabbard, D. (Eds.). (2003) *Education as enforcement: The militarization and corporatization of schools.* New York: Falmer Press.

Sclar, E. (2001). *You don't always get what you pay for: The economics of privatization.* Ithaca, NY: Cornell University Press.

Spring, J. (1998). *Education and the rise of the global economy.* Mahwah, NJ: Lawrence Erlbaum Associates.

Stromquist, N. (2003). *Education in a globalized world: The connectivity of power, technology, and knowledge.* Lanham, MD: Rowman & Littlefield.

On the culture and consequences of bureaucracy for public education:

Apple, M. (1993). *Official knowledge: Democratic education in a conservative age.* New York: Routledge.

Conley, D. (2003). *Who governs our schools? Changing roles and responsibilities.* New York: Teachers College Press.

Hedges, L., & Schneider, B. (Eds.). (2005). *The social organization of schooling.* New York: Russell Sage Foundation.

Skocpol, T. (2003). *Diminished democracy: From membership to management in American civic life.* Norman: University of Oklahoma Press.

Stein, S. (2004). *The culture of education policy.* New York: Teachers College Press.

On the culture and consequences of opposition for public education:

Apple, M. (Ed.). (2003). *The state and the politics of knowledge.* New York: Routledge Falmer.

Davies, L. (2003). *Education and conflict: Complexity and chaos.* New York: Routledge Falmer.

Deckman, M. (2004). *School board battles: The Christian right in local politics.* Washington, DC: Georgetown University Press.

Harber, C. (2004). *Schooling as violence: How schools harm pupils and societies.* New York: Falmer Press.

Kaplan, H. (2004). *Failing grades: How schools breed frustration, anger, and violence, and how to prevent it.* Lanham, MD: Rowman & Littlefield.

Mansbridge, J. (1980). *Beyond adversary democracy.* Chicago: University of Chicago Press.

McAdam, D., Tarrow, S., & Tilly, C. (2001). *Dynamics of contention.* New York: Cambridge University Press.

McLaren, P. (1995). *Critical pedagogy and predatory culture: Oppositional politics in a postmodern era.* New York: Routledge.

Newman, K. (2004). *The social roots of school shootings.* New York: Basic Books.

Saltman, K., & Gabbard, D. (2003). *Education as enforcement: The militarization and corporatization of schools.* New York: Routledge Falmer.

Webber, J. (2003). *Failure to hold: The politics of school violence.* Lanham, MD: Rowman & Littlefield.

Beyond capitalism:

Barlow, A. (2003). *Between fear and hope: Globalization and race in the United States.* Lanham, MD: Rowman & Littlefield.

Bickman, M. (2003). *Minding American education: Reclaiming the tradition of active learning.* New York: Teachers College Press.

Bowers, C. (1993). *Education, cultural myths, and the ecological crisis.* Albany: SUNY Press.

Bowers, C. (2003). *Mindful conservatism: Re-thinking the ideological and educational basis of an ecologically sustainable future.* New York: Rowman & Littlefield.

Crittenden, J. (1992). *Beyond individualism: Reconstituting the liberal self.* New York: Oxford University Press.

Cuban, L., & Shipps, D. (Eds.). (2000). *Reconstructing the common good in education: Coping with intractable American dilemmas.* Stanford, CA: Stanford University Press.

Demartino, G. (2000). *Global economy: Global justice: Theoretical objections and policy alternative to neoliberalism.* New York: Brunner-Routledge.

Frisina, W. (2000). *The unity of knowledge and action.* Albany: State University of New York.

Garrison, J. (1997). *Dewey and eros: Wisdom and desire in the art of teaching.* New York: Teachers College Press.

Goodlad, J., & McMannon, T. (Eds.). (1997). *The public purposes of education and schooling.* San Francisco: Jossey-Bass.

Kahlenberg, R. (2000). *A notion at risk: Public education as an engine for social mobility.* New York: Century Foundation Press.

Kincheloe, J., & Steinberg, S. (Eds.). (2005) *Cutting class: Social class and education.* Lanham, MD: Rowman & Littlefield.

Kohn, A. (1999). *The schools our children deserve: Moving beyond traditional classrooms and "tougher standards".* Boston: Houghton Mifflin.

Koren, L. (1994). *Wabi-sabi for artists, designers, poets, and philosophers.* Berkeley, CA: Stone Bridge Press.

Plumwood, V. (2003). *Environmental culture: The ecological crisis of reason.* New York: Routledge Falmer.

Popp, J. (1999). *Cognitive science and philosophy of education.* San Francisco: Caddo Gap Press.

Rothstein, R. (2004). *Class and schools: Using social, economic, and educational reform to close the black-white achievement gap.* Washington, DC: Economic Policy Institute.

Beyond bureaucracy:

Boyte, H. (2004). *Everyday politics: The power of public work.* Philadelphia: University of Pennsylvania Press.

Matthews, D. (2006). *Reclaiming public education by reclaiming our democracy.* Dayton, OH: Kettering Foundation Press.

Oakes, J., Ryan, S., & Lipton, M. (2000). *Becoming good schools: The struggle for civic virtue in educational reform.* San Francisco: Jossey-Bass.

Oldenski, T., & Carlson, D. (Eds.). (2002). *Educational yearning: The journey of the spirit and democratic education.* New York: Peter Lang.

Osterman, P. (2003). *Gathering power: The future of progressive politics in America.* Boston: Beacon Press.

Palmer, P. (1998). *The courage to teach.* San Francisco: Jossey-Bass.

Purpel, D., & McLaurin, W. (2004). *Reflections on the moral and spiritual crisis in education.* New York: Peter Lang.

Sexton, R. (2004). *Mobilizing citizens for better schools.* New York: Teachers College Press.

Vincent, C. (Ed.). (2003). *Social justice, education and identity.* New York: Routledge Falmer.

Beyond opposition:

Baum, H. (2002). *Community action for school reform.* Albany: SUNY Press.

Bingham, C. (2001). *Schools of recognition: Identity politics and classroom practice.* Lanham, MD: Rowman & Littlefield.

Boyte, H. (2004). *Everyday politics: The power of public work.* Philadelphia: University of Pennsylvania Press.

Bryk, A., & Schneider, B. (2002). *Trust in schools: A core resource for improvement.* New York: Russell Sage Foundation.

Burstyn, J., Bender, G., Casella, R., Gordon, W., Guerra, D., & Lushen, K. (2001). *Preventing violence in schools: A challenge to American democracy.* Mahwah, NJ: Lawrence Erlbaum Associates.

Carr, D., & Haldane, J. (Eds.). (2003). *Spirituality, philosophy and education.* New York: Routledge Falmer.

Florina, M. et al. (2005). *Culture war: The myth of a polarized America.* New York: Pearson Longman.

Forcey, L., & Harris, I. (Eds.). (1999). *Peacebuilding for adolescents: Strategies for educators and community leaders.* New York: Peter Lang.

Freire, P. (2000). *Pedagogy of freedom.* New York: Rowman & Littlefield.

Fung, A., & Wright, E. (2004). *Deepening democracy: Institutional innovations in empowered participatory governance.* London: Verso.

hooks, b. (2003). *Teaching community: A pedagogy of hope.* New York: Routledge.

Kochanek, J. (2005). *Building trust for better schools: Research based practices.* Thousand Oaks, CA: Corwin Press/Sage.

Mansbridge, J. (1980). *Beyond adversary democracy.* Chicago: University of Chicago Press.

Mansbridge, J. (1990). *Beyond self-interest.* Chicago: University of Chicago Press.

Marshall C., & Oliva, M. (Eds.). (2005). *Leadership for social justice: Making it happen.* Boston: Allyn & Bacon.

Mediratta, K. (2004). *Constituents of change: Community organization and public education reform.* New York: New York University Institute for Education and Social Policy.

Meier, D. (2003). *In schools we trust: Creating communities of learning in an era of testing and standardization.* Boston: Beacon Press.

Merz, C., & Furman, G. (1997). *Community and schools: Promise and paradox.* New York: Teachers College Press.

Moses, M. (2002). *Embracing race: Why we need race-conscious education policy.* New York: Teachers College Press.

Reed, C. (2000). *Teaching with power: Shared decision-making and classroom practice.* New York: Teachers College Press.

Rimmerman, C. (2005), *The new citizenship: Unconventional politics, activism, and service.* Boulder, CO: Westview Press.

Rossato, C. (2005). *Engaging Paulo Freire's pedagogy of possibility: From blind to transformative optimism.* Lanham, MD: Rowman & Littlefield.

Sexton, R. (2004). *Mobilizing citizens for better schools.* New York: Teachers College Press.

Shirley, D. (1997). *Community organizing for urban school reform.* Austin: University of Texas Press.

Youniss, J. & Yates, M. (1997). *Community service and social responsibility in youth.* Chicago: University of Chicago Press.

Reflection:
Scarry, E. (1999). *On beauty and being just* (p. 7). Princeton, NJ: Princeton University Press.

Exploratory Democratic Practice: Social Poetry
Cajete, G. (1994). *Look to the mountain: An ecology of indigenous education* (p. 133). Durango, CO: Kivaki Press.

chapter 1 0

Courage

No illusions
the threat is real, adversity ever present
yet danger deepens purpose
serenity in challenge
strength in spirit
persist with renewed intent
worthy of belief, shared aims compel
do not hold back
join together, evolve within, reach beyond.

"*I*t's over! It's all over! The superintendent told me this morning that Grant is just too expensive." Althea waited to compose herself as she glanced at Jim MacIver and Jonathan Caine who sat at the table in her office. After a moment she continued with a mix of sadness and anger in her voice, "He said the District couldn't afford to keep the Grant program going for the four years they promised last spring."

"Test scores?" Caine asked.

"No, not really. They're not back yet. They could even be better than last year. But for Tuscano, it's the budget. He said they'll have to cut services and programs across all of K–12 and Grant's program just doesn't cost out.

Re-Envisioning Education and Democracy, pages 189–212
Copyright © 2006 by Information Age Publishing
All rights of reproduction in any form reserved.

He does have some problems with what we're doing here, but it's really the budget. It's bottom line that's driving this decision."

Jim and Caine both looked troubled but said nothing. When Althea remained silent, Jim asked, "Have you told the faculty yet?"

"No, I just can't do it. Tuscano hasn't gone to the Board yet. He doesn't want to admit defeat with Grant as a failed school. He knows about our progress and our publicity. He hasn't come up with a good way to cover his decision in public."

She paused again and then said with intensity, "This just isn't fair. We've done what we set out to do! He knows that we're moving along on most of our objectives. They promised us four years and now he says there simply is not enough money to cover even one more year. As I said, we may even improve on last year's scores—even though the tests are a little different again this year. We did get Grant, and even the District, good publicity. Jon's press buddy, Karla Morgan, did a flattering feature on us last month."

"You just liked the pictures of you and the kids," Caine said smiling and trying to move Althea beyond her anger.

"Oh sure, Tuscano liked the positive story too. But for the administration, and probably in the end for the Board, it's the money that's done us in. It's over. I know it's over," Althea said softly and sadly.

Jim snapped, "Money! Ha! That's not all there is to it. Whatever they say about money, I bet it's your 'deeper democracy' mission they don't like. When I got the LEAD summer program approved last January, they did worry some about the budget. They were worse than the foundations. But there was also a whole lot of nit picking about the wording of our goals, our leadership recruiting and selection process, and what some referred to as our plans for "teaching agitation." Look, it's actually *not* about the money, Althea. It's about showing another way. For them, if Grant's not about preparing "job-ready, eager consumers," then it's not a funding priority."

"So you're all set for this summer then, Jim?" Caine asked still trying to steer away from the anger and bitterness in his friends' voices.

"The LEAD Summer Academy is on its way. We've got dynamite kids from all around town. We got some good space at the university, plenty of technology, and I have recruited a great staff. And we're going to be about making democratic public policy, not about pandering to the corporate or political establishment! But Althea, we're always hearing about money. Now they say there's not enough money for Grant! That's the standard cop out; the same old story. They want to stop what you're doing."

"But it is the money too, I'm sure," Caine said soothingly. "Education budgets are in crisis across the state and across the country. Superintendents everywhere are forced to cut—to be more cost effective. Most school boards are panicking. We all know teaching the way it's done here at Grant is, in fact, more expensive. Grinding out test takers—even producing really successful test takers—is a whole lot cheaper."

"All this I know, but thanks for reminding me," Althea said a bit sarcastically. "Now look, how are we going to keep this Grant project going? Can we keep it going? We just have to find a way."

Caine looked at a point on the wall a little above Jim and Althea's heads. He began to speak slowly. "We could—I think we must—join with a larger movement for democratic education. Grant is one example—a crucial one certainly—but it's just one very important example of this type of effort around the country. Public education can be about democratic values and practices, as Jim has said right along, but it's about the money too, as Tuscano insists . . . "

Jim interrupted heatedly, "We can make Tuscano and the Board look really bad on this. We've got to go toe-to-toe with them, Jon. Half of the School Board is up for re-election next fall. Grant's got good community support—more than just the LEAD coalition. You've got all that good publicity and you've got all those movers and shakers on the advisory council or whatever you call it. We can mobilize a militant opposition and confront the Board on this. We could make them pay for their betrayal."

Caine still was staring at the wall as he said slowly, "Well, maybe not this time Jim. First, an election focus for next fall will be too late for Grant. Second, our job here and now is to keep moving. Third, I think we've got to consider some non-oppositional strategies."

Jim looked confused.

Althea looked expectant.

Caine looked challenged as he continued, still not making eye contact. "OK, I'm still trying to work this out. None of us want to lose what's been started at Grant. It looks bleak—I know it is bleak—but just because Tuscano and the Board are in crisis mode, it doesn't mean we have to comply. This time, I honestly don't think that our practiced, directly confrontational campaign politics will work. You know, instead of only criticizing or even punishing Tuscano, maybe we can come up with solution paths that he can buy into. Before we unleash our devastating analysis of the corporate culture, right wing influences on public policy, and the tragic disinvestment in public education, maybe we could try to work with the Board in a way that is less threatening—maybe we could find some alternative ways to save this program."

"That's blatantly naïve, Jon!" Jim said sharply. "You're laying down to be co-opted, or more likely to get buried! You should know better than that after all the political battles you've been through."

"Let's hear him out," Althea interjected. "All I can see right now are things we've done before. I sense, maybe I know, that this is a moment when we've got to be imaginative. But honestly, I'm too angry to think this morning."

"Althea, I'm disappointed too, but oddly neither surprised nor very pessimistic," Caine said quietly. He turned to Jim and continued, "All three of us have been through many different kinds of politics. Maybe it'll turn out that I am being politically naïve, but I share Althea's sense of the moment. We need to be more creative. As you say, Jim, we do have some strong resources and we do have momentum. Maybe we can array what we have going for us differently this time. I've learned far more than I expected this year from reading, talking, and especially from working with all the people around this Grant program. Maybe I've even learned more than those lively ninth graders. Maybe this is *our* test—but let's not settle for the standardized one with all the narrow, predetermined answers."

Neither Althea nor Jim responded.

"Sure, money is always a problem and we have to deal with that. And contradictory expectations and demands are always present throughout any democratic venture. Differing visions of goals and ways to achieve them are always swirling around. They're endlessly banging into each other and changing directions. That's always involved in politicking. And, as I have come to see much more clearly this year, it's inevitably and deeply involved in educating too. Look, in putting Grant's ninth grade program together we claimed that neither 'teaching/learning as usual' nor doing 'democracy as usual' would work for us. OK, we've done some not so usual moving in the classroom and out in the community too. Now we must move forward with our politics as well."

"And do what?" Althea asked noting that Jim looked increasingly pained.

Caine continued avoiding Jim's skeptical stare: "Of course I don't know specifically, but our strategy should involve rethinking participation beyond just a few of us. I know this Grant project, even with all of our well-intentioned inclusion talk, was put together and is animated by a relatively small group of people. I think it's time to significantly broaden our base."

"Maybe so," said Althea, "but that will take time—and as you said, we have to save Grant *now*."

Caine nodded as he continued. "Yes, but it's more than Grant. We've been at this point before, in almost all of LEAD's programs over the years, and Althea with your preschool and then with PIP, and for me on countless things in the community and at the legislature. A crisis always turns us into defenders—into goal keepers."

"But Jon, that's exactly where we are. An aggressive defense is exactly what we need. We are being attacked. We have been betrayed! This calls for strong action, not some lofty think tank seminar exercise." Jim insisted.

"Yes," Caine continued, "and over the years we've learned some things about how to hide out, and how to hang on."

"But what more can we *do*?" Althea asked intently.

"I'm not so sure. How about new foundation support?" Caine asked.

"I've already thought about foundations off and on all spring," Althea responded quickly. "The ones that helped us with start-up aren't in a position to carry the full Grant initiative for next year, or to help make up the difference between what the District could come up with and what we actually need. We could go after some new foundation support—although we know that'll be really tough since most foundations want to be in on the ground floor and not subsidize a program that someone else has started."

Althea paused as Caine looked intently at her and Jim looked away.

"We do have many more important things to do, and maybe we could repackage them in a good proposal. And maybe what's coming in these next few years is even more challenging and possibly just as interesting to potential funders as our start-up year. We can truly say we've learned a lot about doing this kind of deeper learning for deeper democracy," Althea said trying to sound more optimistic.

Jim continued to look skeptical as he said, "A minute ago you said it was all over. Maybe so. But let's say a foundation proposal or two is an option. Maybe you can show that Grant's absenteeism has dropped and it looks like retention from the ninth to the tenth grade will be up, right? The teachers have gotten some professional recognition, some of it nationally, for their ninth-grade curriculum and for their innovative teaching styles. We know the community response has been positive, so we can get some key endorsements there. The students' morale is high even though most of my contact with the kids was with Kirk and the new judicial process. I hear parental involvement is up over last year, and as Althea just said, the test scores at least won't decline. So we could have a proposal. It's still a tough sell, and I don't want to let the Board off the hook."

Althea took Jim's pause for breath as an opportunity to reflect. "We can probably make a good case and still remain candid about the continuing problems we, and all inner city high schools, experience on a daily basis. We surely are on our way, but we're not close to solving all of Grant's problems. And let's face it, our program here has created some new problems too. But maybe we could develop a compelling proposal."

"So how could we frame it?" Jim asked. I don't see a new core idea—something that would grab new funders. I still think Tuscano's problem is really about the fact you have a community/school collaboration going on here. Grant has more participation in decision-making than the Board, and maybe most teachers, actually want. And, Althea, you're a great leader, but Grant is not seen inside or outside as a top-down, principal-in-charge type of school. You're not a typical principal, and the Board and the bureaucrats are more comfortable with the old hierarchy. I bet most of those foundations Jon is thinking about prefer those familiar authoritarian forms too."

"Well, we'll just have to see about the foundations, Jim," Caine replied. "I do think we can craft a strong proposal. I don't know now what a new framework would be, but it must be about more than saving Grant for another year. Remember, from the very start, way back when we were hassling over the LEAD Charter School idea, we saw opportunities for more than one good program at one location. As Althea said then, we need more than just another demonstration project. If we really meant that—if our goal really is systemic reform—let's go about reforming the system—starting with *this* school system. Why not propose doing what we're doing here at Grant at the other five high schools in town?"

Althea looked shocked. Jim now appeared well beyond skepticism. They both waited for Caine to continue.

After a long moment he said quietly, "Look, you don't have a faculty meeting until Monday, right? Didn't Tuscano give you at least that long before making an announcement?"

"Yes, he gave me until the end of next week." Althea responded.

"So, let's think more about this and talk around," Caine said. "Can we get together again on Thursday afternoon?"

They both nodded slowly.

*   *   *

Caine and Jim again sat at Althea's office table on the following Thursday afternoon.

Jim spoke before Althea could begin, "If we're going to sketch some new proposal, I hope you two have some new framing ideas. I still don't have a clue. I did get some positive nibbles from several of LEAD's partners including a couple of interesting responses from friends at foundations. It may even be possible to get a proposal turned around so Grant could continue next year. It depends..."

"Althea?' Caine prompted.

"Well," Althea said quietly, "I've thought about it a lot and talked with the ninth-grade staff. I told them we could be in deep trouble for next year and that we need to be imaginative. At first, I got hung up on things that probably are unique here at Grant; things that most likely can't be replicated at the other high schools. This could include some parts of our integrated ninth-grade curriculum, and maybe the intensive community connections we've developed through our service learning programs."

Jim and Caine waited expectantly as Althea leaned forward in her chair.

"But what I think is the bottom line—not Tuscano's or the Board's bottom line—but Grant's bottom line is our continuing struggle with what it means to be responsible for each other's learning. I mean we all continue to struggle with that—but we are moving! The teachers resist being isolated and work hard on sustaining the interdependence that's necessary. But it's so difficult for them when so many things push in different directions. The students get confused. But they're learning with each other and, sometimes, for each other too."

Jim said, "I'm not sure I fully understand this, Althea. But in working with Kirk I heard students, and even a couple of teachers, say that if students were really going to be responsible for each other, they'd need more help. The kids said that if they're supposed to keep their classmates in school and be sure that their friends did their homework, they'd really need more help. I don't think they knew what kind of help that would be. I sure don't!"

Althea nodded as she continued, "Yes, that's the big challenge. I don't know either. Our talk about "deeper cooperation" and "social learning" usually gets dumbed down to just getting along in a group. While that's important, it's not all that we're after at Grant. But I'm still not ready to write in proposal language."

Caine picked up on the opening. "Yes, getting along with others is of course important. But what I'm starting to understand—and I'm late on this one too—is that the radical promise at Grant is about being complexly responsible for each other, while at the same time, being responsible for oneself. That is at the core of what we know education and democracy must be about. But that's not well formulated enough for a proposal yet either."

"Don't worry Jon, we're not proposal writing yet." Jim said. "We're definitely not ready."

> Out of the darkness and into the fire
> energy rises and falls
> again and again, but never the same
> mystery, dissent, creativity, communion
> all is ever in motion.

Roger Flemming began by reiterating his ground rules for their meeting. "You understand Althea, we're here only to talk about possibilities. This is an informal, off-the-record, friendly conversation."

"I understand, Roger, and I really appreciate you doing this for us," Althea said. "Jon Caine and Jim MacIver agree that we need reality checks on how we might keep Grant moving into next year. We sent you some talking points and background materials."

"Yes, I've read those and also reviewed the clipping file we assembled on your program. You've gotten some good press. While you're the first to begin talking with us about next year, I expect we'll be hearing soon from other schools and programs all around the state. This budget mess has pulled everyone up short."

Althea waited and Flemming continued. "As I read this, you're thinking about not only continuing the Grant program, but also extending something like it to the other five high schools in this district. I've rarely seen a funding request under these conditions that proposes expansion rather than just trying to hold on to what they have. I admit this is intriguing. Over the years, and especially during severe budget crunches like this one, our applicants go on the defensive. Here you are proposing to extend what you started. Yes, this is indeed quite unusual."

Althea said, "What you also might find unusual is our focus on the 'middle.' These are ideas—modeled mostly on our Grant experience—to support the majority of the students in public secondary schools. State and federal governments mandate services for the students with special needs and those facing defined challenges. At the other end of the spectrum, powerful advocacy groups are at work to support gifted and talented students. And charter schools and some magnet projects, in a similar way, attract specialized populations. We respect those efforts, but we propose a sharper focus on the rest of the students—what we see as the "underserved middle."

"Yes, I would guess that foundations rarely see a lot what you've been up to at Grant in applications for programs at any level. But honestly, what is most unusual in your talking points is your core objective."

"Unusual?" Althea prompted cautiously.

"Not so much on the surface as stated, but certainly unusual when you play out the implications."

Althea remained silent.

Glancing down, Flemming quoted from the working draft: "*We propose to create and sustain conditions to support students in taking responsibility for each other's learning.*" You set that apart from, but still connected to, the more common exhortations I'm used to hearing about developing student accountability on an individual basis. And you explicitly impose on students a responsibility typically assumed by teachers, administrators, parents, the community, and the state. And furthermore—whatever this is exactly—you propose to extend this vision beyond Grant to all the other secondary schools in the city."

"I think we can show we've made some progress this year," Althea said with a confident voice that surprised her a little.

"I concede that you may be able to document some of the things you claim in this draft, but the test scores aren't back yet, are they?"

Althea shook her head.

"Now look Althea, when you came to us years ago with your early learning project and later when you and May Haun-Crawford presented the first versions of Partners in Participation, the goals were clearly stated and immediately understandable. The means to achieve them were pretty familiar. I'm surprised that you, and cohorts as savvy as MacIver and Caine, are so—what can I say in a friendly way—well so abstract, perhaps fuzzy."

"In those other ventures," Althea said quickly, "we were proposing what was clearly needed, things we knew how to do, but just weren't getting done. They were huge efforts and your help was indispensable. They ended up, I think, more or less successful, but they didn't lead to anything more. They remained effective but isolated demonstrations."

"I know we've talked before about your ambivalence concerning demonstration projects. You know I share your reservations. But you also know that single-site projects with clearly stated and well-framed goals that are assessable with conventional procedures—like your two past successes—are much easier to sell to any foundation board. Your intention to extend to the whole secondary school system is very risky."

"We understand that Roger. We do understand what kind of proposals have a better chance of gaining support and being funded," Althea said quietly.

"So you and your friends are willing to gamble Grant's future on an expanded project?"

"Yes." Althea replied immediately.

Flemming looked at her intently and then at his notes before he continued. "Let's start with the money. Your estimate of what it would take to keep Grant going on into a second phase of the ninth grade program seems to be about right, but we'd need firmer numbers—they are going to be rather large numbers, aren't they? The School Board is tightly constrained, and to make up the difference between their proposed budget cuts and your request will be costly. And your estimate for the planning and development grants for the other five high schools seems to be in the ballpark—but you still lack specifics. This is a big challenge at the funding level. Just coming up with a way to keep Grant going would be significantly cheaper than a systemwide project. So, the numbers must be worked out if and when a budget is actually presented to us."

Althea nodded, took notes, but remained silent.

"Let's say you can be more articulate in stating your core objectives," Roger continued. "Can you help me get a glimpse of how the goals can be accomplished, and what measures for outcomes you will propose? Let me be more direct. How would I know "students are responsible for each other's learning" if I saw it?"

"Some of the things we've achieved so far this year, as you said earlier, are documented—attendance, truancy rates, on-site violence, expulsions, retention, and promotion. The test scores and the other year-end numbers are still a month away, but we'll have them. We will also have detailed descriptions of how the main components of our integrated curriculum and our related activities were actually carried out. We want to provide more than a statement of objectives for each component matched up with results. We have full drafts on our Science for Citizens approach, several detailed accounts of our service learning programs, and some material on how we use video projects to tie together what students are doing in their classes and in the community. We're struggling with how to show students working together and taking responsibility for each other. These narrative case studies are not all positive. There's a lot of trial and error in this. We're pleased with our progress but we're trying to be candid about our shortcomings too."

"Something like that could be quite helpful," Roger said noncommittally. "But you're not specifically proposing your Grant curriculum for the other schools. You are requiring a homeroom approach and it is not immediately obvious to me, for example, how or why the Grant homeroom strategy works. I understand the value of the additional preparation hour for the ninth grade faculty for your so-called integrated curriculum. But you seem to be proposing extending the homeroom strategy as part of the planning grant for the other schools—and that'll be a very expensive move, if it's attempted."

"The curriculum is not "so-called," Roger. It is integrated and we'll be able to show that," Althea said with a hint of irritation in her voice. "Documenting how students become responsible for each other's learning is a lot tougher. We've only begun. That's why it is imperative to continue what we're doing at Grant. We have done things that could be helpful to other schools in their own settings. And, just as important, we could learn from their experience too."

"But if it is not yet possible to fully document what you claim you are accomplishing at Grant, why push the other high schools in the same direction? Some of the programs at those other schools are quite impressive and their test scores have been considerably higher than Grant's. Why should they be interested in developing what you call in these pages "site-specific approaches" to achieve this student responsibility thing?"

"Difficult questions Roger. Why we're willing, as you put it, to "gamble" on trying to do something more than just continue Grant's program is because we now know a lot more about some very important things. At Grant we've called them "core insights." First, focusing support only on government mandated categories of students, and putting scarce resources into programs successfully advocated by special interests, neglects the majority of secondary students. *Most students* will continue to experience underfunded programs in more crowded classrooms with overly stressed teachers and fewer support services. *All students* are put at risk during budget crises."

"I do understand that analysis," Roger said.

"Second," Althea continued, "while we desperately want to have Grant continue to develop its integrated curriculum and homeroom approach, we do not want to become—no matter how successful we are—a standardized model imposed from above. We know that what we're learning at Grant can be transferable, but it must be developed elsewhere, from the ground up."

Flemming nodded but said nothing.

"Maybe I shouldn't say this Roger, but we don't always know what we're doing. We don't think that what we're attempting at Grant is the only answer for all public schools. But we do feel like we're part of a larger vision that needs to be realized, not only at Grant, but also in other places with different ideas, approaches, and programs."

"Modesty is not usually the most prominent attribute of the proposals we review," Flemming said with a broad smile. "Are you through with your 'core insights'?"

"Oh no. Next, it is our belief that the kind of teaching/learning we're evolving at Grant not only enhances education for all students regardless of ability, but also advances a more democratic society. And these are the perennial, the primary, objectives of public education."

"Well, I was saving my confusion about what you call "social learning" and its relation to what you assert would be a "deeper democracy." What do you people really mean?" Flemming asked intently.

"As you've said, this is very difficult to express either clearly or conventionally." Althea continued quietly. "I wish we had a simple case study to present to you, but this is only our first year. We are confident, however, that we can show how students can develop a more complex sense of responsibility that will carry them into a deeper democratic life. We mean by that, Roger, that they will become more than consumers of campaign hype, or passive observers of political entertainment. We mean that they will be experienced with the processes of a more deliberative democracy, with a broader range of skills. They do learn how to listen as well as how to express themselves in several forms—how to be mindful of individual rights as well as how to collaborate with others—and maybe most important, how to be socially and politically imaginative at all levels of their lives. Is this becoming a little more understandable?"

"Perhaps," Roger said thoughtfully. "Let me move to the recommendations on broader community involvement. I'm used to seeing school-community partnership rhetoric. So, what's this about the LEAD Summer Academy?"

"Well, we see it as an essential component that links LEAD's many coalition organizations with this proposal. As you know, LEAD has already recruited ten students from each of the six public high schools. Along with organizing and communication skills, these student-activists-in-training are going to do policy research on community-based initiatives. They will interview community and business representatives about school/community relations, and try to identify new approaches. This could lead to coalition building and lobbying at the Legislature for mutually identified priorities—for example, lobbying to restore funds for neighborhood safety, race relations, youth employment, after-school programs, and extracurricular activities. Another interesting possibility will be their interviews of a representative sample of students from all six high schools, including not only recent graduates, but also recent drop outs. We've learned much from listening to our ninth-graders and we know that all of us—teachers, students, as well as administrators—will benefit from this research. But perhaps most exciting, during his recruiting sessions Jim heard student advocacy for greater integration of students from diverse backgrounds both within and across all city schools."

"You mentioned the staff at the other schools. How can you be sure that there is enough interest in being part of a planning and development grant?" Flemming asked.

"We've met with faculty and administrators at the other schools all along. I see the other principals weekly and am on the phone with them more often than that. Our ninth grade teachers are also in touch formally through their subject emphases, you know, Communication Arts, Social Studies, Science/Math. They communicate with other teachers on-line and through periodic District programs. They also talk with their friends, and not only those in our District. But the real leverage for participation around the District is the possibility of a more meaningful homeroom and the option of an additional prep hour if they do serious curricular integration."

"No opposition?" Flemming asked with a tight smile.

"Oh, there's plenty of that!" Althea responded. "I have strong adversaries within Grant between the teachers and supporting staff in the upper grades. Some have been helpful critics and others, well let's just say, have been strongly opposed—a similar range of responses at the other schools as well."

Flemming shuffled quickly through his papers and then looked up to say: "Let me shift the focus. Let's say I understand all the talking points you faxed and what you've told me so far this morning. Let's also assume you can fill in the blanks and provide the numbers and come up with a full-blown proposal. Why should our group of foundations, or any foundation you might approach, take on such an expensive risk?"

"I thought that's what we were talking about." Althea said.

"No, we were talking about your rather radical proposal. I am asking for your advice on how I could sell something like this to my board."

"It's not so "radical"—I'm leery of that word." Althea said.

"Well, we could use other words, like 'bold' or 'idealistic.' Look, they are intelligent and responsible people, my board. From your perspective they are also rather conservative. They want to back likely successes. That's mostly why they helped you earlier with the your preschoolers and later with PIP. They have a strong track record. They routinely support strong leadership and clear routes toward accountability. That's also why they backed you earlier. This proposal is much harder to understand. It's complex and some will find it vague. For them, it's a long way from your rhetoric to visualizing how what you now propose could actually work. It is in many ways quite controversial—or at least it could become so.""

"They might also be surprised by our provision to have you and some members of your board join an advisory council that would seek and support connections among the planning task forces at each of the high schools." Althea said, "You know Roger, this is all about being responsible for each others' learning on a continuing basis. In this situation we're centrally concerned with a broad re-envisioning of public education for public purposes. At Grant, we're not just doing what we've done in the past, or currently know how to do. All of us have taken risks and learned in the process. We can't go on alone. Other schools need to find what works for them. We need each other's help. Community organizations—like LEAD, like some of the sites our ninth graders are involved with, and places like this group of foundations—all need to be integrally involved."

"You're right, that's not what my board expects," Flemming said with a smile.

"None of us expected what we've gotten into. We did not, could not anticipate what's been demanded of us. That's what a deeper public education and a deeper democracy must be about. Teaching and learning must continually evolve. Democratic life, and, yes, life at foundations too, is all about risk. We are responsible for each other in schools, in our community organizations, and everywhere in public life. We can't just shop it out to teachers, however well prepared or dedicated they may or may not be. We can't just let others with specialized and professional expertise serve us through familiar bureaucratic structures. We can't sit back and wait for charismatic leaders to shape our political choices. We must all be in this together."

"May I use that speech when I present your proposal to my Board? You have less than a month to put it together. I think it's doable, but please try to be clearer on those really vague parts."

*   *   *

Karla Morgan sat across the desk from Jonathan Caine in his law office. With his permission, she started her digital recorder as she began, "I'm working on two angles. First, I'd like your perspective on the proposal from Grant High. I hear they want to have the other five high schools join them in what they call "deeper learning for deeper democracy"—I know you were in on that proposal."

"OK, and your second angle?" Caine asked cautiously.

"My usual interest in the political plans of prominent people," she replied.

"I was privileged to share a little in the drafting of the proposal that the Metro Foundation is currently considering. Folks at Grant are far more knowledgeable sources for the proposal and for your story. Anyway, you have a copy of the executive summary. What do you want from me?"

"Well, I do understand the need to mobilize resources to continue the Grant program. I know the School Board had promised to support Grant for four years. Now there are rumors they're about to rescind that promise. But I'm baffled by what I understand to be plans to adopt similar programs at every high school. That's pretty ambitious when all public and nonprofit sectors are finding that they have to cut back."

Caine paused before he said, "It is *necessarily* ambitious. What started at Grant must not be limited to a single site. This proposal is about system wide changes that need to be developed and sustained in many places. The ambition, as you call it, for "deeper learning for deeper democracy" requires attempts at interdependency across many schools and many communities. It will take the efforts and imagination of many people in many places—and not only those usually connected with public education policy."

"So this is the broadened community involvement that's called for in the proposal that's been leaked around town?" Karla asked.

"It hasn't been leaked." Caine responded. "We sent summaries to several places, including your fax machine. We mean to promote more productive interaction and genuine accountability among public education's many stakeholders. This proposal is about high schools in this city. At the same time, it is part of a broader movement to revitalize, to re-envision, to reform public education—and with that, to enrich the quality of our civic life. This is, or surely should be, part of a national agenda."

"Hmm. That sounds like a campaign speech, Senator Caine," Karla said.

"It could well be!" Caine responded matching her smile.

"OK, then let's get to angle two. Are you going to continue this 'half-time lawyer/half-time visible citizen' life you've been leading this past year? What's next for you?"

"Part-time lawyering for yet awhile. So here's what I think I owe you. I am forming an exploratory committee for a governor's candidacy," Caine said directly. "You know I valued my service in the Senate, but a governor has more opportunities to lead on broad policy fronts. If they are strategically imaginative and politically resourceful, governors can make a significant difference."

"Governor? Well, that's a surprise. Aren't there two, maybe three, major politicians positioning themselves within your party for that race in two years? So, you're going to challenge some of your old friends?"

"Old friends, yes. Challenge them, yes. But...probably not within the party." Caine said quietly.

"I don't understand," Karla said.

"I'm not planning to run within my party. This has been a really tough decision, Karla. As you know, I've been a party regular for all my political life. But now I am deeply involved in what that secondary school proposal is all about," Caine said. "And I'm afraid the leadership required to push the level of change that's needed cannot come from either major political party at this time."

"So, you would like to . . . "

Caine interrupted, "Let me try to explain. While I do know what it takes to run for a party nomination—all the fund raising, all the campaign appearances, the polls, the focus groups, and so on—that's not what's needed. What we need is to find ways to get a wide spectrum of citizens thinking and talking about what's necessary. It will take some time and ingenuity to find the types of venues and forums for these extended conversations. If a campaign does evolve for me, it cannot be one with the usual packaging of issues, or with the usual stereotypes and slogans."

Karla restrained herself and let Caine continue.

"What Grant is about, and what that foundation proposal is about, and what I want my candidacy to be about, is *systemic reform*. I know we talk that talk all the time, but at best we just do small things. Public education is *the* central concern because it the *most* crucial institution we have for building democracy."

"Sure, education is always a campaign issue—even for those who have little to do with it," Karla said.

"But governors have a lot to do with it. And our political parties currently have wedged themselves into static ideologies and policies. They are locked into positions, interest group coalitions, and campaign financing. I am convinced that a different voice and a different vision is necessary. I'd like to move public discourse toward seeing the vital linkage between education and democracy. I'd like to help citizens see that investing in education, rather than disinvesting as we are doing now, is absolutely necessary. And I don't just mean investing more tax dollars. I want my candidacy to be part of a large-scale movement toward making public education truly *the* centerpiece of democratic life. Public schooling must be more than just another decrepit public institution as it is now consistently portrayed. Privatizing, disinvesting, and the like are dangerously wrong directions."

"Sounds like a single-issue focus to me. Single-issue driven third parties don't get much attention. Isn't running outside the two party system sure defeat?" Karla asked.

"On the party side, it was an agonizing realization that my party is not the vehicle for deeper reform. Neither is the competition. I do know the history of third parties, Karla. Usually the best that happens is that the movement becomes somewhat popular and the main themes get co-opted by one or both of the major parties. Sometimes independent candidates do win state-wide offices, although that's infrequent. But I sense that there is an opening in these next few years for some very different kinds of politics."

"Well," said Karla, "even when single issue candidates have a core constituency, that's seldom sufficient to win. As you well know from all the campaigning you've done, there are many other major concerns and important constituencies to appeal to."

"Of course there are," Caine responded, "but public education is an encompassing concern. And it really does relate to all the other issues. At a deeper level than we usually experience during election campaigns, education and democracy are closely joined. Candidates should, or at least I should, try to engage citizens in discussing and eventually acting on these important connections and possibilities."

"I know you've talked about this before and I've read your op-ed pieces this past spring. Why not just do that—speak out, keep writing, appear on talk shows from time to time. You get attention as a public intellectual. A candidacy for governor could make some sense for what you care about, but it sure doesn't look all that promising to run outside the mainstream," Karla said.

"It isn't just because I care about education," Caine continued. "It is necessary to extend discourse beyond those few who tune into a public issues talk shows, or read the op-ed pages—including even those who read your column. We both know that's actually a small fraction of citizens. I can no longer follow an ordinary path because ordinary paths don't lead to comprehensive reform."

"Maybe so, but you have the luxury of working half-time as a high profile lawyer with the other half-time available for what you call 'reading and talking,'" Karla said rather sharply. "What about all those who have a full-time job—and maybe a part-time one too—and have far too little time for politics in their lives?"

"That's a really tough question, Karla. We'll have to find ways to genuinely broaden involvement. Frankly, I don't have a complete answer for you now. I do have what you call the luxury—the flexibility—to push this. I know it can't be done yet within the two parties, or even by any of those able candidates who are now running for nomination. Parties are locked into trying to win elections with the same old strategies."

"But you well know, whoever is nominated will have access to money and all the other campaign resources. The other party is even more well heeled with an incumbent governor who appears to be re-electable. They'll try to ignore you, isolate you, and label you," Karla said.

"Yes, I know. It will have to be a different kind of campaign than what we're all used to." Caine repeated.

"Like what?" Karla asked.

"Come on, Karla. You've got your exclusive already without getting a full campaign blueprint. As I said, I'm not sure about the form yet. Let me continue to work on it. I promise I'll be more specific next time. I know you'll keep asking."

*   *   *

Caine settled uncomfortably on a rickety folding chair near the rear of the very warm and humid Grant High gymnasium. He scanned across the audience for the Graduation Ceremony, taking in the well-dressed families of several races and ethnicities, the Grant faculty and staff, and a few non-graduating students. The members of the graduating class in their bright purple robes were seated in front of the temporary platform. There were too few rows of purple. He knew that only a third of those who started with this class were here to receive diplomas. He also knew that disappointing graduation statistics could be found across the entire state. Despite chronic problems and looming hazards ahead, he was convinced that there must be ways to improve those graduation rates. He felt confident that the percentage would be higher for those who had just completed Grant's ninth grade.

As he shifted on his chair, Caine's attention settled on the importance of initiatives such as Grant's. He tried to be hopeful that the proposal under review at the Metro Foundation stood a fair chance of being funded. He looked up at the platform to see Superintendent Tuscano seated near the center. He knew that Tuscano and several School Board members were lobbying hard for that proposal. Tuscano did not want to abandon a highly publicized effort to turn around a troubled school, especially when it looked like the ninth-grade program was beginning to work. The Superintendent understood that reform across the district was necessary, and that there was much more at stake than a few hundred students at Grant. Caine was reasonably sure that Althea Putnam, who was introducing the platform party, had enough positive visibility with the Metro Foundation to assure their confidence in her leadership. Caine didn't know whether his guarded optimism about the proposal was warranted. But on this graduation evening, he wanted to be hopeful.

He was far less confident that the risks of his emerging campaign for governor would yield results as satisfying as those he now anticipated for Grant. He was past all of the second thoughts that had followed his interview with Karla Morgan. Her story had led predictably to a flood of e-mail, overloaded his answering machine, and had initiated countless conversations. He shared both the enthusiasm and the confusion voiced by those who contacted him. Running as an independent and framing his campaign around public education and democracy was not seen by old political hands as the rational thing to do. Caine sensed that the specifics of his campaign strategy would evolve as he gathered more participants in the "public conversation on education and democracy" he had begun. He knew these conversations were necessary, but not sufficient. In his media interviews and other discussions over these past few days, he found himself becoming more articulate in expressing his vision. Even more important, he had become much clearer in his understanding that the vision would require continuing engagement with others' ideas, experiences, and situations. It was, he knew, not his vision that was being worked out. He was, along with many others around the country, trying to build and sustain a broadening democratic discourse—a movement that included his candidacy.

Looking around the high school gym, Caine knew that his guarded but growing optimism was in part based on his experience at Grant. Here, teachers and students had begun to learn *with* and *for* each other. He needed to expand on their achievement. There must be ways to build even more broadly—within this state and across the nation—a civic movement to ensure deeper democratic learning.

Given intensive and inevitable resistance to systemic democratic reform, how can we persist in the face of pressures to diminish aspirations or concede defeat?

Those engaged in comprehensive reform unavoidably face loss of confidence, resolve, and hope. Frustrations surface in response to formidable opposition, chronic passivity, and recurrent scarcity of crucial resources. To yield to unsatisfactory compromise; to become mired in protest or lost in despair; to retreat, to hide, to reluctantly surrender are familiar, though tragic, reactions.

Yet the future of public education and democratic governance is at stake. Change is neither easy nor safe. Paths toward beauty, truth, and justice always entail risk. The spirit of democracy is forged in contexts of civic courage, and liberated through expressions of principled thought and action. The courage required to sustain systemic democratic reform is *social, informed, inquiring, responsible,* and *expansive.*

Social courage emerges as a composition of diverse insights and efforts, beyond the capacities of any one person. Courage may begin with the individual, but becomes politically effective only when extended to involve and inspire others. Resilience and renewal are found in interdependence. Mature interdependence is grounded in an understanding of the radically social nature of systemic reform. It requires continuous searching for intellectual, spiritual, and material resources gained only through interaction with others. In the face of serious resistance, it takes courage to refuse tendencies to fall back on individual heroics or to relinquish responsibility to a charismatic leader. Especially during moments of disappointment and stress, we must remain open to others' thoughts and feelings, willing to share responsibility, and ready to exchange trust. Immersed in the daily struggles required to implement even small-scale changes, it is essential to develop broader connections with potential allies, in addition to deepening relationships with immediate collaborators. By remaining engaged with an ever-widening network of like-minded others, the risk of unnecessary compromise is reduced; the likelihood of demoralization and burnout is diminished.

Informed courage is centered in the highest possible quality of knowledge and interpretation. In the face of significant opposition, reform activists can neither seek solace in wishful illusions, nor refuge in preferred ignorance. Reform deliberations are impeded by efforts either to simplify and exaggerate, or to diffuse and minimize challenging concerns. While selective attention to a failed strategy or seemingly decisive loss is perhaps inevitable; blame, despair, and evasion are not useful in arraying a knowledge base sufficient to support continuing reform. Courageous awareness and resolute honesty are required to maintain realistic appraisals of personal and civic intentions and actions. Fully comprehending the complexities and contradictions of the status quo, activists must persist in asserting coherent, compelling, and truthful representations of reform programs and prospects.

Inquiring courage necessarily flows from the heightened awareness gained in pursuit of knowledge. Courage is required to move beyond familiar cautions and criticisms to explore uncharted territory. Ambiguity, complexity, and uncertainty are always present. Reformers always need to learn more. They need to experiment with multiple and diverse approaches to expanding social insight. Inquiry that is inclusive and integrative, creative and resourceful, is necessary to move beyond immediate obstacles. Courageous engagement in the dynamics of deep learning is required to sustain systemic innovation.

Responsible courage entails unwavering attention to the fundamental purposes of democratic reform. Whether struggling to save a precarious organization, working to protect a limited success, or daring to propose a new initiative, reform efforts must embody the defining aspirations of the movement. Treatment of fellow activists, and especially reform opponents, must meet high standards of compassion and justice. The politics of 'education as usual' emphasizes neither public transparency nor interpersonal ethics. It takes courage to act with determined integrity in all the phases of high stakes politics. It takes courage to engage non-oppositionally when aggressive response seems merited. In the short run, brave accountability increases vulnerability. In the long run, it is essential for principled social change.

Overall, the courage required to sustain systemic democratic reform is an *expansive courage*. Proponents will always operate in contexts of scarcity and injustice. In spite of limited access to conventional resources—political position, public acknowledgment, time, and money—they will always be called to push beyond the constraints of past action and present resistance. They will be challenged to outperform those in positions of power, and to accomplish more with less. It takes courage to imagine and enact bolder, more beautiful visions. But by expanding interdependence and ingenuity, surprising integrations are likely to occur. Aspirations are strengthened and action enriched as reformers weave insights framed by rigorous research with perspectives forged in specific struggles. Descriptions of lived experiences blend with intuitive glimpses often expressed in aesthetic vocabularies. As any reform initiative evolves, it is imperative to connect local efforts with broader social movements. To avoid retreat, to refuse defeat, *reformers must always seek more*—deeper solidarity, renewed understanding, evolving inquiry, and greater responsibility.

Coda

The future of public education and democracy is at risk. Powerful forces are eroding commitment to public schools and weakening democratic resolve. Significant challenges confront progressive efforts to enhance the quality of public education and to enliven democratic culture, politics, and governance. Contemporary social and political landscapes are aggressively shaped by comprehensive reform initiatives *not* intended to promote authentically democratic social inquiry and public life. Shifting momentum away from pervasive individualism, irresponsible consumption, and entrenched power runs contrary to the prevailing culture.

A deeply democratic civic vision is necessary. An inclusive, coherent, and compelling progressive vision is needed to counter economically-driven, elite-dominated public life. Thoughtful social assessment and interpretation must continue. Yet trenchant analysis and scathing critique are insufficient. Tireless efforts aimed at maintaining hard fought progressive gains are necessary. Yet incremental and isolated successes are not enough. Disciplined preparation—responsive to an articulate and aesthetic appraisal of the common good—is required to sense and to seize comprehensive reform opportunities.

A deeply democratic civic vision is possible. In a democratic society, promoting the common good is a fundamental aspiration. Stated intentions to develop personal and social potentials are realized and sustained through broad and active participation in shaping public life. In a democratic society members move beyond self-regarding choice and material acquisition to find meaning and fulfillment in complex responsibility, skilled interaction, and civic solidarity. Public education and political processes must nurture these potentials across the full life span of engaged citizens.

To accomplish systemic progressive reform of education and democracy, now, at this most difficult time, is to:

Re-envision . . .
to engage in a sustained process
of imagining new possibilities and bringing these into existence
centered in teaching and learning
radically social, always exploratory, necessarily creative
inherently aesthetic, profoundly ethical
deep cultural and political change
becomes possible
envision, then envision again . . .

Exploratory Democratic Practice: Oracles

Across time, place, and cultures, people have worked to extend their understanding deep into the past and far into the future. Seeking out revered persons (prophets) or processes (divination) to foresee specific events or to guide efforts toward desired ends is a widespread social phenomenon. The tradition of *consulting oracles* offers a metaphor for the time-honored *civic practice* of grappling with the unknown.

A pilgrimage to the priestesses on the mountain at Delphi, a journey into northern forests to witness the reading of runes, or casting yarrow stalks before scholars of the *I Ching* vary significantly in experience and interpretation. Yet study of these and other prophetic traditions suggest that the *civic purpose* of consulting oracles was generally *not* to seek reliable predictions, but instead to participate in an exploratory and interpretive form of social inquiry. Oracular 'ways of knowing' were engaged on the public's behalf in order to:

- deepen and extend collective wisdom concerning significant social issues;
- integrate intellectual, emotional, intuitive, sensory, kinesthetic, and spiritual dimensions of human experience;
- challenge assumptions of certainty—to de-center, destabilize, and surprise;
- bring new elements, relationships, and possibilities into play; and most important,
- inspire principled social action.

Here, in the concluding chapter of our book, we propose that this paradoxical tradition can be used to offer distinctive insights at critical junctures experienced over the course of working to promote systemic reform.

Phase 1—*Prophetic Dispositions:*   Social movements are rarely motivated or sustained by commitments to narrow objectives aimed at solving specific problems. Reform efforts must remain centered on notions of high purpose and profound value. The practice of 'consulting the oracle' begins, therefore, by negotiating focal concepts (e.g., 'community,' 'equity,' 'democracy') as lenses through which to guide further inquiry.

- Participants are organized into small working groups (3–5 members).
- Group members are encouraged to reflect individually on the status of the reform initiative. Each member is asked to identify one focal theme that reflects a critical experience or prevailing concern associated with a significant stage in initiative's development.

Phase 2—*Query:*   Reform movements require continuous reflection and deliberation on questions of depth, complexity, and challenge. The quality of questioning expressed in civic and political forums shapes understanding and response to pivotal social concerns. Questions can be formulated in a manner that opens new solution paths by framing complex issues in novel ways.

- Each individual is asked to formulate one question of primary importance to the reform initiative.

Phase 3—*Negotiation:*   At the heart of democratic deliberations is the challenge of reaching consensus—agreement beyond simple majorities; ideally, agreement that approaches unanimity.

- The small working groups convene to consider each member's *prophetic disposition* and *query.*
- Group members then negotiate a shared *prophetic disposition* and *query* reflective of both individual priorities and group consensus.

- The full collective is reconvened to consider the contributions of each small group. Participants negotiate across small group proposals to arrive at consensus on one shared *disposition* and *query*.

Phase 4—*Response:*   Reform requires its proponents to move beyond illusions of certainty and control to anticipate and constructively utilize ambiguity and indeterminacy inherent within all aspects of democratic learning and life. It is important to repeatedly exercise and refine social imagination—to develop change-related knowledge that is creative, systemic, and provisional.

- Participants return to their small groups to craft a response to the consensus query.
- *Responses* to oracular queries are particularly effective if expressed in multidimensional ways. Poetry, imagery, metaphor, etc. can be used to engage social, educational, and political processes in ways that draw from, but also enrich and extend, linguistic and logical analysis.

Phase 5—*Interpretation:*   Upon receiving an oracular *response*, the community assumes an ethical responsibility to work together to interpret and enact their oracle's counsel. It is understood that the meaning of the oracle's prophecy can only be discerned if approached with sincerity and solidarity, through diverse perspectives, and across the full spectrum of human perceptual capacities. Communal understanding and appropriate response also requires continual refinement achieved through acts of collective creativity, risk, exploration, and renewal.

- The full collective is reconvened to consider the *response* generated by each small group.
- Participants identify and reflect upon insights gained through the oracle process.
- Participants identify and negotiate specific actions to be taken.

Reform is intrinsically future-oriented, as well as connected to the past. Consulting 'the oracle' as an *exploratory democratic practice* can help us to more fully understand how we conceptualize, and then move toward, visions of the common good that are possible even under the most challenging circumstances. The oracular metaphor provides a *prophetic* and *poetic* approach to social inquiry, democratic decision-making, and principled action.

Thematic Bibliographic References

Exploratory Democratic Practice: Oracle
See Prelude

Printed in the United States
62973LVS00001B/208-210